INFILTRATION MARKETING

BOOKS BY THE AUTHOR

Total Marketing: Capturing Customers with Marketing Plans that Work,
(Dow Jones Irwin, 1989)

How to Bring a Product to Market for Less than $5,000
(John Wiley, 1991)

Marketing Magic
(Bob Adams, 1994)

Entrepreneur Magazine: Bringing Your Product to Market
(John Wiley, 1997)

Streetwise Marketing Plan
(Adams Media Corporation, 2000)

INFILTRATION MARKETING

Achieve astounding

sales increases on

a very low budget

by entering your

customer's world

Don Debelak

Adams Media Corporation
Holbrook, Massachusetts

Published by
Adams Media Corporation
260 Center Street, Holbrook, MA 02343. U.S.A.
www.adamsmedia.com

ISBN: 1-58062-263-1

Printed in the United States of America.

J I H G F E D C B A

Library of Congress Cataloging-in-Publication data
available upon request from publisher.

This publication is designed to provide accurate and authoritative information with regard to the subject matter covered. It is sold with the understanding that the publisher is not engaged in rendering legal, accounting, or other professional advice. If legal advice or other expert assistance is required, the services of a competent professional person should be sought.
— From a *Declaration of Principles* jointly adopted by a Committee of the American Bar Association and a Committee of Publishers and Associations

This book is available at quantity discounts for bulk purchases.
For information, call 1-800-872-5627.

Visit our exciting small business Web site: www.businesstown.com

TABLE OF CONTENTS

Chapter 5: Finding the Actual Prospects / 61

Section Two: Engaging Prospects / 73

Chapter 6: Creating Awareness in Potential Customers / 75

Chapter 7: Understanding the Customer's Buying Process / 87

Chapter 8: Matching Your Efforts with Prospects' Buying Activities / 99

Section Three: Arousing the Interests of Prospects / 111

Section Four: Demonstrating that You'll Deliver on Your Promises / 149

Section Five: Enticing Customers to Buy / 175

Chapter 14: Establishing the Price/Value Relationship / 177

Chapter 15: Using Promotions to Generate Sales / 189

Section 6: Replicating Sales Activity / 201

Chapter 16: Building a Loyal Customer Base / 203

Chapter 17: Setting up Cross-Promotions and Alliances / 215

Appendices

PREFACE

I've been involved in marketing for over 25 years, much of that time working with small companies ranging in size from one to 200 employees. I've spent some of my time over the last five years working with a small business development center, consulting with and offering seminars to a vast variety of clients with almost every type of company. My experience has taught me that small business entrepreneurs know that marketing is the most important ingredient to business success, but they aren't really sure exactly what marketing is about. They can't relate to marketing's traditional definition of the four Ps—pricing, promotion, product, and placement—or they tend to think of marketing in one-dimensional terms, such as advertising or sales.

I like to think of marketing in very simple terms. It's targeting a customer group that's big enough to support your business goals and then developing customer loyalty, either from having the best products, best promotions, or developing some other strong ties with the customer. Figure P-1 shows what marketers have been trying to do for the last 25 to 50 years, and are still trying to do today: Top of the mind awareness in the customer. That's how marketers get and keep sales momentum strong and produce significant profits.

The problem marketers have is their customers' world has been changing rapidly. People have become increasingly busy; they have an incredible number of options, both in what to buy and where they learn about products, services, and retailers. Customers have become demanding, buying only those products that give them the features and benefits they want, at a price they want to pay

Marketing has changed over the years from mass marketing of the '50s and '60s where all marketers had to do was blast a message out to consumers through TV and radio ads to niche marketing of the '70s and '80s where marketers targeted smaller market segments and positioned their products to appeal to a subset of consumers. The

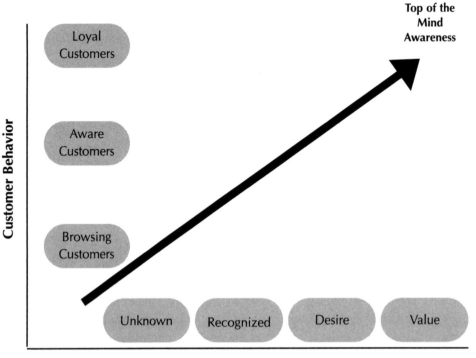

1990s saw the rise in relationship marketing, where companies like Nike related to their customers through superstars like Michael Jordan. The world of "I sell, you buy" marketing gave way to the "we know you and what you want" style of marketing.

Infiltration Marketing

Today marketing is evolving into what I call infiltration marketing. Companies are no longer just marketing their product, they are going into the customer's world. Campbell's Soup puts big barrels in grade schools to collect soup labels that schools

> Marketers need to adjust to the customer's rapidly changing world.

can use to buy a wide variety of computers and other school equipment. Think of the impact that the big barrel with the Campbell's slogan "Soup is good food" has right next to the front door of a school. That has a big-time impact on parents every time they walk by. General Mills offers a similar program with its Boxtops for Education program. Schools that collect the box tops from the tops of cereal receive 10 to 20 cents for each one.

Infiltration marketing isn't a new concept. Accountants that serve on the boards of entrepreneur clubs are practicing infiltration marketing. Companies that have sponsored top researchers' "how-to" seminars and classes at conventions are practicing infiltration marketing. The change today is that everyone is doing it. Fort Dodge Veterinary Products provides a complete quality control system for ranchers so they can meet government standards. As an off shoot, the company sells some of its products, but that's a result of the company being willing to help its customers solve their problems.

Infiltration marketing isn't just limited to big companies. Garden centers offer courses on how to create an English garden that blooms from March till October. Consultants band

> Marketers are starting to go into their customers' world.

together to present complete courses on the use of nickel alloy steel. Ski manufacturers sponsor cross-country skiing events. People selling dog care products are setting up booths with free grooming at dog shows. Small companies benefit the most from infiltration marketing because its tactics are the only ones they can use to build a dominant market position.

Infiltration marketing has two big advantages for every business. One is that its tactics are, for the most part, inexpensive. Campbell's Soup could have a strong impact on 500 to 1,000 parents for about $2,000. Most tactics can be implemented just as easily by a one-person firm as they can be implemented by a major corporation. The second is that these tactics can be used by almost every business. The customers' world, after all, is the same for every type and size company.

The Book's Format

The biggest question I get asked by small business owners is: "I know I need marketing, but I'm not sure what to do?" That's a question that's tough to answer because every business is different, with its own set of problems. There is not one all-

> Marketers with tiny budgets can effectively implement infiltration marketing tactics.

encompassing strategy that always works or is even right for every situation. Unfortunately marketers don't have the resources to just try every marketing strategy. Marketers need to limit their marketing and sales expense to 15 to 20 percent of their sales dollars. That limit requires marketers to concentrate on the marketing tactics where they will produce the greatest benefit.

I've found that the easiest way to determine where the marketing dollars should be spent is to break the entire marketing and sales process down into easy to understand steps so that you can easily determine where your marketing efforts need to be improved. This book covers how to break down the marketing process into six objectives so you can focus your marketing efforts on the one that will produce the quickest return for your business. This book also discusses a wide variety of tactics that work best to achieve each marketing objective.

The margins in each chapter will also contain one of these codes (100), (500), (1,999), and (2,000+). These numbers stand for how much a tactic will cost to implement: under $100, under $500, under $1,999, or over $2,000. The amount listed is the lowest implementation cost for each tactic. Larger companies may spend more when they implement a tactic on a broader scale, and marketers will pay more when they hire outside people to perform the work.

My Goals

I formatted this book so it can be a valuable reader resource for years to come. Marketing is not an exercise you do every once in a while. Things in the market change, your goals will be modified, and your marketing situation will be in state of constant flux. You need to constantly monitor your situation and be prepared to try a new strategy. And when one tactic doesn't work as you had hoped, you have to be prepared to switch to a new one

I've tried to do achieve several goals with this book:

1. Introduce the concept of infiltration marketing and explain why its use is increasing and why it is so effective.
2. Provide an overall understanding of what objectives marketers are trying to accomplish and an understanding of all the various tactics marketers have available to them.

3. Offer an easy-to-use process for readers to refer to when they try to discover what marketing issues they need to resolve.
4. Chronicle a vast array of infiltration marketing tactics that can be used by a marketer to address every marketing situation.

The main point to understand is that I didn't write this book for you to read one time and then put on your bookshelf. I wrote it to be referred to and used constantly, both as a problem solver and a source of creative new approaches to your marketing situation.

Who Is this Book For?

I must admit I'm quite partial to small businesses. They are able to implement creative new strategies that often have an explosive effect on their business. As you read through the book, you are sure to notice that I like to look at marketing in new ways and, for the most part, don't like to automatically apply tactics and strategies that have been used for years. I want to understand the situation from a marketing point of view and know that the tactic I employ is directly related to the current situation.

Small businesses have an easier time than larger companies at taking fresh looks at old situations, employing new strategies, and engaging in nontraditional thinking. But the book is not exclusively for small businesses. It's for anyone who wants to learn the new approaches marketers are currently taking, understand why those approaches are working, and have a guide on how to implement these new strategies.

> This book is designed to be your desktop marketing reference guide.

The Appendices

The last appendix in the book contains a form to help you understand your specific goals for each marketing tactic you employ. You are free to copy this form and use it as often as you wish. I believe this form will help keep you focused on what your objectives actually are. I find that most people can see a marketing tactic and decide to implement before considering what the tactic is designed to do and whether that tactic meets one of their objectives. The appendices also include a section that discusses strategic alliances and partnerships, which are a key component of infiltration marketing, and there is an appendix on how to write a strategic alliance or partnership proposal. Many of the companies you may wish to partner aren't going to immediately understand all the benefits of working with you. The proposal format is a method you can use to clearly explain what you are trying to accomplish in your partnership.

The Budgeting Process

Traditionally marketers have developed yearlong and, in some cases, three-year marketing plans with budgets, responsibilities, and implementation dates. This was a critical step when most marketing tactics were expensive, and it is still an important step in larger companies. But infiltration marketing tactics are frequently very low in cost. Try and use as many of the ones as you can that apply to your situation. There is no need to wait an entire year to see what happens. Try them and then evaluate the results. The answers of why they worked or not let you quickly fine-tune your marketing program.

> Fifty percent of your marketing budget should be for infiltration marketing tactics.

If you do use a budgeting process (which is still a good idea), have a budget line item for infiltration marketing tactics. I believe infiltration marketing tactics should be budgeted at a minimum of 35 to 50 percent of your total marketing budget. But don't lock yourself into a year's schedule of activities. Instead, list the tactics you may employ depending on the situations that develop. This strategy still gives you budget guidelines to follow, but offers you the flexibility of creating a strategy that is focused on your marketing situation as it develops. You won't succeed in today's market without the ability to move fast.

My goal is to help you have fun marketing, to help you create a highly profitable business, and to help you grow your business so it meets your own personal goals. The great point of an infiltration marketing approach is that you can succeed in a big way no matter how small your budget is. All you need to do is get started. I'd also like to know when your programs work great or when they miss the mark. The great new marketing programs are coming from small independent marketers, not from big companies. Netscape, after all, was a pipsqueak company when it decided to give its product away—free. Any traditional marketer would have told you Netscape was crazy. And it was. Crazy like a fox. The greatest break from marketing tradition that I've ever witnessed was an incredible example of infiltration marketing, and it produced a company capable of making Microsoft, the behemoth of all behemoths, sweat. Let me know when you observe marketers stepping outside traditional thinking, and I'll try to share them with everyone either in a new book or a magazine column.

Don Debelak
DSD Marketing
P.O. Box 120861
New Brighton, MN 55112

CHAPTER ONE

A New Era of Marketing is Already Here

Levi's was king of denim in the 1980s and early 1990s. In 1998 Levi's sales plummeted, the company slashed 4,700 jobs, and the company closed 11 of its 27 U.S. manufacturing plants. A pretty devastating performance at a time when the economy was running at record levels. What happened? Levi's lost its image of "cool," and with that loss its market share slipped over to jeans from stores like the Gap, Sears, and Wal-Mart and to fashion designer jeans manufacturers such as Tommy Hilfiger.

Levi's did an outstanding job of mass marketing their products to teenagers and young adults. They had the right product, they promoted it well, and people bought it. But then Levi's tactics stopped working. Levi's is in the process now of "reconnecting" to their customers. They are doing promotional tie-ins to movies featuring young Hollywood actors, and they are sending their marketing people out to infiltrate mainstream America and learn what the young people of today really like.

Marketer's traditional tactics were to choose a target market, develop products that the market needs, and then use promotional tactics to sell the brand name to consumers. The emphasis was having the right product and delivering a message that connected with consumers—two things that marketers still need to do. But that is no longer enough. People are just too busy today and have far too many choices for a marketing message to produce significant results, no matter how many times the message has run.

This is the hard reality that Levi's succumbed to, along with any number of companies including AT&T, Cadillac, and Hardees. Today marketers have to go further and infiltrate their customers' world and become part of the fabric of their lives. Even more so, companies need to stop just looking at customers as buyers and start to look at them as partners.

The bad news is that marketing is changing and that marketers need to adjust. The good news is that the new marketing era allows small marketers to compete on an equal footing with the largest customers, and it allows them to create a dominating market position from even the smallest sales base.

> Marketing methods are changing because people are too busy and have too many choices.

When I was a marketing manager for a dental company, we had what we felt was a viable product for cleaning root canals. Rather than a big advertising campaign, we instead had the product tested by several respected endodontists. They responded very favorably to the product, and rather than introduce the product with a traditional marketing program, we had the endodontists give continuing education seminars on root canals that mentioned our product. We received 8,000 requests for information out of 110,000 dentists the first 30 days the product was available. That was almost a 2,000 percent increase from our previous introduction of a fiber optic lighted drill, for which we received less than 400 responses. And our introduction costs on the root canal cleaner were 50 percent less than for the fiber optic lighted drill.

$2,000+ →

Our dental company went into part of our customer's world—continuing education credits. We didn't dictate the course material, and our product was only briefly mentioned by the endodontists. Our only blatant marketing efforts were that we were listed as the sponsors of the seminars and we typically had a table set up in the back of the seminar with our new product. This campaign was a true example of less is more; the less we pushed our product, focusing instead on education, the more our product sold.

As an added bonus, the endodontists we used for the seminars recommended some changes to our product that we incorporated. Those changes helped sell the product. We also let the endodontists mention the changes they suggested. This stroked our presenters' egos, and they increased our sales.

More importantly, the dental company strategy could have been used by a three-person company or by the largest companies in the industry. The greatest example of infiltration marketing is Microsoft. You can't even buy a computer anymore without a Microsoft operating system. It is no wonder that Bill Gates, Microsoft's founder, is the richest man in the world. He may have taken infiltration marketing a little too far; he not only infiltrated the customer's world, he has tried to take it over.

Infiltration marketing can produce astounding sales increase on a very low budget.

Compare the tactics of Microsoft, a true infiltration marketing company, versus Pepsi, a traditional mass marketing company. Microsoft has contracts with manufacturers to install their operating systems. Pepsi pays slotting allowances, which are up-front fees for premium shelf space to grocery stores. Microsoft gives away the details of its operating system to companies that write computer software. Pepsi spends hundreds of millions of dollars on consumer advertising. Microsoft bundles more and more products into its low cost start-up software, which it licenses to computer manufacturers. Pepsi purchased Taco Bell and Kentucky Fried Chicken in order to have more sales outlets for its products. There is no question that Microsoft's strategy is both more effective and less costly than Pepsi's.

$500

$100

Big Results for Small Companies

Large companies are practicing infiltration marketing with success, but the real wonder is what an infiltration marketing strategy can do for small companies. It can create a market niche that a small company can thrive in for years. It can increase sales of a small start-up venture over 1,000 percent per year. And it can give marketers an effective strategy even when they don't have a large marketing budget.

Infiltration marketing succeeds with even a tiny marketing budget.

George Quam is a life insurance salesman who found the going tough. He decided to concentrate on dentists, who were a good size market in his hometown. Now, starting to sell insurance to dentists already in practice is tough. They typically have a decent disposable income and everybody is trying to sell them something. George succeeded by concentrating on the dental students when they were in college. He'd go to dental meetings, work through the dental fraternity, and help out at the dental school. He'd

$100 →

sell the students a low-cost convertible term policy, which could be turned over into a full-life plan once the students had income. George's presence at dental meetings, and his association with all his dental buddies, let him be first to know what other investment products were being pitched to dentists, and George has been able to keep on top of all the long-term investment needs of his clients. As a result, George has built a great career out of serving dentists.

George Quam's story also points out that infiltration marketing tactics aren't totally new. Salespeople like George, stockbrokers that are members of the local country club, and other businesses where networking is a prime marketing tool have all been involved in what I consider infiltration marketing. What's different today is that infiltration marketing is stretching out to virtually every corner of the marketing arena. Results similar to Quam's can be found in virtually every type of business.

> Every facet of marketing is being influenced by infiltration marketing tactics.

Retail Store Layout. Real Goods is a California retailer that promotes products that save fossil fuel. It sells its products through the Solar Living Center, which, in addition to being a retail store, is also an education and demonstration center. The Solar Living Center is not just a retail store, it is a fully functioning solar building, without air conditioning. Heating costs about 10 percent of what it would be in a normal building of the same size. More important, turning the retail store into a demonstration center has boosted sales to $3.1 million in 1998 (up from $700,000 in 1995).

$2,000+ →

Retail Store Location. PC Club markets its own line of custom personal computers. It places its stores nearby giants in the industry like Computer City and CompUSA. Why? So when a customer can't find something they need in a PC Club store, the salesperson can tell them what to buy over at the competitive store. PC Club knows that marketing in today's world dictates that meeting the customers' needs comes first, and selling products comes second. The results? In 1998 *Inc.* magazine rated PC Club as its 108th fastest growing small company.

$100 →

Service Business. At first glance Custom Research Inc., a market research firm, looked pretty promising a few years ago with 157 clients, many of them household name consumer marketing companies. But sales weren't growing and profit margins were thin. The company looked at their accounts and found that only 10 were high profit margin, high sales  volume accounts. The rest weren't profitable at all when the company charged selling costs against revenue. Custom Research responded by drastically cutting their customer list and concentrating on the remaining customers. They learned the customers' businesses, created individual plans, and became a partner in the companies marketing efforts. The result: five years later their sales jumped 45 percent to $16 million.

Clean Shower, competing against consumer giants like Proctor & Gamble and Lever Brothers, generated $100 million in sales in less than five years.

Product Manufacture. Clean Shower was started five years ago in the garage of Bob Black. Today its sales exceed $100 million. All Clean Shower did was give away its products to radio hosts around the country. Those hosts used the product, loved it, and became irresistible sales-  people when they'd rave to their listeners about how easy it was to keep their showers clean. Clean Shower used advertising, but they stepped out-side the envelope of the traditional marketing message and communicated in a new and effective way to their listeners.

Internet Business. Amazon, a book store on the Internet, had in 1998 a greater market value, based on its stock price, than Barnes and Noble, the world's largest chain of bookstores. What is Amazon's secret? Its Web site doesn't try to sell books; it provides information. The Web site lists detailed information about each book, the book's relative sales ranking,  reviews and comments from other readers, editors, and authors; and other similar books the reader might want to look into. Amazon has compiled the ultimate self-service environment.

Sporting Goods Manufacturer. Barney Adams invented the Tight Lies golf clubs, fairway woods (and now drivers) that are easier to hit than other fairway woods. Sales are projected at over $30 million in 1998, and Adams's golf club is clearly a big business. But it didn't start that way. When Adams first started out, no retailer or pro shop would carry his

clubs. He was too small, and the shops were content carrying the brands of the big manufacturers. He created demand for his product by traveling the country and setting up shop at driving ranges and golf shops. He offered to custom fit clubs for golfers after analyzing their swing. He kept this up and, lo and behold, he started to get 20 to 30 calls a week from people who knew one of his customers and wanted a Tight Lies club. It wasn't long before he started getting calls by the pro shops hoping to catch a piece of the action.

Business-to-Business Supplier. There was a time that Ridger Chemical just sent its salespeople out with information about their products' features and benefits. But then the company discovered their customers were quite interested in just how Ridger Chemical manufactured their products. It turned out that their processes were ones customers wanted to duplicate on their own products. Rather than hide behind a curtain of proprietary secrecy, Ridger trained its salespeople in its own manufacturing processes and shared the information in an educational partnership that benefited both Ridger and its customers.

$100 ➡

Distributor. Nailco Salon Marketplace is a distributor to beauty salons. Checking with its customers, it found most didn't have a strong business background, a drawback that created a high rate of business failures. Nailco decided their job was to help its customers, and it partnered with them to provide a business ecosystem providing services like malpractice and liability insurance, 401(k) plans, credit card financing, and marketing support. The $32 million wholesaler offers the services at *its* cost. The results: 15,000 salons participate in the program; retention of current customers is up 30 percent; and order size is up 35 percent.

$1,999 ➡

One thing you'll notice about all of the small business stories is that none of them are small businesses today. But they all started out small. Some, such as Clean Shower and Adams Tight Lies, were actually produced out of a garage. The reason the products have done so well is first that they were good products with a target market. But just as important is that the companies used infiltration marketing tactics to grow their business.

Infiltration Marketing—a Definition

This book will cover dozens of tactics that I define as infiltration marketing, which is entering the customer's world in a new way. A simple way to look at the topic is that marketing used to be defined by the concept "I sell, you buy." The whole concept was based upon marketers figuring out what a customer's hot buttons were and then exploiting those hot buttons to convince consumers to buy their products.

With infiltration marketing, marketers take a different approach. They assume that customers are going to make up their minds from information, discovered in their own way. I like to define infiltration marketing as communicating with customers in their world, on their terms. Which means marketers have to both communicate with customers where they look for information and communicate with customers in the customer's preferred format. Marketers who do infiltration marketing extremely well not only do those two steps, but their and the customer's goals appear to be one and the same.

> Infiltration marketing is communicating with customers in their world, on their terms.

This process is just as important for industrial companies, whose customers aren't consumers but other companies. One company I worked for sold equipment that measured the depth of electroless nickel, which is used for corrosion protection. We combined with an electroless nickel manufacturer, a producer of corrosion resistant steel, and a manufacturer of solvents designed to enhance the adhesion of electroless nickel to offer seminars on improved corrosion resistance. Companies who weren't that interested in any one company's products were attracted to a complete informational seminar. Combining forces with other manufacturers offered potential customers what they needed to know about a product benefit, corrosion resistance, that was very important to them.

While the variety of infiltration tactics is almost infinite, there are a few guidelines that most tactics follow. The most important ones are:

> Marketers need to help customers meet their goals.

1. Be in the customer's life in a nonintrusive way. Sponsoring of events, holding seminars, conducting research, and joining associations are just a few of the ways that you can be non-intrusive. Remember that marketers can't just worry about selling product. They need to worry about advancing their and their customer's common goals

2. Provide self-service information. People don't trust marketing messages that are oriented towards just one product. Instead they want to look at information from their peers about all their choices. People want to be educated to make their own choices.

3. Be everywhere you can. Consumers absorb very little on each contact, even if it is nonintrusive. So the trick is not to spend money on expensive ad campaigns but to do strategic alliances and partnerships with other companies, associations, and customer groups to make your visibility as high as possible.

4. Match your goals with the customer's goals. Companies are feature, benefit, or product oriented while customers have a goal in mind. Consumers want a complete solution. As an example, they do not want a crash-proof, easy-to-enter inventory control system. They want a foolproof, safe running plant.

5. Provide the complete solution. Customers may want to make their own choices, but once made they want it executed completely by someone other than themselves. If that means you need to expand your product line, coordinate with other suppliers, or install equipment that is not yours, that's what you do.

6. Look the part. When George Petrides opened his first Wild Bird Center, he set up a miniature bird sanctuary on the grounds. There are now 102 wild Bird Centers across the country, with sales over $25 million. The key to success was that George looked and acted the part of a bird watching enthusiast, primarily because he was.

7. Be real. Don't think for a minute that the customer will fall for any manipulative tactics. You have to not only look the part, you have to believe the part. The customer today lives in a media-saturated world and won't be fooled for long. Often marketers have to go out of their way to prove they are real. Frozen Fusion, for example, is a retail store that features fruit drinks. The middle of the store has fresh fruit, and the drinks are blended right in front of the customers. Customers know the drinks are fresh because they see them being made.

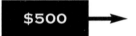

8. Show respect. The greatest danger in infiltration marketing is sometimes marketers start to think that they know more than their customers. Microsoft has certainly been guilty of being this cocky. It is always good

to remember that the customer always knows what he or she wants, and you should always give them the respect that "your boss" deserves.

Infiltration marketing requires a different mindset. Amazon doesn't focus on convincing people to buy from them. It focuses on giving people the facts they want to know when looking for a book. And if they order, great, if not, Amazon is happy to have helped out a reader. That's the mindset of an infiltration marketer: I'm going to help you. The lesson is that if you sell less aggressively, you are going to sell more product in the long run to customers who really do appreciate your efforts.

> Marketers will sell more with less aggressive sale tactics.

Infiltration Marketing Tactics

This book covers a wide variety of tactics. Marketers in the past have used all of the tactics but not in the same way. The key is to use the tactics in a cost-effective way to infiltrate the market. These tactics will be covered in depth in later chapters, but I've listed next some of the more important ones to give you a better understanding of the scope of this new marketing direction.

ALLIANCES

It is hard for any one company to present a total solution to any individual customer goal. That's especially true for small companies. So they need to coordinate in a wide variety of ways from doing seminars together, promoting each others businesses, to a more formal marketing or sales alliance. If several companies with complementary products are all trying to reach the same customer, they can do it more cost effectively and produce a far greater impact when they work together rather than working alone.

◄ $500

THE INTERNET

The Internet is a great marketing tool for providing information to customers in a self-service format, for combining the educational expertise of several companies, for united presentations with associations, and for putting together forums

$2,000+ → for customer groups to communicate with each other. The Internet is the ideal tool for marketers to let widely scattered or otherwise hard to locate customers come to them.

WRITING PROPOSALS

$100 → The secret to low cost marketing success for small companies is to strike as many alliance and partnership arrangements as possible. The problem with achieving that goal is that many small business owners are highly self-reliant, and associations tend to pride themselves on being independent. A key skill for infiltration marketers is to know how to put together a proposal whose appeal will be obvious to everyone.

ADVISORY COUNCILS

> Consumers will support companies that focus on their concerns.

Innovative marketers have long used advisory councils of customers as a sounding board for their proposed programs. But the concept is even more effective when the advisory board's duties are expanded into industry- or market-related concerns. A manufacturer of personal watercraft, as an example, would benefit from an advisory group recommending rules and regulations for personal watercraft that would benefit fisherman, boaters, water skiers, and per-

$1,999 → sonal watercraft users.

DATABASE MARKETING

$500 → This is a tactic that has been used for the last ten years primarily to pepper prospects with targeted direct mail messages. But the tactic can be improved on when joined together with the databases of other companies, and even associations, for industry or market relevant information. People will read a newsletter that focuses on key industry issues long before they will read a newsletter promoting a company or product.

ADVERTISING

In the fall of 1999 Chrysler and *Car and Driver* magazine produced a newspaper supplement on the new cars of 1999. Most of the supplement was a discussion of new cars from a variety of manufacturers, but it also included press releases **$2,000+** from Chrysler on its new products. This was an ideal advertisement. It was informative, identified with customer goals, and presented Chrysler's name and message in a nonsales oriented format.

This book will cover a wide variety of infiltration marketing tactics. As the examples above point out, these tactics themselves are not totally new, but rather how they are used has changed. Instead of sales-oriented marketing methods, they have been reformatted to meet the goals of infiltration marketing. These tactics can be used by every type and size company, and they provide a solid foundation for marketing success in today's highly competitive business environment.

Putting It All Together

Spinergy Inc., a high performance bicycle wheel manufacturer, started from virtually no sales in 1994 to nearly $10 million in 1998, primarily with infiltration marketing. The range of tactics that Spinergy, which was founded by Martin Connolly, used to promote its Rev-x wheels demonstrate how quickly low cost tactics can build a powerhouse company. Some or Spinergy's tactics were to:

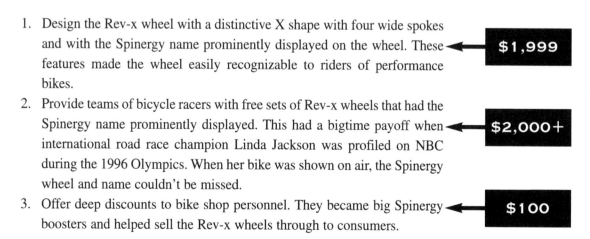

1. Design the Rev-x wheel with a distinctive X shape with four wide spokes and with the Spinergy name prominently displayed on the wheel. These **$1,999** features made the wheel easily recognizable to riders of performance bikes.
2. Provide teams of bicycle racers with free sets of Rev-x wheels that had the Spinergy name prominently displayed. This had a bigtime payoff when **$2,000+** international road race champion Linda Jackson was profiled on NBC during the 1996 Olympics. When her bike was shown on air, the Spinergy wheel and name couldn't be missed.
3. Offer deep discounts to bike shop personnel. They became big Spinergy **$100** boosters and helped sell the Rev-x wheels through to consumers.

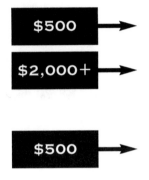

4. Sponsor bicycling seminars at big name companies like Hewlett Packard, Microsoft, and Boeing featuring champion cyclists such as Dan Casey who gave in-house, lunchtime motivational talks.

5. Give complimentary wheels to TV shows appealing to younger viewers, including *Pacific Blue*, the USA Network's "Baywatch on bikes" series.

6. Sign deals with high-end bike manufacturers for them to include the Rev-x wheels on their bikes. The result was that at the 1998 Interbike Show, Rev-x wheels were everywhere, including demonstration models by leading bike manufacturers like Cannondale.

The Rev-x wheel is a good product or it wouldn't keep selling. But the Rev-x took off, with a modest marketing budget, because of an effective marketing approach. My goal is that after reading this book you too will be able to generate the success you are looking for, no matter what type or size business you have.

CHAPTER TWO

A DIFFERENT LOOK AT MARKETING FUNDAMENTALS

Infiltration marketing is a cost-effective method of creating strong links between customers and products, services, stores, and other business. But it doesn't change the fundamental job of marketing; it just accomplishes those goals with a different twist. The fundamental goal of marketing has always been to create a close link with the customer. All infiltration marketing does is to find a better way of creating that link. To effectively implement the entire range of marketing tactics, small business people need to understand the marketing function and when and how to use each marketing tactic.

I've had opportunities over the last five years to present many marketing seminars to small business owners and marketers, and I've consulted with a wide variety of small business clients. One thing I've learned is that people often have a poor understanding of marketing. Part of the reason is that marketing is hard to define succinctly, and many definitions such as creating closer links with customers are too broad to provide much understanding. Another part of the problem is that many people (including me) have trouble grasping the marketing concept from the traditional academic definition, which is that marketing consists of four Ps: product, price, placement, and promotion. The final issue that confuses people is that there appear to be dozens of definitions of marketing in use today, and there really isn't a consensus that one definition is any better than the next.

I've found in working with and for small business over the last 20 years that people need a framework to help them understand the marketing process, diagnose where their marketing efforts need improvement, and prepare an effective marketing

> The process of marketing to customers can be broken down into six steps.

plan. I have found that defining the steps in the marketing process, which lead to profitable sales, is the easiest and most effective guideline for small business marketers.

Becoming the Marketing LEADER

I define the marketing process with the acronym LEADER. The letters in the acronym stand for:

- L—locating customers, which includes discovering the right customer group for your products or services, learning what the customer wants, and then determining what people are in that customer group.
- E—engaging prospects, which includes making prospects aware of your product, understanding the customer's buying process, and matching your marketing efforts to the prospects' timetables.
- A—arousing prospect's interest, which includes finding out what prospects want—but aren't getting, communicating quickly that you deliver what the customer wants, and contacting the prospects enough times so that they will take action.
- D—demonstrating that your product will deliver what you promise, which includes creating immediate credibility through your product and promotional materials, offering complete solutions to customers' goals and expectations, and proving the support customers need to buy.
- E—enticing prospects to buy, which includes establishing the right price/value relationship, creating an emotional impact, and using promotions to create greater sales.
- R—replicating sales activity, which includes building a loyal customer base, using your customer base as a source of referrals, and sharing customers with noncompeting businesses.

> Infiltration marketing enhances every step in the marketing process.

While the impetus behind many of the new marketing tactics has been how to effectively engage the customer, all six steps in the process can be enhanced with infiltration marketing tactics. The added plus for small business owners is that many effective tactics can be done for less than $500, and sometimes less than $100.

One step that stands out from the others is replicating sales activity through referrals, repeat sales, and through the judicious use of your customer base. Many people won't consider this a key step in the customer buying process or fundamental to marketing. The reason I include it is that repeat and referral sales are high-profit sales that require a minimum amount of marketing and sales effort. Most companies can't succeed without at least 30 to 50 percent of their sales coming from repeat and referral customers. The cost of making an initial sale is too high. One of the benefits of infiltration marketing is that you are forming a partnership with customers, which will greatly enhance your repeat and referral business. I list replicating sales activity as a key step because without it, most companies will fail.

Today's Marketing Challenges

Infiltration marketing tactics started in response to the two biggest problems marketers have today: first and foremost, engaging customers and, secondarily, enticing customers to buy. Potential customers, who are just too busy or skeptical to notice, largely ignore ads, direct mail, and other traditional methods. Engaging prospects in a cost-effective way so they notice your product is a never-ending battle for all marketers. Companies need to engage prospects in a way where the customer feels in control and where the customer feels his or her goals resonate with yours.

> A marketer's biggest challenge today is engaging prospects in a meaningful way.

Another difficult task for marketers is enticing customers to buy. This problem has two sides. One is that prospects today have been conditioned to always look for the best sale, and they will often wait for a sale. The second is that the customer has many choices of where and what to buy. The result is that when a company engages customers and arouses their interest, they better be able to complete the sale quickly. If they don't, the customer can easily end up buying from someone else. Then all the marketing effort and expense expended on that prospect are lost.

Infiltration marketing tactics have become an essential element for marketers who want to avoid price discounts. They establish a comfort level between the customer and marketer, create a product or service that has a price/value relationship that appeals to the prospect, and build a positive emotional impact on the prospect that encourages them to buy. People are comfortable with you when they feel you are giving them a fair deal every day. When you frequently discount prices on short-term promotions, you imply to your customers that you can settle for less profit than you normally make. Its no wonder consumers wait for a sale, because to them your sale price is the market price.

Completing All Six Steps

Spinergy, the high flying bicycle wheel manufacturer discussed at the end of Chapter 1, had success not only because of its infiltration marketing tactics, but also because it completed all six steps of the marketing process.

1. *Locating customers.* Spinergy decided that its target customers were high-end bike racing enthusiasts and determined that they could easily be reached through bike shops specializing in racing equipment and through a visible presence at major bike races.
2. *Engaging prospects.* Giving away product to top bike riders immediately caught the attention of Spinergy's target customer, especially when those riders won races or were profiled on TV. A second tactic was offering wheels to bike shop salespeople, who are typically bike enthusiasts, so they could give testimonial support for Spinergy's products.
3. *Arousing prospect's interest.* Top racers winning races on Spinergy's wheels was all it took to arouse the prospect's interest. To be sure the target customer realized it was a Spinergy wheel, the company designed a distinctive X-wheel spoke alignment and prominently displayed the company name on the wheel.
4. *Demonstrating that the product will deliver.* Top racers using the wheel certainly validates the product's effectiveness. But the point is made even stronger when the Spinergy wheels are on the winning racer. The point is driven home even more when the bike shop salespeople, who could use any wheel, choose Spinergy's.

5. *Enticing customers to buy.* Bike racing enthusiasts are willing to spend whatever is necessary to give them the best chance to win a race. The more targeted prospects see Spinergy's wheels on winning bikes, the more they want to buy the wheel. Spinergy's tactics were a close tie-in to the target prospect's goal: winning races. Spinergy's corporate seminars with Dan Casey, a well-know bike racer, demonstrated that the product would work and gave additional motivation to buyers to purchase immediately.

6. *Replicating sales activity.* This requires first that the wheel is a technological advancement and people do win races with them, which it does. The second tactic is to make the wheel available in as many places as possible, including bike shops and on new bikes, as original equipment. The tactic that really sent Spinergy's sales soaring was building momentum, demonstrating that in marketing nothing succeeds like success.

There are two important points to note in the Spinergy example. One is that many tactics can accomplish several steps in the marketing process. Having corporate motivational seminars at big companies engages prospects, arouses their interests, helps demonstrate the product will work, and entices prospects to buy. Many tactics can do double, triple or even quadruple duty in the marketing process. Marketers don't have to worry about having separate tactics for each step; they just have to worry that each step is accomplished.

> Many tactics can accomplish more than one step in the marketing process.

The second important step is to note that the steps one through five must be accomplished sequentially. Missing any one step in the process will stop the customer's buying process. And when you stop the process, more than likely you will lose all the impact of your previous marketing efforts.

The Funnel Effect

As you go through the six steps you will find the number of prospects you relate to shrinks (Figure 2-1). You can't get every prospect you locate to continue on to be a customer. I've found that the funnel can range from 80 percent of prospects passing from one step to the next for a low cost fun item that appeals to a large group, to as low as one-half to one-third of prospects continuing on to the next step for higher cost items. As an example, look at the marketing consultant's customer flow below:

Number of viable prospects located	320
Number of prospects engaged in a meaningful way	160
Number of prospects we can arouse their interest	80
Number of prospects we document that we can provide the service they need	40
Number of accounts that are enticed to buy	20

This prospect flow chart will change for each business. But as a marketer you want to have a rough idea of what the chart is like in your industry. Knowing this helps you in two ways. First, it determines how much marketing activity you need to project for the proper level of marketing activity. For example, if the marketing consultant needs $250,000 in sales per year and his or her average sale is

Prospect flow charts are a critical marketing tool.

$5,000, then he or she needs to make 50 sales per year. Working backwards, that dictates that a consultant, without any repeat or referral business, must locate between 700 and 1,000 potential prospects per year. If the consultant can count on 20 repeat or referral orders per year, he or she needs to locate 500 potential prospects per year to generate the 30 additional customers needed to hit 50 total customers.

The second way this prospect flow chart can help you is in determining where your marketing efforts are breaking down. If the industry typically needs 200 prospects to get 50 sales, and you need 400, you have a marketing problem. Following the percentages, you can determine where your efforts are falling short. As an example, let's look at a retailer of women's clothes. The chart below shows a comparison of a market research study of similar retailers and the retailer's actual results.

	Average	Actual Store
Number of people who walk by the store: (Locating prospects)	1,000	1,000
Number that walks into store (Engaging prospects)	45	49
Number that spends more than 3 minutes in store (Arousing customers' interest)	25	15
Number that spends more than 10 minutes in store (Demonstrating product will perform)	12	7
Number of Buyers	6	3

Looking at the numbers it is obvious the women clothing retailer isn't arousing the interest of people once they are in the store. The owner needs to evaluate why there is a problem. It could be any number of reasons including the clothing styles, sizes available, prices, or color selection. But the breakdown chart helps the owner determine where the marketing and sales effort is failing.

If you don't know the breakdown in your industry you can typically find at least a rough breakdown by following these steps:

Knowing where your marketing efforts are breaking down allows you to solve your problems.

1. Determine what to call each step for your business. For example, an industrial customer might call locating customers bingo card responses from magazine publicity, engaging customers might be prospects they either call on directly or talk to on the phone for over five minutes.
2. Call marketers selling to the same market and ask them what percentage of their prospects advance from one step to the next.
3. Check with industry associations to see what data they may have published on sales tracking. They will often have articles or studies that they will share with you.
4. Check in industry trade magazine for articles on sales tracking.

If you don't know the name of your associations and trade magazines, you can get their names from *Gale's Source of Publications* and *Gale's Source of Associations* at larger public libraries.

LEADER as a Tool for Marketing Breakthroughs

I've found that most businesses have most of their marketing problems related to just one or two of the six steps in the marketing process. The prospect flow chart helps you see where you are not performing up to marketing norms. But it can also show you how to produce a marketing breakthrough by showing you where the marketing process is breaking down for everyone in the industry.

Once you solve the riddle that is holding everyone back, you can develop strategies that will grow your business in a big hurry.

> Determining major industry bottlenecks creates opportunities for rapid sales growth.

The six stories of real life situations discussed next show how this strategy can work for every business.

MANUFACTURER OF HIGH-END CHILDREN'S CLOTHING

Situation: Company has grown at a sales rate of about 50 percent per year. About half of the stores they sell to order repeatedly and are very happy with the line. The other half of the customers only order once and are disillusioned with the product and its sales results. The stores that buy only once are a huge drain on the company, as sales costs per store are much higher than the profit from one-time orders.

Analysis: Manufacturers who sell through distribution to consumers can have three customer groups: the final consumer, retailers, and distributors. In this example the manufacturer sold direct to retailers, so it didn't have to worry about distributors. Manufacturers must evaluate each customer group separately when attempting to identify problems. When you have multiple customer groups, start your evaluation with questions involving the final customer.

> Products don't sell well unless they are grouped with other similarly priced products.

Why do customers buy at some retail stores and not others? The company's investigation turned up that the stores where the product sold well were high-end specialty shops where all the products were expensive. The shops where the product sold poorly were midrange stores where the company's products were higher priced than other products.

The company is doing a poor job locating and identifying customers in the retail customer group. The company needs to do a better job locating and qualifying stores that sell upper-end merchandise. The store will increase sales by concentrating their sales efforts on its target customers. ◄ **$100**

If the company wants to increase its sales dramatically it needs to figure out a way to sell more products to midrange stores. For the consumers in midrange stores, the problem is enticing the consumer to buy. It is very difficult to sell a high-priced product without merchandising to a midrange store, and it is hard to effectively merchandise a small product line. My recommendation to the company was to band together with four to five other upscale children's goods manufacturers and put together a merchandise program for high-end clothing. That way the manufacturers might get a good size area of the store to promote their products. This loose alliance would be a good deal for everyone. The upscale manufacturers, who had trouble selling at midrange stores, would be able to properly merchandise ◄ **$1,999** their products. The retailers, who would like to expand their customer base, would have products to offer to more upscale buyers.

INDUSTRIAL SUPPLIER OF CUTTING TOOLS

Situation: Kennemetal makes tools that are used to machine steel parts. These tools can range in cost from $5 to $200 and can represent anywhere from 5 to 30 percent of the cost of a manufactured part. Kennemental's sales presentation was that customers using its products could lower their cutting tool budget 10 to 30 percent. But customers weren't buying. Kennemetal looked into why the customer wouldn't buy, as a 10 to 30 percent savings in a major budget item appeared to be a meaningful sales point. The company discovered that first their prospects hear the same cost-saving message for hundreds of suppliers, and second, that their target companies didn't have a good system to verify that they were in fact saving the money suppliers had promised.

> You must distinguish your features and benefit proposition from your competitions'.

Analysis: Kennemetal had two problems. First, it wasn't arousing interest from prospects because it had the same benefit statement as dozens of other manufacturers. The second problem was that companies weren't convinced Kennemetal could deliver on its claimed cost savings, and even if they could the company wouldn't be able to verify it.

Kennemetal tried at first to implement some simple verification procedures. The problem it ran into was that most manufacturers produce a wide variety of parts, some requiring heavy machining and other light machining. Another variable was that cutting tools have a very short life span on some tougher metals, while they can last weeks on softer, easy to machine materials. So the prospects couldn't set up a "head to head" comparison of tool life.

Kennemetal succeeded when it offered two additional features to large potential accounts. First, it would guarantee a cost savings. And second, it would put an engineer in the customer's plant one day a week who would develop a verification system that would satisfy the prospect's management team. Once Kennemetal has documented success at larger customers, it should be able to use that data to generate business at smaller accounts where it can't afford to put in an engineer one day a week.

$2,000+ ▶

RETAIL SHOP SELLING CLOTHING ITEMS FROM MOVIES

Situation: It's a Wrap was a small struggling shop selling clothing items from movies that had been completed. The store wasn't generating enough revenue primarily because it wasn't pulling in the number of prospects it needed to be successful.

Analysis: The store wasn't locating, engaging, or arousing the interest of enough prospects to be successful. The problem was that the store wasn't big enough and didn't have enough inside appeal. The store had never expanded because it didn't have a secure source of sales items.

> Consumers expect specialty stores to be entertaining.

The storeowner brought in her daughter, Tiara Hallman, who had recently graduated from the University of Southern California's undergraduate program in entrepreneurship. Tiara first increased the supply of products. She offered a service to movie studios to store their cast-off wardrobe items and props after production and make them available for reshoots or promotional purposes 24 hours a day. Once the clothes and props were no longer needed, Tiara would sell them and give a percentage to the studio.

With a secured source of supply, she then created an interesting store that would attract customers. She moved to a 7,000 square foot location, hung movie memorabilia from the ceiling, and put an information card with the movie's name the piece came from on each garment. In 1997 the formerly small struggling store ← **$2,000+** had sales of $1.28 million.

SOFTWARE COMPANY SELLING SALES FORCE AUTOMATION PRODUCTS

Situation: Siebel Software opened its doors in 1993. It offered a product that was fairly new to the market that allowed marketers, sales representatives, and support people to share customer information. The software allowed sales representatives to call up customer data in the field and for every support person to have instant access to important information in the field. The product wouldn't be available until 1995, and Siebel Software needed to have an effective marketing plan in place to launch the product.

> Companies need credibility when marketing products where failure can't be tolerated.

Analysis: Virtually all major companies want to make sales and service people more productive. The problem is that those same companies aren't willing to waste a month or two of their most valuable employees' time on a system that doesn't work as well as promised. Siebel

Software, which was a new start-up, knew it would have credibility problems that would prevent it from engaging the customer effectively.

The company attacked the problem with a two-prong strategy. First, it formed alliances with Charles Schwab Discount Brokerage and Anderson Consulting, one of the top consulting companies in the country. Charles Schwab bought a 2.5 percent interest in Siebel Software, and today 4,000 Schwab brokers use the product.

$500 ➤ The company also convinced George Shaheen, managing partner of Anderson Consulting, to join the company's board, a move that convinced Anderson's employees to recommend Siebel Software's products to its customers.

The second part of Siebel's strategy was to hire the very best software salespeople in the industry, luring them with attractive commission packages that in 1998 averaged almost $200,000 per year. Hiring top salespeople who had built

$1,999 ➤ their own credibility with other products gave an implied credibility to Siebel's products, which accelerated sales to the tune to $120 million in 1997.

SMALL MARKETING CONSULTANT

Situation: OutSource ConneXion is a one person marketing firm run by Tracey Lowrance. She markets her services to small companies that need marketing services but can't afford to hire their own marketing person. Her specialty is developing marketing programs that give companies a competitive edge.

Analysis: Service companies selling to companies have problems enticing the customer to buy. Small companies know they need marketing but typically don't have time to implement marketing programs and/or aren't sure that the marketing program will deliver what they want, which is more profitable sales.

Lowrance solves this problem by not only designing the plan but also implementing it for the customer. When a customer needs to open up a distribution

$100 ➤ channel, Lowrance designs and implements a plan, and her standard of success is not writing a plan but how many stores started to carry the product.

MEDICAL PRODUCTS DISTRIBUTOR

Situation: Alan Bagliore worked for a medical supplies distributor where every company sold pretty much the same products. In 1988 he decided to go into business for himself. The problem was that his services were pretty much like everyone else's. He couldn't get people to listen to him.

Analysis: Engaging customers is always difficult when you don't have anything unique to sell. You as a marketer or salesperson only have about five to ten seconds to interest a prospect to really listen to you.

Bagliore solved his marketing problem in a very straightforward manner. He didn't try to sell his services or products. He called up prospects and told them, "Let's look at this as a partnership. You tell me what you need, and I'll do my best to make it happen." This is a different approach that concentrates on solving near-term problems that are on a prospect's desk that very moment. People want their problems solved and are happy to listen to people who can solve them. The results speak for themselves. After only ten years in business, Bagliore's company, Cypress Medical, had sales of $50 million.

> Prospects buy products to meet their needs, not your needs.

$100

Balancing Expenses

Marketers have limited resources that have to be carefully spent to meet their objectives. I've found that the LEADER marketing process is a great help in knowing what activities you should focus your spending. Siebel Software, for example, offers its salespeople the opportunity to make commissions that average $200,000 per year. That expense is a wise investment because it attacks Siebel's number one marketing problem—credibility. Siebel is buying credibility by hiring the software salespeople with a proven track record selling to major corporations.

You should analyze your marketing expenses carefully to ensure that you are spending the money where it needs to be spent. You also need to be sure that you are providing enough effort in each area of the LEADER process. It doesn't do any good to spend all your money locating prospects if you can't spend the money or effort required to engage customers and generate their interest. Our children's clothing manufacturer was a good example. The company was actually losing money selling to the wrong stores. That was money that could have been spent concentrating on the right customers or setting up alliances and merchandising programs for stores concentrating on intermediate-priced merchandise.

The next 15 chapters cover each step in the LEADER concept in more detail. This chapter's job was to first acquaint you with the overall LEADER marketing philosophy and how it integrates with infiltration marketing. More importantly, this chapter hopefully helped you realize that these concepts do not produce incremental improvements in your marketing. They are designed to produce significant and even monumental increases in your marketing performance, sales growth, and profit performance.

SECTION ONE

Locating Customers

CHAPTER THREE

TARGETING THE RIGHT CUSTOMER GROUP

Infiltrating a customer's world requires you find a customer group that you can locate, afford to penetrate, and whose members have a goal you can help them achieve. It is better yet if you can also find a group whose goals are not being met. This is step one in every marketing process because finding an ideal target customer group to sell to is the single most important task of marketing. The simple fact is that great marketers can't sell anything to anyone. Customers in the end determine which products they buy and for what reasons. Marketers can achieve results when they combine the right product with the right customer base. This doesn't mean that there is only one target customer group for every product. Each product might have many profitable target groups to sell to. But for every profitable group there may be a dozen unprofitable groups. Your job is to find a group that will meet your sales and profit objectives.

This chapter covers step-by-step how you determine the right customer group for your business. The topics covered include how to:

Divide potential customers into customer groups;
Decide which customer groups are ideal target customers;
Use industry information to find potential alliance partners;
Locate opportunities for infiltrating the customer's world.

Segmenting Customers

A customer segment is a group that has similar needs, desires, and behavior. For example, we could divide bike customers into the following segments:

Racing enthusiasts

High-end, midrange, and low-end mountain bike users

High-end, midrange, and low-end buyers of comfortable bikes

High-end, midrange and low-end buyers of road bikes

Trick and show bicycle riders

Midrange and low-end trick bike riders

High-end, midrange, and low-end BMX bicycle riders.

Rarely will a marketer have a product that will appeal to everyone. Marketers only need to select one particular market where they can infiltrate the customer's world and give them what they want. Companies may serve more than one customer group, but typically they will use different marketing strategies for each group.

In the bike example, customers are segmented by the type of bike they like to ride and the price range of the bikes they like to buy. There are dozens of different ways that you segment customers. There is no one right way of segmenting customers. What is important is to find a way of segmenting customers that separates them into groups where they have similar needs, desires, or behavior.

> There are typically several profitable customer groups for every marketer to choose from.

METHODS FOR SEGMENTING CUSTOMERS

Age

Young couples without children, senior citizens, and middle-age people all have different tastes. Restaurants frequently target different age groups, as do car manufacturers, vacation destinations, and clothing stores. Movies, records, and radio stations also target a customer group based on age. Marketers will also segment by families with young children versus families with older children, and even grandparents of young children.

Appearance

Some people like traditional clothing, others like fancier clothing, while others favor a grunge look. People also care about the appearance of their homes, cars, hair and a wide variety of other items. Businesses will also often rent space based on the appearance of the property.

Application method

Paint customers could be segmented by whether they like to use a brush, roller, or spray method of application. Cooking techniques, such as microwave, frozen food, or quick stove-top meals are another example of segmenting by application. Cellular phones may be used for business purposes, talking to friends, or a means of communication in case of emergencies.

Benefits

Products or services can be differentiated by the benefits that are important to the customers. Some businesses may hire a marketing consultant to handle a large influx of business, others may be looking for a new strategic direction, while still others may want an impartial party to conduct a market survey of their customers.

Company vs. individuals

Landscapers might have large companies, corporate business parks, shopping malls, or individuals as clients. Carpenters, plumbers, and electricians can specialize in new construction, repair work on major buildings, or the individual home market. Office supply companies might specialize in direct sales to companies or sales to home based businesses and individuals.

Decision-makers

Marketers selling to industrial accounts will often segment customers by who they have to work with to make a decision. For some accounts the key influence might be purchasing, for others it could be engineering, manufacturing, or the president of the company.

Desires

Customers might want environment-friendly detergents, or they might want one that can get out stubborn stains, is gentle on clothes, or is ready to use without any dilution. Customers of garden store products might want to buy a variety of products and coordinate their own garden, or they might want to buy a preselected group of plants.

Distribution channels

Some customers buy products for their hair from salons, others from drugstores or discount stores, and still others from major department stores. Where they buy their product typically determines a price range and a feature/benefit package. Catalogs and TV products also have a different set of customers than department stores.

Family size

Singles, families with no children and two incomes, single moms with children, families with one or two children, or families with many children can all be a customer group. Some companies, such as event planners, photographers, and family tree publishers will target large extended families.

Geography

Companies might sell to customers in the United States or limit activities to a region or state or even part of a city that is located within a five-mile radius of their business. In the Upper Midwest you can buy Lefse, a traditional Norwegian potato bread, and in Philadelphia you can buy scrapple, a breakfast meat dish. Sporting goods, outdoor gear, boating, and fishing equipment can all have targeted customer groups based on geography.

Image

My son tells me the boys in his middle school have the following images: smart, popular, normal, druggie, and grubby. Each group dresses and acts differently to distinguish themselves from the other groups. Adults are really no different. We have an image of ourselves that we want to project, from an outdoors type to a person of culture and class. Projecting an image is one of the most powerful buying motivators people have, and it should be considered more often than it is when segmenting customers.

Income

A chain of day care centers might be targeted at high-income people, certain cars such as the BMW are targeted at high-income consumers, and the Saturn is clearly targeted at midrange income consumers. Marketers of other products such as vacations, homes, and stock brokerage services segment customers at certain income groups.

Innovation

Some people, as well as some industrial companies, pride themselves as always having the latest innovations and being on the cutting edge. Others won't buy until a product has proven to be useful or until the latest innovation has all the kinks worked out. A third group might always purchase the last generation product in order to get a lower price.

Lifestyle

Some people love the outdoors, other people enjoy art museums and the symphony, and still others follow a Christian or environmentally sensitive lifestyle. Young families, rural families, urban families, and soccer moms all are considered to have their own lifestyle.

Occupation

This is a frequent method of segmenting customers in business-to-business and business service marketing. Doctors, dentists, accountants, and engineers could all be target customer groups based on occupation. Some consumer products are also targeted at occupations. Examples include high-quality tool sets targeted at mechanics and motivational stickers and awards whose target customer group are teachers.

Performance

Kitchen blenders, cars, bikes, and golf clubs are all targeted at customer groups that want a certain performance. For example, some golf clubs add distance, others keep the shot straight, and still others make it easier to loft the ball. Industrial marketing also commonly uses performance as a segmenting tool. Some large volume manufacturers with long production runs might want the highest speed production equipment, while a manufacturer with short runs would be more concerned with new equipment's setup time.

Personality

Some people are fun loving; others are practical, studious, risk taking, or very conservative. Industrial marketers also know that companies have personalities. Some avoid risk at all cost, others are anxious to seek out breakthrough opportunities, and others are oriented either to marketing or manufacturing issues.

Predisposition

Some people want to buy products from recycled material, others buy the same products their parents bought, and others won't buy what their parents bought. Manufacturing companies are often predisposed to stick with a production method, an inventory control system, or certain product features.

Price

Consumers can always be broken down into premium, midrange, and economy priced buyers. Some manufacturers are low-cost buyers, while others will purchase based on the economic benefit of the product. Retailers are also separated by the cost of the products they sell, from dollar stores to high-priced specialty shops.

Product type

Some people like gourmet pizza, others pizza with the works, and still others just like pepperoni or sausage pizza. People might buy Victorian wallpaper or heavily flowered wallpaper. Some people like Berber carpet, while others prefer plush carpet. One manufacturer might only buy carbide cutting tools, while another will only buy diamond coated cutting tools.

Process

Service and industrial suppliers can segment by the type of manufacturing process they use. For example, plastic manufacturers might use vacuum forming, injection molding, rotational molding, or a hand lay up process.

Repair options

Some large computer users have contracts with their suppliers for complete maintenance of their equipment. Other users like to be able to repair the unit themselves. Products sold to dentists, automotive shops, or manufacturing plants often have features that allow self-maintenance, while others must be factory serviced.

Sex

Male or female; marketers will also segment customers by alternative lifestyles.

Size

Clothing comes in small, medium, large, plus, and extra small sizes. Other firms segment customer groups by the number of employees, number of stores, or by the number of students. Telecommunication equipment suppliers segment potential landlord customers by the number of telephone lines their buildings have. Agricultural suppliers might rank farms by the number of acres they have, and veterinarian suppliers may have segmented by the size of feedlots.

Type of business

Service and industrial manufacturers often target one type of business. For example, they might focus on home-based business, boat manufacturers, hardware stores, insurance companies, or another type of business.

Usage

Some homeowners only use their personal computer for accessing the Internet, others for word processing and accounting, while others may use it for games. A fax manufacturer might target engineers and architects sending blueprints, and a horse saddle manufacturer might target people who ride recreationally or for show. In industrial accounts, the volume of products used or sold can determine a customer group.

I've found that it is ideal to separate customer groups by two to three characteristics. One is usually not enough to get a customer group that possesses similar buying behavior. For example, a customer group is fashion conscious preteen (ages six to 13) girls. Three characteristics—sex, age, and image—segment this group. Another consumer customer group is middle-class families with school-age children. Income and family size are the items that differentiate this group. A service company might target a customer group that contains solo obstetricians practicing in rural areas. Size of business, occupation, and geography are the key categories segmenting this group. One last example for an industrial company would be a group that consists of electronic manufacturers producing PC boards for high-volume consumer products with surface mounted technology. Usage, type of manufacturer, and size of production are the three characteristics used to identify this group.

> Your first marketing task is to separate your customers into groups.

Your first marketing task is to break down your potential customer groups into segments. You aren't ready to choose your target groups just yet. In the next steps we will analyze which groups are easiest to market to. So list as many potential customer groups for your product as possible.

Potential Target Customer Groups

1. _____

2. _____

3. _____

4. _____

5. _____

6. _____

If you sell through a distribution channel, remember that every link in your distribution channel also needs to be carefully chosen. If you sell to distributors that then sell to retailers, you need to categorize both what type of distributor you want and what type of retailer your want to carry your product. There will be several different types of distributor groups you could use, and you will also have a variety of retailers to use and segment. You also need to be concerned that all the target groups you select are well coordinated to meet the same goal. The best method of doing this is to identify the target customer group that will actually use your product and then work backwards to choose your distribution channel based on how and where your target customer group selects and buys products.

> Match your distribution network to your target customer group.

Copernicus is an educational toy company that produces science toys such as anatomically correct skeletons. Its target customer group is high-income parents of young children that want to provide their children with educational stimulation. To determine a distribution channel the company has to evaluate where its target customer group shops for its type of product. The best retail store group is educational toy stores such as Noodle Kidoodle and Imaginarium. Since the educational toy retail market is fragmented with many smaller retailers, Copernicus also needs a distribution network to sell to those stores. Typical toy distributors sell to more traditional toy stores, drug stores, and small discount houses. They will carry educational toys, but they don't specialize in them. Copernicus instead can sell through a system of manufacturers sales representatives that specialize in educational toys.

Industrial and business-to-business marketers would follow the same course: first choose a final customer group and then choose a distribution channel that already serves that market. Chapter 6 covers how to set up and use an alternative distribution channel when current channels won't work well for your product.

Choosing an Ideal Customer Group

Big businesses have to sell to many customer groups to meet their sales and profit goals. Small businesses have a big advantage because they typically only need to sell to one customer group. There are certain characteristics that make a customer group easier to market to. If at all possible, a small business should select a market group that is easy to sell to.

> Small businesses have a big advantage: they only need to appeal to one customer group.

The characteristics of an ideal target customer group are that they:

1. are easy to locate;
2. allow you to charge a profitable price;
3. can be swayed to try your product with minimal expense;
4. will meet your sales and target objectives.

CUSTOMERS ARE EASY TO LOCATE

Hard-to-locate customers are difficult for marketers because they have to invest a great deal of money to find the customers either through trade shows, advertising, seminars, or events. The only really low-cost option for finding customers is to put together alliances with other companies where you can share your leads. Your marketing costs are low when your target customer group is easy to find. Racing bike enthusiasts are easy to locate: they read magazines, go to bike races, and register for entry information. Plus, since they are often together, they are a customer group where infiltration marketing can easily be implemented by sponsoring races, offering trail rides, and by attendance at big events.

Consider the case of RC Enterprises, manufacturer of Painter's Helper, a painting aid that makes it easier to paint corners. I've listed the targeted customer groups for this product along with an analysis of how easy the customers are to locate.

1. Professional painters that do subcontracting work for contractors. Fifty to 70 percent of this market can be located through union memberships or through the distributors that serve this market. The others will be hard to find.
2. Professional painters that work with interior decorators or homeowners. Over 90 percent of this customer group can be reached through trade magazines, distributors, mailing lists, or yellow page listings. This group has to promote its business, which makes it easier to locate them.
3. Homeowners that enjoy decorating their homes. A part of this market can be reached through press releases and ads in magazines, and another part can be reached through high-end painting and decorating shops. Although only 50 percent of this market can be easily reached, 50 percent is still a good number of people since the group is so large.
4. Homeowners that only paint their homes when necessary. This group can only be effectively reached with displays at the stores where the group buys their paint. Even then it is unclear whether the group would notice the product.

Customers are easier to find when a product or service is important to them.

Groups two and three are the clear choices when considering how easy customers are to find. I'll continue to use the example of RC Enterprises and the Painter's Helper for all the criteria in determining which customer group to choose.

A PROFITABLE PRICE

You can charge a profitable price when customers feel your product helps them achieve an important goal, when emotions dominate the purchase decision, and when the product meets a specialized need.

1. Achieve an important goal. Groups two and three have a goal of a well-decorated room, a goal the Painter's Helper helps meet. Group one's goal is speed, and they already know speed tactics for corners, while group four is interested in speed and cost. The Painter's Helper helps this group paint faster, but the product has the drawback of costing more.

2. Emotion dominates the purchase decision. Consumers typically place high priority on satisfying their emotional needs. Price becomes a bigger concern when features dominate the purchase decision. The features need to offer enough value to justify the price. Tommy Hilfiger clothes, for example, satisfy an emotional need to have the "in" clothes and be part of the popular group. Clothes with the Tommy Hilfiger label are consequently able to charge a hefty premium.

3. Satisfy a special need. Painting corners is awkward, but it is not a major or special need. Products that meet special needs would be Victorian wallpaper for a Victorian home, a punch press that could stamp out an unusually shaped part, or a printer that could print a six-foot Santa Claus on corrugated paper.

> Buyers will always pay more when the decision is based on emotion.

MINIMAL MARKETING EXPENSE

Your job is to convince prospects to try and buy your product. This task again can be easy or difficult, depending on just a few points. I've found that few small business marketers do even a preliminary evaluation of how hard a customer group will be to convince. This is a major mistake. Why try to make money on a group that is difficult to market to when you can make much more money targeting a group that is easy to market to. The questions you need to consider are:

1. How many choices? The more choices a group has to accomplish the same objective, the more difficult they will be to sway to your marketing

viewpoint. None of the four groups has many options to paint corners other than just using a paint brush.

2. Do they see a need? Groups two and three will be upset by the slightest imperfection in a room and will probably see a need for the Painter's Helper. Groups one and four won't really care if there are a few mistakes in their painting jobs.

3. Are they predisposed for or against your product? In some markets, consumers are reluctant to make any changes. This is especially true if several companies have tried to introduce products or services similar to yours in the past. In other markets, a group of consumers will be predisposed toward your product. Only a few years ago, there were very few educational toy stores. Yet many parents were predisposed against standard toys and anxious to have educational toys available. That group supported the rapid growth of educational toy stores over the last few years.

> Small business should try to chose a group which will require minimal marketing expenses.

4. How much product support is required? When consumers or some small businesses buy a computer, they are tolerant of the computer occasionally crashing or needing repairs. Companies selling to this market often have limited support, which is low cost. Large retailers who rely on computerized registers can't afford even the slightest glitch. Companies selling to that market need a great deal of support, both at the point of sale and for technical backup.

5. What distribution channels are available? Some markets have ready-made distribution channels that greatly cut marketing expenses. The high-end paint and wallpaper stores such as Sherwin Williams, which serve homeowners concerned about decorating, are easy to find and easy to market to. The professional market buys from a variety of sources and isn't as conveniently served through a distribution channel. This is a major question mark for group two. Group four has a distribution channel set up with home improvement stores. Those stores require more advertising and promotional support than the specialized paint and wallpaper stores. This is because the paint and wallpaper stores attract consumers because of their specialized, quality merchandise, while home improvement stores attract consumers because of their price.

> The quality of the available distribution channel has a large impact on your marketing expense.

MEET YOUR SALES AND PROFIT OBJECTIVES

This is a decision that has to be met by each company. A chosen customer group needs to be able to support your sales and marketing objectives for the next two years. After that you will be able to attack other customer groups to meet higher sales and profit objectives. In the case of RC Enterprises and its Painter's Helper, the two best target groups are two and three. Group two, professional painters who work with homeowners and interior decorators, may only be 10 to 20 percent the size of group three, homeowners who enjoy decorating. Group one, professional painters that do subcontract work for contractors, is also smaller, while group four, homeowners who only paint when necessary, is by far the largest group.

CUSTOMER GROUP EVALUATION CHART: THE PAINTER'S HELPER

	Group 1	Group 2	Group 3	Group 4
Easy to locate	No	Yes	Yes	No
Charge a profitable price	?	Yes	Yes	?
Minimal Marketing Expenses	No	?	Yes	No
Meet Sales and Profit Objectives?	?	?	Yes	Yes

In the case of RC Enterprises and the Painter's Helper, group three, homeowners concerned about how well their homes are decorated, is clearly the best target group. In other markets, there can be two or more ideal markets that you can chose from.

CHOOSING A CUSTOMER GROUP DICTATES PRODUCT FEATURES

If RC Enterprises chooses to target the homeowners for whom home decoration is important as a target market, that decision impacts its product and marketing program in many ways, including:

> The target customer group decision impacts every market and product decision.

- The product itself should be made with high quality materials and the design should indicate its function—a corner guard—as much as possible. Producing the cheapest possible product would be a big mistake.

- The product needs a package with detailed instructions done in a professional way.
- Endorsements on the package from past users would increase sales.
- Marketing programs should concentrate on placing the product in as many high-end retail paint and wallpaper stores as possible.
- The company should seek alliances with companies that display at home shows in major cities.

SEGMENTING WORKS FOR EVERY BUSINESS

RC Enterprises is a painting aid manufacturer, and I segmented the market from RC Enterprises's perspective. But the exact same segmenting process works for everyone in the market.

Retail Stores. Paint and wallpaper stores need to segment the market. They could target:

- professional painters, offering contract pricing to the painters who paint upscale homes;
- interior decorators who select the wallpaper that the professional painters apply;
- homeowners who are concerned about how their home is decorated;
- homeowners who decorate only when required.

> Very few products or services will appeal to every target customer group.

Distributors of paint and paint products would also need to segment their product lines to appeal to one of the four markets. They would have an additional option of selling to contractors or painting subcontractors. Other people in the decorating market, such as drapery suppliers, color-matching coordinators, and carpet stores all need to make a similar segmenting decision.

Can you picture one product line that would equally appeal to every group? Probably not. Every target customer group has different needs. The company that tries to appeal to everyone with one product concept will in the end appeal to no one. That is why you must segment your customers.

Potential Alliance Partners

The first two sections of this chapter, segmenting your customer group and then picking a group to target, are traditional marketing choices. The next two sections of the chapter deal with how easily the market can be infiltrated. Alliance partners are an important concern for a small business because often you don't have enough impact on your own to attract customers. RC Enterprises, for example, isn't going to be able to put on much of an event by itself.

There are several market conditions that indicate that many of the suppliers will be willing to join in alliances.

◄ $500

1. Many small suppliers in the market. I saw a seminar on decorating a Victorian home at a home show where eight small companies joined together to offer broad-based information on decorating.
2. No dominant suppliers. A dominant supplier doesn't want to share the limelight and wants to host its own events, and it may punish companies who don't cooperate with them. Netscape, for example, was unable to get any computer manufacturer to feature its products because of Microsoft's dominant position.
3. Holes in many suppliers' product lines. Manufacturers specialize in just one or two aspects of semiconductor production. None of the suppliers supply a turnkey system, and they are willing to work together. Suppliers to metal plating plants, on the other hand, supply a turnkey solution and are less likely to form an alliance.
4. Products need to work together. Mountain and rock climbers, for example, need many different items to meet their goal, which is reaching the top of the mountain. Alliances are a natural in this industry. Wind surfers on the other hand, don't need much besides a wind surf board and a carrying rack.

> Alliances work best when consumers buy a variety of products to meet their goals.

5. Customers belong to an identified market segment. Rock climbers, wind surfers, and owners of Victorian homes are all members of a recognized customer group that many suppliers are trying to sell to. Other products, like halogen lights, are sold to a broad market segment. Companies with

products like the halogen light will have a harder time finding other companies with similar goals to align with.

6. Markets served by a fragmented distribution system. Fragmented distribution systems give all suppliers fits. For example, suppliers of high-end children's clothes will sell to some high-end children stores, some midrange stores that include an exclusive section, and some department stores. Fragmented distribution leads to higher marketing costs per sale, a cost an alliance can help lower.

In the case of the Painter's Helper, group one, the professional painters, would not have the sixth characteristic that suggests alliances would be easy to arrange. Distributors to construction trades are almost always full-line suppliers, and distribution is not fragmented. Groups two and three, professional home painters and homeowners for whom decorating is important, probably have all six characteristics true for them. Group four, homeowners who just decorate as necessary, probably need fewer products to meet their goals and tend to buy in home centers where large suppliers dominate. Probably only number five, being in an identified market segment, will apply to group four.

Opportunities Exist for Infiltration Marketing

Infiltration marketing requires that you go into the customer's world and make an impact. Some target groups are much easier to infiltrate than others because they have events, meetings, or other occasions where they get together and where you can go. Other groups don't present those opportunities. Professional painters that do subcontract work virtually never get together or do anything that a marketer can infiltrate. Professional home painters that work with interior decorators have to be alert to all the new changes in the market and are likely to attend shows, read trade magazines, and be open to learning about new ideas. This group is much easier to become a part of. Marketers can infiltrate homeowners that are serious about their decorating by working with the retail stores they frequent. Those stores will be happy to hold classes, provide counseling, or offer additional services that benefit their customers. Homeowners that only paint when needed are hard to infiltrate because they don't care enough to learn much about what's new.

There are several traits that make a group easier to infiltrate:

1. Group's active association in running trade shows, seminars, regional meetings, or other activities that bring people together.
2. Rapid changes in usage or technology in the industry.
3. Wide interest in the customer group in trade shows, races, or other large events where the target group attends.
4. Consumers are passionate and want to constantly learn more about what is happening.
5. The product or service provides important benefits to the users. This is especially true in business-to-business marketing where you must impact a significant customer problem or goal if you want to succeed with infiltration marketing tactics.

> The more passionate customers are, the easier they are to infiltrate.

CUSTOMER GROUP EVALUATION CHART: THE PAINTER'S HELPER

	Group 1	Group 2	Group 3	Group 4
Easy to locate	No	Yes	Yes	No
Charge a profitable price	?	Yes	Yes	?
Minimal marketing expenses	No	?	Yes	No
Meet sales and profit objectives?	?	?	Yes	Yes
Possibility of forming an alliance	No	Yes	Yes	?
Infiltration opportunities	No	Yes	Yes	No

Before moving on, rate the customer groups that you had identified earlier in the chapter, then choose the best group as your target market. A great marketer always does best in markets that are responsive to good marketing tactics. That rule applies to you, too.

CUSTOMER GROUP EVALUATION CHART

Your Product Service or Store: _____

Potential Target Customer Groups:

1. _____

2. _____

3. _____

4. _____

	Group 1	Group 2	Group 3	Group 4
Easy to locate	_____	_____	_____	_____
Charge a profitable price	_____	_____	_____	_____
Minimal marketing expenses	_____	_____	_____	_____
Meet sales and profit objectives	_____	_____	_____	_____
Possibility of forming an alliance	_____	_____	_____	_____
Infiltration opportunities	_____	_____	_____	_____

Conclusion

Marketing is a process, and when you follow the process, all the answers will become clear. You'll find marketing does not require creative genius, just a willingness to listen to what your customer group is telling you. The first, and far and away most important step, is to decide what customer group you are going to serve. Once you know that, as you are about to find out, marketing becomes a whole lot easier.

CHAPTER FOUR

DISCOVERING WHAT MOTIVATES YOUR CUSTOMERS

People are so inundated with marketing messages that they often just block out all messages sent to them in traditional ways. Ask people what commercials they see in an evening of TV viewing and they probably can't remember more than one or two. Business-to-business direct mail typically gets recycled before it's even read. People attending trade shows often are there with a specific purpose in mind—for example, buying new kitchen cabinets—and there is no guarantee that they will walk the rest of the show and see your booth. To counteract this marketers need to find customers in new places and communicate with them with new methods.

3Com is a large company in the networking and modem industry that primarily supplies modems, routers, other networking devices for small businesses. 3Com had a marketing challenge when it developed a new set of network products for larger companies to compete with a well-entrenched competitor, Cisco Systems. The buyers of these larger systems were unlikely to pay much attention to 3Com's trade journal advertisements or direct mail campaigns because they were pretty much content with Cisco products. 3Com identified its key target for selling its product—network managers at companies with over 500 employees. The company knew that those managers were 98 percent male, and it also knew that it would need to find adventuresome managers who were willing to see what a new supplier had to offer.

3Com ran two simultaneous Web advertising programs to find customers. One was through computer networking content sites, the other through participant-oriented, sports-related sites. 3Com's click-through rate to its own site was higher from the sports-related sites. The program was so successful it generated over 5,000 leads in just 60 days. 3Com would have had unimpressive results if it had just stuck to conventional sites. 3Com increased the effectiveness of its program tremendously by knowing its customers and some of their personality traits. That information let 3Com go to totally noncomputer related sites it knew would be popular with its targeted customers.

> Marketers find many more prospects when they break free of conventional marketing tactics.

> **$2,000+** ➔

The point of this chapter is learning to find more customers by looking for them in different ways. There are two big advantages in knowing how to break free of some traditional approaches. One is that you'll be locating customers at sites where they are actively engaged. In the 3Com example, when network managers visit a computer network site they may have just been looking for one piece of information. If they are looking for information on new products, 3Com would probably be just one of 10 or 20 companies trying to attract the attention of the network manager. At the sports-related sites, visitors may have a higher degree of interest because sports is their avocation and not their job, plus 3Com might be the only company displayed for networking products. That engages the visitor in a much more powerful way than the networking site.

The second advantage is that 3Com can go to sites where there is a high probability that the prospects will buy what they find. 3Com knows many network managers are not going to try a new supplier until they have a proven record with their new products. 3Com needs managers willing to take a chance. The network managers who go to sites for sports like kayaking, rock climbing, or mountain biking are likely to have a risk-taking

> Knowing what motivates your customer will help you get both more, and better prospects.

mentality. Prospects from a computer networking site will have a lower percentage of people with risk-taking tendencies. 3Com was able to get prospects, and get better prospects, by understanding their likely buyers' personal motivations.

3Com's strategy seems simple to follow, except for one small problem that I've found over the last 10 years. Small businesses often don't have a good understanding of what really motivates their customers. Their motivations, both for personal or business reasons, are often only indirectly related to their products they buy. Marketers succeed in finding customers when they understand what appeals to their customers and then go to locations, magazines, trade shows, seminars, or anywhere else that offers that same appeal to the marketers target group. The whole process starts with understanding what motivates your customer.

I did consulting work for a small manufacturer that made equipment for washing trucks. The company sold a mobile truck washing vehicle that was about the size of a small forklift. The vehicle had a large brush that washed the side and front of the truck, a high-power rinse spray, and could turn at 90 degree angles to zip around an entire truck in about 10 minutes. The vehicle could move around the truck yard, going from truck to truck to keep them clean. The company's competitors were fixed bay truck washing equipment and service companies who would come in to a truck depot and wash the trucks with their own spray equipment.

The owner of the manufacturer had invented his equipment in response to environmental regulations that mandated that truck companies collect their wastewater rather than just flush it down into city sewers. His product collected and filtered dirty water as the truck was being washed. The filtered water was then reused to continue washing the truck. Fixed bay washing equipment could also collect and filter the wastewater, but the truck washing service companies sent all the wastewater down into the sewer system. The owner marketed his business based on two assumptions about truck company owners: one, that meeting environmental regulations was important, and two, that truck owners were concerned about how clean their trucks were.

The true situation was actually quite different. The truck company owners were not really worried about environmental features. Nor were they concerned about how well the truck was cleaned. Their number one concern was marketing their business. Fortunately for the manufacturer of truck washing equipment, the owners felt that their customers believed a clean truck indicated that the truck company had good customer service. The truck owners were much more receptive to the company's new message, "Never send a truck out dirty again." Truck owners started to take

notice when marketing focus changed from promoting the benefits of "environmentally friendly" to "make a better impression."

I tell you this story for only one reason. Most small business owners and marketers believe they know their customers. And some do. But most often they are so caught up in thinking about the features and benefits of their own products that they are unable to focus on what the customer really is looking for. You can't succeed at infiltration marketing without knowing your customer groups' real motivations. Who would come if our truck washing equipment manufacturer ran a class with other companies on meeting environmental regulations? If anyone came, it would be the yard foremen, who can't make a major purchase decision. Instead of finding customers, the truck washing company would have been wasting money.

Small business marketers often don't understand what really motivates their customers.

Starbucks Coffee and Bruegger's Bagels are great examples of the power of knowing what motivates customers. Starbucks and Bruegger's both find customers by placing their stores in locations nearby where their potential customers either work or live. These stores sell coffee for $2 to $4 along with bagels for $1.50. Inside many of the office buildings that Starbucks's and Bruegger's customers work at are coffee stands that sell coffee, donuts, and probably bagels at a much lower price. Many of Starbucks's customers can get free coffee at their office.

What is the motivation for a Starbucks customer? A better tasting cup of coffee? I don't think so. They are looking for a status symbol. Something that shows that they are important in their company and a person who is "on the move." With the advent of computers, companies cut way back on their number of secretaries. Having a personal secretary in the pre-computer era was a symbol that you had arrived. So people have to look for new symbols.

Starbucks and Bruegger's placed their stores near office buildings that were populated by lawyers or big companies where they were likely to find a large number of people anxious to make a good impression. The other location for the two stores are upscale neighborhoods where people own big houses and fancy cars and have the propensity to want to show off. Starbucks and Bruegger's are perfect products for the times.

This chapter covers finding out what motivates customers. That knowledge will help you find alternative places to find your customers. It will also help you find ideal alliance partners, companies with noncompeting products that satisfy the same motivational urges of your customers. Later chapters will talk about how to use these same motivations to engage prospects, arouse their interest, and finally entice them to buy. I want you to think like a high-end men's retailer that realized that Starbucks's customers are his customers. Working with Starbucks is a pretty good choice for finding customers for that retailer. What would be a better marketing activity for the men's retailer, belonging to the chamber of commerce or being a member at an exclusive business club? The business club would be better ◄— **$500** because that is where people go who have a desired image of high achiever.

One of the difficulties in finding your customers' true motivations is that they often don't admit their true motivations even to themselves. I can't believe ◄— **$500** Starbucks Coffee customers believe they spend $3 a day to look successful in the office. Similar examples of people not knowing their true motivations also exist in business-to-business marketing. At one time I was marketing manufacturing equipment against a larger, more established company. Our product was 10 percent less in price and had better features and faster performance. Customers would buy the higher priced equipment. They always had a feature/benefit reason for their purchase, but the fact was they just felt more comfortable buying from the established company. People make company purchases, and they will often make purchases based on emotional decisions.

> People always try to give logical reasons for their emotional decisions.

Small companies can't afford expensive research, but I've found that they can usually pick out the personality traits of people who are buying in their product or service category and can understand what different psychological motives people base their final decision on. They can do this by understanding what personality trait their customers operate under, knowing what their interests are, and under- ◄— **$100** standing what the customers desired image is.

The Personality of the Buyer

As it relates to purchasing behavior, I've found that most buyers fall into one of four personality traits for any given purchase. People may change traits for different purchases depending on how important they are to them, but on each particular purchase, people behave in one of these four ways.

1. Optimizing. People in this mode purchase whatever gives them the most satisfaction. They eat at the finest restaurants, buy the most expensive production equipment, and drive the cars that appeal to them the most.

2. Risk Adverse. People in this mode take action to avoid unpleasant consequences. Companies may put in a quality control system to avoid losing customers. People may buy a car model that has been out for several years because the kinks are worked out, or companies will get high-priced consulting advice from Arthur Anderson because they are confident that advice will be sound.

3. Judicial. Every decision has positive and negative aspects. People in this group try to balance the possible positive and negative outcomes for their situation. These people may buy a Jeep Cherokee instead of a more expensive sports utility vehicle to balance their desire for status with their economic realities. Many business decisions are primarily judicial, although those decisions can still be heavily influenced by the company's culture and interests.

4. Maintaining. People just buy what is necessary to get by. They may buy used cars, eat at home, and live a very modest lifestyle. Many businesses and professional groups operate with a maintenance outlook.

One of the comments I often get from business-to-business marketers is that they see how personality traits play a part in consumer marketing, but it doesn't apply to companies. That is totally untrue. Companies have cultures, which can be dictated by the CEO or have evolved over time. Those cultures have the same distinctive personality types that buyers have. Some companies want to be leaders (optimizing), others spend as little money as possible (maintaining), some are risk adverse, while others try to decide the product with the best price/value relationship (judicial).

For example, Frontier Communications sells phone systems for small businesses. One customer group is companies that need between four and 12 incoming and outgoing lines. Some members of this segment would be companies that are optimizing-oriented, judicial, risk adverse, or want as little change as possible. If Frontier's system has the latest technology, it will appeal to optimizers. So Frontier

$500

will want to look for customers at high-tech fairs, companies that purchased high-end copy equipment, or companies that have installed expensive brands of com-puter networking equipment. Frontier might want to do an alliance with Novell, a top-of-the-line computer networking company, because both companies serve optimizing customers. Frontier would do a similar analysis if it sold systems that had redundant backup and were guaranteed not to fail. Here they might target risk adverse companies and would look for companies with that same risk adverse tendency.

$500

Business-to-business marketers could dramatically improve sales by observing company personalities.

Psychological Motivation

I don't really like applying the word psychology, or as marketers more com-monly call it, psychographics, to marketing. Marketers aren't really interested in understanding all that is involved in a customer's psychological make-up. They only want to know what will motivate the customer to buy, to help find the cus-tomer or to help convince the customer to buy a product or service. It is impor-tant to understand a little bit of psychological motivation because consumers often do buy to support their desired image or to make themselves feel good. A parent, for example, who is frugal in every other way may buy extravagantly for his or her child. That act supports the parent's desired image of a good parent, and it makes the parent feel good for spending on what he or she feels is most important, a child. This motive in the case of the parent is strong and dominates the buying decision. While businesses buy primarily to support their image or goals, which could be increased market share, increased productivity, or improved cash flow, each person involved in the purchase decision will have psychological motivations. For example, a young engineer might recommend the newest equipment with high-tech features because he will understand it better than older engineers.

People have various interests and desired images of themselves that dominate the types of products they buy, which can lead marketers to better ways to locate their potential customers. I've listed just a sampling of the possible interests or desired images people may have:

Interests	**Desired Image**
Family	High achiever
Home	Unconventional
Social events	Progressive
Vacations	Outdoors person
Hobbies	Family oriented
Sporting activities	Fast climber
Entertainment	Financially savvy
Fitness	Dedicated volunteer
Community activity	Intelligent
Achievements	Good social skills
Recreation	Hard working
Job advancement	Party animal
Technology	Romantic
Knowledge	Adventuresome
High income	Cutting edge
Security	Technology savvy
Environment	Low profile
Investments	Conservative
Yard and gardens	Frugal

As an example, follow the purchase decisions of a fireplace for the home. One target customer group would be people who have a strong interest in their home and in entertaining. The two most likely personality traits of this purchase are optimizing and judicial. The members of the groups' desired image can vary, but more than likely it will be one of these four: high achiever, outdoors oriented, technology savvy, or romantic.

> Customer groups have a wide variety of interests and desired images.

This really puts your target group into several subsegments. What you want to do is look at each subsegment and see which one dominates the customer group. That's the group you'll want to appeal to, and that's the group you'll want to figure out how to find.

MOTIVATIONAL PROFILE

Product: Fireplaces

Customer Group: People who have a strong interest in their home and entertaining

Personality Trait	Desired Image	% of market
Optimizing	High achiever	25
Optimizing	Outdoors oriented	5
Optimizing	Technology savvy	15
Optimizing	Romantic	5
Judicial	High achiever	25
Judicial	Outdoors oriented	5
Judicial	Technology savvy	5
Judicial	Romantic	15

In this example, it is clear that the fireplace manufacturer wants to appeal to consumers who are high achievers. For the marketer this means he should focus on locating customers at country clubs, from lists of people who attend expensive social functions, and people who subscribe to magazines for high achievers like *Fortune* or *The New Yorker*.

$500

I can't emphasize enough that knowing your prospects desired image and interests is the quickest way to huge sales gains. And the first big gain is in knowing how to locate customers. That is one of the biggest advantages of infiltration marketing; you develop a great sense of exactly what your customers want to achieve and how to locate them.

Paying attention to customers' motivational profiles helps you locate ideal prospects.

When I worked for the dental company we developed a new product that made it easier for dentists to do root canals. This allowed the standard dental practitioner to do more work in-house instead of sending patients off to the endodontists. The customer group we were targeting were dentists who wanted to do more specialty work, primarily as a means to

$1,999

earning more money. We targeted dentists that had attended seminars, purchased books, or hired consultants to increase their business. This cut our prospect lists down to about 12,000, (out of over 100,000 dentists) and allowed us to focus on our true prospects with enough marketing effort to generate sales. Our program would have been a lot less effective if we had tried to promote our product to all 100,000 dentists.

Desired Image

I have already mentioned that personality traits play a role in business-to-business marketing. Desired image also plays a decisive role. The only difference is that business's interests and desired images are different than consumers'. Consider these four managers' desired images:

- cost conscious, frugal, a good manager with a keen eye on the bottom line
- a great motivator, gets results by generating peak performance from employees
- an innovator, always on the cutting edge, able to lead the industry in new directions
- customer service oriented, always looking for ways to enhance the company's relationships with its customers

Does anyone really believe that these four executives will make the same buying decisions? Of course not. Their decisions will be based largely on reinforcing their own desired image. Every employee, from the top of a corporation to the bottom, has a desired image that they will, at least in part, base their final decision on.

> Desired image plays a big part in business-to-business purchase decisions.

Listed below are some of the potential interests and desired images that come into play in business-to-business marketing.

Interests	Desired Image
Market leader	Financially savvy
Cost saving	Cost cutter
Quality conscious	Manufacturing expert
Productivity increases	Sells unique, hard to get, products
Employee satisfaction	Well connected in the industry
Holding down variable costs	Marketing leader
Maximizing cash flow	Innovator
Community image	Industry expert
New products	Mistake free
Increased market share	Employee friendly
Containing overhead costs	Customer friendly

Clearly businesses of all types, including manufacturers, retailers, service businesses, and distributors and wholesalers have companies and executives with all of these interests and desired images. One difference between companies and consumers is that companies will change their image and interests each year to coincide with their own business goals for that year. For example, in some years a business may have as its goal to increase productivity. That interest will dominate their thinking that year.

Motivational Profiles

You want to fill out your own customer groups' motivation profile, along with your guess at what percentage of the market that group makes up. The only difference between consumers and business customers is that you should use desired image as the primary motivational driver for consumers, with interests being a secondary concern, while using interest as the primary motivational driver for businesses with desired image a secondary concern.

Your customers' motivational profile should cut your costs of locating customers in half.

MOTIVATIONAL PROFILE

Product: _____

Target Customer Group: _____

Personality Trait	Desired Image (for Consumers) Interests (for Business)	Percentage of Market
_____	_____	_____
_____	_____	_____
_____	_____	_____
_____	_____	_____
_____	_____	_____
_____	_____	_____
_____	_____	_____
_____	_____	_____
_____	_____	_____
_____	_____	_____

Your final decision is to decide which of the psychological profiles dominate your target customer group, or if your customer group is very large, what subsegment of the market based on its psychological profile you will choose to market to. For example, a manufacturing consultant may have as a customer group plastic injection molding manufacturers with 50 to 100 employees. His target customer might have the personality trait of maintaining, and its prominent interest may be improving quality. The consultants' marketing focus for finding customers would be to find companies that are looking for low cost methods for improving quality control with the subsegment personality trait of maintaining.

List your target customer group(s): _____

List the predominant personality trait of your chosen subsegment:

_____

List the predominant desired image (consumers) or interest (business):

_____

You should keep a copy of your customers' group motivational profile handy as you will be referring back to it in several later chapters when we discuss how to design your product features and marketing messages.

A Big Payoff

For nine years Sherpa Corporation was the market leader in manufacturing software. But then sales stopped growing and new competitors entered the market, offering products that they claimed were more innovative and daring than Sherpa's. The company took a look at their customers and realized they had concentrated their efforts on technical savvy buyers who were on the leading edge of manufacturing technology. These buyers were no longer impressed with a nine-year old company but instead wanted the newest software available.

Sherpa realized it had the wrong customer target inside of the company. They switched over to targeting top executives, who were risk adverse and liked the fact that Sherpa had software with a nine-year proven track record. None of its competitors could come close to the number of installations and success stories that Sherpa had built up. The result of the new strategy: Sherpa's 1998 first quarter revenues were 41 percent higher, and its domestic revenues grew 71 percent.

$100

Recently young entrepreneurs have started to dominate markets aimed at young adults. Some of those markets are beachwear, snowboard gear, and kayaking equipment. The reason the young entrepreneurs succeed is that they know their market because they are a member of the market. To succeed as an infiltration marketer you need to know your customers and markets as well as the young entrepreneurs know theirs. The first step in achieving that goal is to understand what motivates your customers.

CHAPTER FIVE

FINDING THE ACTUAL PROSPECTS

You know who your target customers are and their motivational profile. Now you need to actually go out and find the names of as many people as possible that are in the target customer group. You can do this with a wide variety of cost-effective tactics. You can buy, trade, or barter for names; piggyback promotions with larger companies; give your product to experts; run contests or promotions; do surveys at events you sponsor; pass out coupons; use advisory groups; fund programs like seminars or festivals; do cross promotions with companies serving the same customer; use the Internet; start a club or association; and initiate an active networking program.

Buying or Acquiring Names

You can buy a list of names from mailing list brokers (listed in your Yellow Pages) who acquire the names from any number of sources, including magazines, catalogs, attendees at trade shows, and association membership lists. The list brokers have lists for virtually any type of customer group. They have lists of bicycle shops, doctors, mothers with newborn children, drivers of four-wheel trucks, as well as thousands of other categories. These lists are large and were formerly useful for direct-mail campaigns. Today their usefulness is less because the lists are chosen from venues where large numbers of people go and are typically not seg- ◄ **$1,999** mented enough for infiltration marketers. If you do use these lists you need to send out a screening postcard or mailer that will help you identify the target customer. For example, if you want to sell an egress window, which allows people to easily exit a basement through a window, you could buy a list of people who attended a home show. Most of those people would not be interested in a window.

The most effective tactics can be very inexpensive.

So you need your mailer to have an offer that will cause your prospects to call you. For example, you might offer a reprint of a magazine article on "Sunlight and Fresh Air for Your Basement Rec Room."

$500

A better tactic is to buy a specialized magazine or newsletter mailing list or the names of the attendees at an event, seminar, or convention. Trade and specialty consumer magazines targeted at your customer group are the best way to keep informed of all the magazines, shows, newsletters, and events that might sell you a list. Trade magazines are ones directed at retailers, distributors, or manufacturers, while consumer magazines are directed at the final customer. Every customer group, whether it's a professional, consumer, industrial, or business group, has many magazines and newsletters that you should subscribe to. Some of the newsletters may only have 5,000 to 10,000 subscribers. But those lists can be valuable if they are appealing to your target customer. You won't find these magazines at your local newsstand. There are two resources at larger libraries that contain a comprehensive list of consumer and trade magazines. One is the *Standard*

$100

Periodical Directory, and the other is *Gales' Source of Publications*. Get a list of those magazines and newsletters and ask for samples or subscribe to as many as you can. Consider buying the list of any magazine or newsletter that is focused on

$500

your target customer. You'll also read about events, seminars, association meetings, standards committees, and other helpful groups that you might be able to buy a list from. Trade magazines often have press releases from other small companies

$100

who might make excellent alliance partners.

Catalog lists that cater to your customer group are another cost-effective way to get consumer lists. You can start collecting the names of catalogs by simply subscribing to them.

Every target customer group has specialty magazines and newsletters directed solely at it.

You can find the names of specialty catalogs by going to the library and looking in one of the directories of catalogs. They contain the names of literally thousands of catalogs. Order copies of as many catalogs as you can find that fit your target

market. Those catalogs will sell your names to other newsletters and other catalogs aimed at your target customer group. Those catalogs in turn will put you on their prospect list and start mailing you catalogs. To get the names of people receiving

$500

any of the catalogs or newsletters just call up the catalog and ask if they will sell or trade their customer lists.

The cost-effective industrial lists I've found are primarily from associations and seminars sponsored by associations. You can get the name of most of the associations from *Gale's Source of Associations*, which is available from major libraries, or from industry trade magazines, which can be found in *Gale's Source of Publications*. Again, just contact the associations and ask if they will sell or trade their customer list.

$500

Another free tactic for getting names is trading for names with other businesses serving the same customer group. This is one of the most cost-effective ways to get names. Jewelry stores, fine fashion stores, and high-quality restaurants have all been known to trade customer names. When I was selling industrial equipment for measuring the thickness of electroless nickel layers, I often exchanged leads with an electroless nickel supplier. We both learned of names of prospects we hadn't heard of before, and we were able to increase our prospect list by more than 50 percent without spending a dime.

$100

> It's not cost-effective to buy names that aren't focused solely on your target customer group.

If you are a new company and don't have any names to share you can always offer something else of value for another company's names. I've provided free tests in a metallurgical laboratory, prepared press releases and marketing plans, offered testimonials about products, and given away products all in exchange for other companies' customer lists. If companies don't want any free products or services, you can offer them a sponsorship in a seminar or event at a favorable price. For instance, I might offer a seminar on getting angel investors featuring a panel of successful entrepreneurs. The seminar could be targeted at emerging young companies. I could offer to list banks, accountants, attorneys, and other marketing consultants as sponsors of the seminars provided they send invitations to the seminar to all of their customers that are new businesses.

$500

$1,999

Piggybacking with Larger Companies

Small companies can also obtain names by leveraging off of a larger business. Retailers and distributors frequently utilize this tactic. Dry cleaners will locate their store next to a large liquor store or drug store in a strip mall. Hardware stores will run ads or sales of a major brand name like Black and Decker to attract cus-

$1,999 ➤

$100 ➤

tomers into their stores. Record stores will often feature major displays and other promotions offered by major record labels to build their own credibility. In all of these examples, retailers are bringing in new customers by piggybacking off the larger company's name recognition.

$500 ➤

Distributors can follow the same path by setting up special promotions for retailers. Bicycle distributors, for example, will set up a fall promotion. They will get accessory and bike manufacturers to make special products available or offer special package discounts that the distributors will promote in their catalogs. The promotion goes out with the distributor's name, who also gets the business, but the distributor is really piggybacking its efforts on to the major manufacturers brand names and discounts that are in the catalog. The distributors will pick up new accounts and customers by coordinating their efforts with a well-known manufacturer.

$500 ➤

This is a tactic that can also be used by small manufacturers or service providers. One of the best ways to do that is to offer coupons for free product samples, seminars, or free attendance at a trade show. For example, a group of small bridal suppliers, catering services, and dance halls were hosting a bridal show. They passed out two-dollars-off coupons to nightclubs, bowling alleys, flower shops, bakeries, and any other business where their target customers might go.

$1,999 ➤

$100 ➤

A new quality control consultant decided to put on a seminar on some new testing procedures for manufacturers of close tolerance plastic parts. He had two university professors, two vendors, and himself as speakers in a four-hour program. He had a distributor of testing equipment give out free passes to all of its customers. The distributor was listed as a sponsor of the seminar, which enhanced its credibility. The distributor's involvement also guaranteed that most of the target customers knew about the seminar, a key factor for significant attendance at the event.

$1,999 ➤

Paper Direct is a specialty manufacturer of letterhead, brochure, and newsletter paper. Their target market is small and home businesses. I purchased a package of My Marketing Materials software and found that Paper Direct had several free coupon offers in the box, plus a catalog and some free samples. All I had to do was send off the coupon to receive some other free sample items.

Giving Your Product to Experts

Nu Medics produces a medical monitoring system for diabetics. The system includes a palmtop computer on which a diabetic logs in information about what they are eating, how they are exercising, and medications they are taking. The patient also logs in their blood sugar levels, which they get from a glucose meter that is also part of the system. Periodically, the patient transfers the data to his or her doctor's office through a special modem. The doctor, after reviewing the information, could advise the patient on any recommended changes that he or she needs to make.

    Nu Medics sold full systems to the five major diabetes centers in the country for $2,500, which was less than 50 percent of the systems' total cost. In return for the rock bottom price, the centers agreed to write a report on the system, show it to visitors, and even keep a literature rack next to the system. People who saw the system at the centers could call Nu Medics and request a complete information package. Not only did Nu Medics have prime candidates call them, they also positioned their product as cutting edge technology that had at least tacit approval of leading medical researchers.

 **$500**

Run Contests or Promotions

Customers remember you when they see you in noncommercial ways at places they frequent. The number of ways this can be done are almost limitless, and all can help you not only locate customer names but position your product or service in a positive light. A tactic that works very well is a contest or promotion where several companies combine their efforts to attract customers.

    I was recently at a fishing contest sponsored by several manufacturers, resort owners, retailers, and distributors. The contest also had a large tent set up where local stores combined to put on a demonstration on how to best use some of the new lures on the market. Everyone was a winner. The show promoter had better **$500** attendance: the stores, distributors, and manufacturers enhanced their image; and customers could learn about new products. The added bonus for the sponsors was that they ended up with a complete list of attendees.

$500

This same tactic can be used in a wide variety of other ways. An outdoors and camping store could team up with parks, guides, canoe stores, and other related businesses to offer a free wilderness vacation to Alaska. The cost would be shared, the promotion would be a great tool for collecting names, and all the businesses could share the leads.

$2,000+

Contests can be very cost effective when they generate free publicity. Hammacher Schlemmer, the catalog of high-priced gadgets, runs a contest every year looking for the most innovative new products. People can send in entries of their own products or products they've found on the market. The catalog also promises to send interested people (who are ideal target customers for Hammacher Schlemmer catalogs) a list of the top 25 qualifiers for the most innovative new product of the year. I've seen groups of retailers run contests for trips to Hawaii, and associations will often run contests for cruises or vacation trips that they sponsor. Recently I saw a contest in *Meeting and Planner* magazine seeking entries for the worst meeting story. A company offering fulfillment services for meeting planners ran the contest. Every entrant got some sort of promotional item, and the winning story would be published in *Meeting and Planning* magazine.

> Contests locate customer names for a very low cost per name.

$500

> See writing proposals in Appendix B.

If you want to put together a contest or promotion with other companies you should be prepared to approach other companies with a proposal to solicit their support. Appendix B, on writing proposals, offers a format for submitting a partnership idea to other companies. Putting together a contest or promotion is work for you, but it also gives you two big advantages. First it puts you in the driver's seat for collecting names and other pertinent information about customers. Second, it allows you to be in charge of future partnerships or alliances. A contest is a good starting point, or test, for what could turn into a more profitable long-term partnership arrangement.

Conduct Surveys at Events

Fozfruit is a frozen fruit bar manufacturer that targets young people who are health conscious. The company collected both names of consumer prospects and the names of stores that served its prospects by passing out samples and taking surveys at over 100 small health-conscious events per year. The events were 10K runs, 25K bike rides, hikes, walkathons, and triathlons. Fozfruit's representatives asked people to fill out surveys as they gave away sample bars, coupons, T-shirts, and hats. Fozfruit chose small events because the cost was low and the company could have a prominent position. Fozfruit learned two things with its survey: the name of potential consumer customers and the stores where they bought healthy foods. Fozfruit then used the positive survey results to sign up stores as retail outlets. The total cost was about $1,000 per show.

◀ $1,999

Pass out Coupons

One time honored tactic that still works is passing out coupons that people can send in for a free item or gift. You don't want to offer a discount to an item. Every one does that. Hewlett Packard likes to give away coupons for a free mini-publisher's kit. The kit contains a variety of aids for publishing newsletters, greeting cards, and business cards. Avery, a supplier of labels that can be printed on a computer, does the same thing when it gives away with certain purchases coupons for a free sampler kit of every label they make. Avery does this both to find out customers' names and to help sell its products. It advertises on the outside of its package that you can obtain a free sample kit when you buy select packages. That free offer acts as an incentive to get customers to purchase the product plus it gives Avery the name of people using its products. Inside the package is a coupon you need to mail off to receive the free merchandise.

> Give away something valuable and you'll not only get a name, you'll make a friend.

Marketers selling to teenagers and young adults are using the same tactic with street teams, which are a group of people who go out to where the customers are to pass out samples and coupons. They usually are also part of the customer group. Hugo Boss Fragrance, for example, sponsored a yearlong, nationwide marketing tour that started in 1997. For the tour a Hugo Utility vehicle, manned and driven by the "Fragrance Police," traveled to concerts, nightclubs, parties, and other events. The vehicle stops, and the "Police" join in the festivities. As they party, the "Police" also pass out samples and coupons to prospective customers.

$2,000+ ➤

Use Advisory Groups

Advisory groups are great for providing input into your business, but they can also be used for getting customers' names. CLS is a New England electrical distributor that has grown over 400 percent over the last five years. CLS created customer advisory boards in each of the company's seven sales regions. CLS advisory groups bring together eight to 10 customers to discuss CLS's service, new promotions, and new product offerings and to offer suggestions on better ways for CLS to conduct business. They can also talk about different programs that CLS can launch to get new customers, and they can even give prospect names that CLS's programs will appeal to.

> Advisory groups can tell you the names of prospects who will respond to your offers.

$1,999 ➤

Seminars and Events

You will get prospect names anytime you put on a seminar or event that appeals to your target audience. I have found that more target customers respond to an informational meeting that features an expert speaker to talk on a subject of interest. You can have a table in the back of the room where you display products and have a chance to talk to people. But more importantly, you can get their names when they register. One tactic I use to get even more names is to send out materials from the seminar to people who can't attend. The people just have to call up and leave their names and addresses to get the information.

$1,999 ➤

You can take a similar tack with sporting events, parties, theatre shows, or other events. A friend of mine is a graphic arts designer. Every year he sets up a tournament at a local golf club and gets about two hours worth of tee times. He then joins with a marketing firm, advertising company, and printer to sponsor the

tournament. Everyone invites their best customers, and the suppliers all pitch in to pay for prizes, greens fees, and dinners. It costs my friend $75 to $100 for every ◄— **$500**
good customer he invites. By combining his event with other suppliers, he also learns the names of the other suppliers' good customers. Some of those businesses may call him the next time they need a graphic artist. If he decides to approach the prospects from the golf outing for business, the prospects should remember him favorably. Small companies use this same strategy when they combine with other companies to

> Combining with other companies produces better events and increases a company's exposure to more prospects.

rent a super box or pit area at other sporting events like the Indy 500 and the Super Bowl. Taking advantage of entertainment and sporting events is a marketing ◄— **$2,000+**
activity attorneys, accountants, and other professionals have long practiced.

Cross-Promotion

Cross promotion is a tactic where companies offer each other's services or offer both of their services together. Companies typically use cross promotions as a publicity tactic to generate more product exposure. Industrial companies and service providers can combine their products to provide a complete solution for customers and to cut marketing costs. For example, Xerox was having trouble selling high-speed laser printers because customers also needed items like binders and booklet production equipment to produce the final product—massed produced information for three-ring binders. Customers simply didn't buy until they had decided on every piece of equipment. Xerox partnered up with several other manufacturers so that customers could buy a total package. As a result, Xerox cut its sales cycle in half. The bonus for Xerox was that it received an influx of new prospect names. ◄— **$500**
The names were leads that their partner companies had already obtained through their own marketing efforts.

Using the Internet

Jeff DeLong came up with the idea of his C-ya greeting cards during a divorce five years ago. The cards tell the other person why, at least from the person sending the card's perspective, that the relationship is over.

DeLong uses nontraditional artwork on the cover that depicts misery and non-sentimental wording like "Before I was alone—I was happier then" and "There can never be a new beginning—without a final ending." All cards then end with a large bold final statement, "C-ya."

Delong worked on his greeting card line for five years before he hit upon the winning formula of finding customers on the Internet. Today DeLong is averaging 2,300 hits per day, and he is selling 2,000 to 3,000 cards per week, averaging $30,000 per month from his Internet site. DeLong has also been able to set up distribution through beauty supply shops who have contacted him as a result of his Internet Web site.

$2,000+ ➡

You can greatly boost your Web visitors, interlinks, and people who register with your company by giving away something free. C-ya Greeting Cards has a few cards on its site that people can download for free. 3,000 people a month take advantage of that offer. C-ya gets prospects' names by requiring them to register. Free items are also a tremendous traffic builder at linked sites, where you can promote your free promotional item to help get people to surf over to your site. The great thing about giving away something free on the Internet is that it doesn't have to cost you anything. You can simply let people download an informational report or, in C-ya's case, a greeting card.

> You can double or triple the number of customers you find by offering people something free in return for registering on your site.

$500 ➡

Start a Club, Association, or Chat Room

Patent attorneys originally started the Minnesota Inventor's Congress, and patent attorneys still play a big part in running the organization, which helps inventors get their products to market. This, coincidentally, often requires the inventor to obtain a patent. This is a great marketing strategy for customer groups where the people in a customer group change constantly. A person who invents a product one year may not invent another for five or 10 years, if ever. The Inventor's Congress sponsors seminars, educational courses,

> Sponsoring a thriving club gives you credibility and a steady source of new customers.

and an annual convention. It charges dues and has admission fees, and the patent attorneys actually don't have to spend much money to keep the group alive.

This tactic is used by restaurants and theatres that support single's groups; garden stores that have clubs for groups like rose growers or people who have rock gardens; and hobby shops that support clubs by giving them space to run their meetings and display their models and craft projects. You can take this tactic one step further by forming the club along with leading experts and other related companies in your area. Don't try to run the whole club yourself, you only need to be **$500** a member. Your club will be more successful as you get more people and companies involved and you'll cut down the financial risk to any one company.

Networking Programs

Scott Turner, of Philtec Instrument Company, received $200,000 to $300,000 in overseas orders for his $750,000 per year business that sold testing equipment to semiconductor manufacturers. He didn't run promotions, rarely advertised, and had a tiny marketing budget. All of his overseas business was the result of networking. He worked together with industry groups setting standards for what semiconductor quality tests should be run. One of those standards required one of Philtec's products. Every time a new semiconductor manufacturing plant was built **$1,999** overseas, it automatically purchased one of Philtec's products for its quality control department.

You can network in a wide variety of ways that put you in contact with potential customers. Some of the methods you can use include:

> The best way to network is to contribute your time and talents.

1. Become a member and keep close contact with clubs and associations that are related to your business in any way. Serving on **$500** committees will generate a high number of good contacts. This is a great way to meet a mentoring contact that may know many top prospects for your business.
2. Be a volunteer at local, city, or state government groups that affect your business. For example, an environmental consultant can be a volunteer **$500**

$500

$500

$100

$100

$100

advisor to the state environmental agency on waste tires. This helps the consultant gain exposure and credibility.

3. Retailers can network with customers that can't visit the store. My grandmother's nursing home had a retailer bring out clothing samples once per month to sell to its patients.

4. Serve on standards committees for key industry groups. This technique builds credibility and produces many leads. I've been able as a small business marketer, to penetrate companies like IBM, Chrysler, Ford, and Carpenter Steel with contacts I've made on standards committees.

5. Develop contacts in complementary businesses that can help you. Stockbrokers, for instance, network with accountants and attorneys. Consultants frequently network with manufacturers' sales agents who sell products to their targeted customers.

6. Encourage your customers to be your advisors. When I first start marketing any product, I ask people I'm talking to if they think I'm on the right track or if they could see any way that I could improve what I'm doing. Not everyone helps, but I've found that at least 50 percent do. I found that customers respond to requests for help all the time, even on the first call. Tell the customer what you are trying to do, how you are trying to accomplish it, and ask for the customer's help.

7. Run classes at neighborhood community education departments for local business and vocational colleges or offer to speak at various business meetings. At some point every community newspaper lists a calendar of community events. Look those over every week for groups that might be interested in your products or services, then offer to give a class, speech or demonstration. If the group has the right target market you might even be able to offer the class or speech at no cost.

This chapter has covered many different low-cost techniques for locating customers. You can also use high-cost tactics such as direct mail, advertising, and trade shows. I believe infiltration marketing tactics are typically much more effective as well as being less expensive. The tactics discussed in this chapter not only get you prospect names, they give you credibility in the prospect's mind, which is a tremendous marketing advantage.

Infiltration marketing produces prospects that typically turn into customers.

CHAPTER SIX

CREATING AWARENESS IN POTENTIAL CUSTOMERS

The result is that you should be able to turn a high percentage of infiltration marketing prospects into customers.

The *Detroit News* took a group of young adults, ages 18 to 30, to the Auto Show in Detroit. The newspaper wanted to see how the group would respond to the hundreds of marketing messages delivered by what are supposedly sophisticated high-tech marketers.

The results were pretty astounding. The group actually despised the booth from Toyota, who had a "youth booth" with jugglers, blinking lights, blaring music, bobbing balloons, and even cheerleader-like presenters. The group felt the marketers were talking down to them, and they were not happy that they were being targeted with a blatant marketing attack. Other than the Toyota booth the group was bored with the current crop of cars being displayed. For the most part, the group is still waiting for the car that is "right for them."

Another group of cars scorned by the group were the retro cars like the VW Beetle and Ford Thunderbirds. The group thought these cars were relics from their parent's generation. The only exhibit that produced a universally positive reaction was the Hummer booth, a vehicle with a $93,000 price tag, beyond the price range of any of the group's members.

One point the group repeatedly pointed out, in between their cell calls to friends, is that they disliked cars that try to be something they are not. The

Beetle's oversized spoiler was just one example. The group felt the spoiler went against the car's purpose as an economy-class car. Another example is Chrysler's PT cruiser, a cross between a car and a sports utility vehicle. According to the group a sports utility vehicle should be a sports utility vehicle, and a sports car should be a sports car.

One 19-year-old panel member's comment about the whole show was, "I'm bored. It seems like I'm seeing the same stuff over and over again. I haven't seen anything that stands out."

> Customers are bored with the same old routine. Marketers need to break tradition if they want to engage customers.

Unfortunately, this panel group of young adults is no different than most of your potential customers. Consumers are bombarded by so many marketing messages that it is hard for them to remember a commercial or ad they have seen dozens of times. The new creative tactics that are now emerging are not only effective but also far cheaper than traditional marketing tactics. Breathe Right, the nose strips that open up nasal passageways to prevent snoring, gave its product to NFL football teams and told the team trainers to use the product when players had a cold. Breathe Right told the trainers that its product would improve breathing. When Jerry Rice of the San Francisco 49ers used the product on national TV, sales took off, and the company had a virtually free publicity program.

This section of the book on engaging customers covers first in this chapter how to get customers to notice your company and your products. The next two chapters discuss the customer's buying process and how you can match your activities to their buying habits so they will check you out when they are ready to buy. The goal of this section is to help you expose your company to as many prospects as possible, and then help you keep up a two-way, ongoing relationship with prospects until you convert them to customers.

Building Awareness

The ideal tactic for building awareness both introduces the product and engages the customer. In the course of three years, Bob Black, the creator of Clean Shower, took his product from his garage to over $100 million in sales. His tactics were very simple. He gave his product away to radio hosts. After they had used the **$2,000+** product for a few weeks, they could go on the air and say anything they wanted about the product. Black didn't even bother offering the hosts a prepared script. The results were stunning. The hosts told funny stories that their listeners soaked up, and then the listeners went out to buy the product. Today, Clean Shower's sales are greater than Windex's, and Black is holding off challenges from consumer giant companies like Proctor & Gamble and Lever Brothers.

> Infiltration marketing tactics took Clean Shower from a garage to $100 million in sales in just three years.

Nike uses a slightly different form of infiltration marketing to penetrate its target customer group, which are teenage and young adult males. They pay college and pro teams to have their **$2,000+** players exclusively use its products. They also use endorsements from great sports heroes like Michael Jordan and Tiger Woods. Nike's commercials weren't product oriented but instead only listed Nike's name at the end.

Companies are getting their names across to the public in new ways, from buying naming rights to sports stadium to sponsoring individuals, teams, research programs, conventions, contests, and a whole host of other tactics. Any size company can use these techniques. A one-person graphic designer can offer community classes, give seminars, and write a newspaper column. A favorite tactic of **$100** mine is to offer free classes for the Small Business Development Center (SBDC) on introducing new products. The SBDC promotes the class, I include the SBDC's flyer in all my promotional mailings, and everybody wins. When I was with a dental company we hired the top endodontist in the country to give a series of seminars at a dental trade show. Over 1,000 dentists appeared and it was a great success. **$2,000+** Our products and information were available on a side table, and the product was launched nationwide for $20,000 in an industry where just one full-page ad cost $15,000.

The most successful, cost-effective programs for creating awareness are all **$2,000+** infiltration marketing tactics. These tactics are not necessarily brand new. Duncan, the producer of yo-yos, for example, had a fabulously successful campaign in the **$500** 1950s. Duncan hired young yo-yo experts to go to schools and shopping malls to demonstrate yo-yo tricks. They also sponsored contests for kids about once a month at my local shopping mall, where the kids could win prizes. What's new about infiltration marketing is that it is more widely used than ever before, and big and small companies alike are beginning to recognize that in many instances it's the only cost-effective tactic available.

> Marketers are all starting to recognize that only infiltration marketing tactics are cost-effective.

Some awareness programs, such as seminars and cross promotions, are similar to programs for getting customer names. The difference is that the tactics to be outlined in this chapter are used to get a company's name in front of customers to create awareness. The tactics used are going into the customer's world, creating events that customers want to attend, cross promotions, and letting your customers spread your message. An important point to remember in all of your marketing activities is to share your message without being blatantly commercial. And as the young adults in the *Detroit News* story point out, don't try to fool your prospects.

Going into the Customer's World

I mentioned in the preface that Campbell's Soup and General Mills had programs that help schools receive free computers. Campbell's puts big containers that look like soup cans in the entry way to grade schools. Parents can drop soup can labels into the container and the school can turn in the labels for a computer or other school supplies. General Mills puts coupons marked Boxtops for Education on top of their cereal boxes. Those coupons can also be turned in for a variety of computer-related supplies.

$2,000+

These programs do several key things for both Campbell's Soups and General Mills. First, the schools ask parents to save their soup labels and box tops. That leaves a positive impression with the parents and gets them to participate in the programs. Second, the companies have collection boxes in school entries, with their names prominently displayed, where parents and children can see the companies' names on display. Third, every time parents see a Campbell's Soup or General Mills product, they'll remember the promotions.

$1,999

$500

$500

I once helped a company that was marketing a new hairbrush for horses. Its greatest marketing tactic was attending horse shows where they set up a booth and offered free grooming classes and even gave demonstrations on horses that would bring people over. The company gave top trainers brushes to use and in some cases paid the trainers to use only their brushes. The company also was listed as a sponsor for certain grooming awards at each show. At the same shows, people producing shampoos, riding apparel, and riding accessories also had booths. The booths had products for sale, but those sales were not the key focus of any of the booths. The key focus was helping horses look good at the show.

> You engage customers when you focus on helping them meet their goals.

The next chapter deals more extensively with how to figure out where your customer goes for information so you can know where to go. The point is it doesn't matter what type of business you are in, from retail to service to industrial accounts, once you know where your customers go, be sure to go there.

Kik-Wear Industries is a manufacturer of young men's wear. They feel that the ◄ **$2,000+** best way to show its clothes is to associate their product with music acts. So it works with City of Angels, a record label, to sponsor a tour of electronic music. Kik-Wear's name appears on all the tickets for concerts, on promotional CD's from bands on the tour, and on tour posters.

I mentioned in the last chapter that Hugo Boss Fragrance sent Fragrance ◄ **$500** Police out to get prospects' names. You can use the same infiltration marketing tactics to create awareness of your product. Manufacturers of new candy bars, cigarette manufacturers, and other consumer product manufacturers often hire people to give their products away at games. Some companies, particularly companies targeted at teenagers and young adults, take this a step further by using ◄ **$2,000+** what are sometimes called street guerillas to create product awareness. Street guerillas usually are groups of four to eight people who infiltrate a crowd and pass out stickers, logos, and free samples. These teams go out to music events, in-line skating or skateboard contests, nightclubs, and any other event where young people congregate.

Creating Events Your Customer Wants to Attend

When EvansGroup Technology, a marketing communications firm, wanted to strengthen its relationship with Hewlett Packard and other major companies, it decided to host an afternoon of "idea provoking, out-of-the-box thinking." The day included a feature presentation by Gordon

MacKenzie, author of *Orbiting the Giant Hardball: A Corporate Fool's Guide to Surviving with Grace.* MacKenzie spoke for an hour and a half about how people can use creativity and originality in their professional and personal lives. EvansGroup also had snacks, a get-acquainted activity, and a mini-trade show in the back for people to learn about some of EvansGroup's activities. The program was great and the attendees enjoyed the day off from their day-to-day routine.

$2,000+ ➤

Customers always appreciate a break from the daily routine.

I've already mentioned seminars several times, but they work in a wide variety of ways to put your company's name in front of your customers in a very positive way. You can host events, contests, fairs, and a wide variety of other events that bring people together. I've found that people will even have a favorable response to a mostly commercial event as long as it has a significant noncommercial activity. For example, many areas of the country have ski swaps that are sponsored by ski shops in the area. The shops allow people to come in with their old equipment and sell it to other people. People can do this themselves, or they can leave it on consignment and the shops will sell it. The ski shops also have their own booths set up and they have a large amount of equipment available at special promotional pricing. When you attend the shows, about one-third of the floor space is ski swap equipment and the rest is taken up with ski shop displays. The important point is that people appreciate the ski shops hosting the event, even though most of the equipment sold ends up being new equipment. Distributors will also host major events like a ski swap, inviting their retail store customers to attend. Bridal fairs, hunting and game fairs, and similar events are another service distributors sometimes offer to improve their relationships with their retailers.

$500 ➤

$1,999 ➤

Retail stores and malls are increasingly turning their actual location into a destination event. Oshman's Sporting Goods has batting cages, golf ranges, basketball courts, and a wide variety of other demonstration areas. Cabella's, a retailer of outdoor products, has started putting up large destination stores that contain virtually every item in their catalog. The goal is to turn the store into a fun destination. The entire concept reflects a national trend called entertailing.

$2,000+ ➤

A new marketing trend in retail is entertailing—adding elements from the world of entertainment to retail stores.

In 1996 the MARS (Music and Recording Superstore) opened. The store specializes in music equipment such as guitars, amplifiers, and drums. Traditionally, music stores have placed instruments in glass cases and asked customers to keep the noise down so as not to disturb other customers. Not at MARS. The instruments are out in the open where everyone can pick them up, and people can play as loud as they like. The store has a stage for impromptu performances, a fully functioning recording studio, and music clinics on everything from drums to recording equipment. The store's founder, Mark Begelman, built into his store the ability of his customers to perform and record their music.  MARS goes one step further by inviting famous guitarists like Pat Travers or Butch Trucks of the Allman Brothers band to jam sessions at the store. In the end customers buy lots of products. MARS has opened 11 stores between 1996 and the end of 1998. A further testament to the effectiveness of MARS's strategy is that its two fastest growing competitors, Guitar Center and Sam Ash Music Corp., use very similar strategies in their stores.

Cross-Promotions

Another cost-effective tactic for creating awareness is cross-promotions with companies that are serving your same target customer. This doesn't necessarily get you the customer's name, but you can still expose the customer to you at very little cost, and the customer may start buying from you. Tommy Hilfiger, the popular hip clothing line for teenagers, signed a deal with Nintendo to have all the skiers in 1080, the popular Nintendo 64 snowboarding game, attired in Tommy Hilfiger clothes. Cross-promotions are commercial efforts, but they help companies get their name repeatedly in front of target customers.

Kiss My Face sells soaps and shampoos for men that are made with natural ingredients that gently tenderize men's faces. When Bic introduced a new disposable razor, Kiss My Face bought 200,000 razors for eight cents each. They then combined their soaps with the new razor and placed them in 3,000 store displays that they sold to retailers. Kiss My Face sold out

and made money, primarily because Bic's lavish promotional spending helped people notice the Kiss My Face displays. More importantly, Kiss My Face signed up hundreds of new retail outlets who took on the product because of the Bic promotion. Even if the company hadn't made money, this would still have been a great promotion. The company exposed its product to both retail and consumer customers that provide a base for its future business growth.

> Piggybacking onto a larger company's promotion is a low-cost way to achieve significant exposure.

Cross-promotions are also used by a wide variety of more traditional companies. Simek's, a supplier of frozen entrees and meats in Minneapolis, has opened up stores inside of Super America, a chain of gas stations/mini-marts. Being together in one location helps both companies. Simek's shows its products to all the customers coming into Super America, who are prime candidates for its easy-to-prepare dinners. Super America finds a new set of customers in Simek's loyal customer base. Arby's Roast Beef and Sbarro Italian Food also market their products together under one roof, which helps customers of each learn about the other's offerings while cutting down on overhead expenses.

$1,999

$500

Cross-promotions can be as simple as having your card or brochures in other stores or locations where your target customer goes. Upscale restaurants will sometimes have artwork from galleries displayed, and the galleries will have restaurant brochures available. Antique dealers in Minnesota have a brochure that shows the location of 20 dealers within a five-mile area. The dealers all have an incentive: it makes them look bigger and makes a customer trip more worthwhile.

> Small companies gain valuable exposure from cross-promotions.

Cross-promotions aren't limited to agreements where both companies are involved equally. They can also be situations in which one company does all or most of the work and the other company product or name is used to add credibility. The Kiss My Face story is an example of how a small company did all the work. Often retailers and distributors will put on a fair or event and do all the work and have a major manufacturer pay a sponsorship fee. Of course, the major company's name behind the program attracts visitors, but the work is still done by the smaller retailer or distributor.

$1,999

Speeches, Classes, Columns, and Other Publicity

Your neighborhood continuing education program or technical college will have courses on topics like starting a day care business, advertising and public relations for small companies, and bringing birds in your back yard. This is great exposure if you are a neighborhood-based retail or service business. Many, if not most, of the courses offered by community education are ones suggested by area businesses. **◄ $100**

Association meetings and trade shows also offer classes or discussion groups on various topics. This is a great spot for a small business to make a presentation on a new process or to simply get its name in the spotlight. The number of attendees is not as important as the number of people who read about the speech and see the presenter's name. Sometimes trade shows will have a call for papers about a year in advance, and other times they are open to suggestions from businesses in the industry for speeches. Giving speeches at trade shows has the additional benefit of giving you a lot of new network contacts. **◄ $100**

Every midsize to large community around the country has a large number of special groups that have meetings. These can range from single's clubs to hobbyist groups, such as people interested in gourmet cooking, to professional groups such as freelance writers. Check with your newspaper every week and you'll find a section on upcoming meetings. On any given month most businesses will have several groups they could make a free speech at. I've found these groups are happy to have speakers, provided they don't have a fee. They like it even better if you have free samples to give away.

Another way to create awareness of your business is to write columns for newspapers and magazines. You'll often see question and answer columns in local papers on items like funding your retirement or maintaining your home. Local business people write those columns. Even if you don't

> You can gain plenty of exposure if you are willing to share your knowledge.

receive a fee, the columns provide plenty of exposure for you. Just contact the editor, who will often be willing to try out a new column if you offer a few months worth of columns for free.

You can also use this tactic in magazines if you have a national market. I write a column for *Business Start-Ups* and *Entrepreneur* magazines on inventions. The columns help keep my name out in front of my targeted audience, and I also get paid for writing the column. Small trade magazines to most industries will also accept articles from businesses that are well written. If you are a florist wholesaler, magazines targeted at retail florist shops might be willing to publish articles on the care of unusual flowers in the store or on how to save money and provide more variety by staggering the types of flowers carried throughout the year.

$100 ➤

The Internet

The Internet is a useful tool that can help keep your name out in front of your customers. There are several tactics that help keep your name in front of the people who use the Internet.

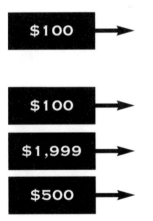

1. List your Web page address on every piece of literature you send out.
2. List the Web pages where another group mentions your company in a directory or in another way. For instance I'm on the Web with *Business Start-Ups* and *Inventor's Digest* magazines, as well as in about 25 other inventor and small business-related Web sites. This builds credibility for me as well as arousing people's interest.
3. Be listed on or linked with as many other sites as possible.
4. Change your site frequently so you will be listed near the top of search engines like Yahoo and Excite.

The Internet, for all its success stories, hasn't produced positive results yet for most companies. Even Amazon, the wonder company of the Internet, hasn't produced profits as of early 1999. So don't go out and spend too much of your marketing efforts on the Internet. It is a tool that works very well for businesses with widely scattered, dedicated customers that may be otherwise hard to reach. For example, inventors are a good target group for the Internet. They are hard to find, and the people who are active inventors change every year. This makes it difficult for marketers to cost-effectively locate the inventors, which it turn makes it hard for inventors to find the help they need. The Internet is a perfect marketplace for a group like that. Another example is leather bomber jackets similar to the ones worn by crewmen in World War II. These are expensive at about $250 each. There are people who want those jackets, but not enough for most retailers to want to carry the product. A person a friend of mine knows sold 1,000 of the bomber jackets at a profit of about $100 each on the Internet before Christmas 1997. Another product that does well on the Internet is expensive cigars, again a product where the buyers are widely scattered throughout the country.

But people won't look on the Internet for products they can easily find. The products they want aren't likely to be found on an Internet search. Try looking up hitch balls, a product that can be found in most auto parts stores, on the Internet. You won't be able to find them listed anywhere. The point is not to go out and do a big Internet push until you know your product category is well covered on the Internet.

$1,999

The Internet's success has had a huge impact on marketing, primarily because of its users' rule of community before commerce. People don't want the hard sell, they want information first, they want to associate with people who have the same interest, and they want to be a valued member of the group. Web sites that succeed follow these rules.

> The Internet is an ideal marketing tool when customers are hard to find.

Go to eBay's web site *http://www.eBay.com* to see a successful site that accomplishes this mission. The company even makes money, hosting online auctions for people selling any number of products. The company makes its money by taking a small percentage of each transaction. eBay has succeeded because it has been able to create a community for its most popular auction categories. If you are a beanie baby collector, eBay has chat rooms, online bulletin boards where you can post specific requests, and news sites for new interesting stories. The site contains all the information it can find on beanie babies and lets people freely converse with one another to the point where they can even arrange for private sales transactions. Does eBay care? Not at all. It doesn't post rules to stop transactions, it wants a community of beanie baby customers coming to its community. The community gets potential customers interested in the site, where they eventually buy.

> Infiltration marketing follows the same rule as Internet Web sites: Community before commerce.

What about advertising, direct mail, publicity, and other traditional tactics. Why spend a lot of money on marketing tactics that can produce an uncertain outcome when so many of infiltration marketing's tactics are free, or have a very low cost. In the past, marketing has revolved around how much money you spend. Today, it revolves around how much time you can devote to going out into the market, making your presence known and developing a core of key relationships that keep your name constantly in front of the customer.

CHAPTER SEVEN

UNDERSTANDING THE CUSTOMER'S BUYING PROCESS

In order to infiltrate the customers' world most effectively, you need to understand how people actually go about buying a product. Marketers make the most foolish mistakes when they don't understand customers' behavior. The manufacturer of truck cleaning systems I mentioned earlier in the book promised a one-day training for any truck line owner purchasing his $50,000 piece of equipment. Unfortunately, by emphasizing the one-day training program in its marketing program, the company inadvertently pushed the first decision on buying the product to the shop manager instead of the truck company owner. That one-day training program convinced shop foremen that the product was hard to use, which was a negative feature since the people running the equipment tended to leave the job after six to nine months. A sales feature promoted by the company was actually killing sales.

This chapter covers understanding customers' initial, intermediate, and final selection process so you know what to do to influence the right buying behavior. Finding out the process people go through before buying a ◄ **$500** product can be done by any company, for the price of 100 to 200 phone calls, and it frequently will lead to innovative and profitable marketing tactics.

I worked on the early marketing of a motorized golf pull cart that has a target customer group of older men and women golfers who prefer to walk but do not want to actually pull their own golf cart. The company was selling about $1 million per year of the $500 product, but its marketing costs per sale were too high for it to make a profit. The company's sales cost were high because ads in golf magazines cost anywhere from $5,000 for a small ad to $80,000 for a full-page ad, and the total cost of having a booth at a trade show was $15,000 to $30,000 per show.

When given the assignment of cutting marketing costs, my first step was to call up customers and find out how they went about buying the product. I found out that customers fell into two categories: pioneers, who were the first people in a golf club to buy a product, and the followers, who only bought the product after a friend at their golf club had purchased one. The task was quite simple: first, motivate the pioneers to sell more to their friends, and second, find more pioneers.

> Small business marketers often misunderstand the buying decision process.

We could actually have accomplished both tasks at the same time by running a cross-promotion with a manufacturer of a driver with very flexible shaft, which gave older golfers more distance. I proposed a program where pioneer buyers could get a free, state-of-the-art driver if they had six friends also buy a cart. In return for offering the driver (which the company paid for) as an incentive, the driver company would provide us names of all of their buyers, who for the most part were both older and innovative buyers.

The days of putting a product on the shop shelves or in a mail order catalog and watching the money pour in are long gone. Marketers need to find out more information about their customers and then tie in programs that fit their customers'

> Effective programs are easy to create once marketers understand customers' behavior.

lifestyles. Our survey also showed that motorized golf cart customers played on average 35 to 50 rounds of golf per year. Promotional tie-ins with trips to golf vacation resorts, or even playing cards for the men's locker room, are all additional ways of promoting the product that were obvious once we understood customers' behavior.

The Initial Selection Process

People have hundreds, if not thousands, of purchase options. They respond to that by scanning and categorizing choices in just a few seconds. They then scrutinize their final choices more closely before actually deciding what to do. For example, the truck owners mentioned at the beginning of this chapter saw the phrases "cleans trucks" and "one-day training" and immediately decided the product was one to pass on to their shop foremen. In three seconds the company was out of consideration by the truck owner. The picture wasn't any prettier when the literature went to the shop foreman. Unless he had a severe problem with washing trucks, the literature ended up in the trash can in less than 10 seconds. Nobody would read the literature and no one would remember the product after two days, let alone two weeks.

> Passing the initial selection process can increase sales 100 percent.

Over 90 percent of the marketing literature I see is targeted at the final selection process, when people are deciding what to buy. This is a huge mistake. I've done studies of people attending trade shows and have found that they typically throw away a minimum of 70 percent of the information they pick up seconds after they actually look at it. I've also surveyed engineers who receive a large amount of information for a project. The engineers quickly discard at least 75 percent of the information without even reading it thoroughly. The best final decision literature in the world won't help you if it is sitting in the trash can.

People go into a buying mode on their own for their own reasons. You have to tie into that reason or you won't pass the initial screening process. For example, consumers might buy a lawnmower because all the neighbors have new lawnmowers, their lawnmowers have stopped working, or their lawnmower isn't cutting their lawn fast enough. The first group of consumers might want a deluxe looking lawnmower, the second a simple functioning lawnmower, and the third a lawnmower with a wider cutting blade. In the consumers' initial screening process, they will quickly rule out any product that doesn't meet the reason that they have decided to buy.

This screening process applies to consumers and to all types of businesses. Retail stores may want more impulse items, more upscale items, or want to diversify into a new market. Distributors may want to fill out a line, add products with higher margins, or have an innovative product they can use to take business from competitors. Manufacturers may be focusing on lowering costs, increasing productivity, improving quality, or adding new products. Your prospects' initial screening process depends on their particular needs, goals, and concerns at the time they decide to buy.

In Chapter 3 I discussed how to target the right customer, and Chapter 4 covered how to uncover the customers' goals. Those facts are the information you need to formulate what I call the initial customer response, which is what message will initiate a positive customer response in five seconds. Once you know that you then need to be sure that everything you do, from your literature to your storefront to your initial sales openings, reinforces the correct initial prospect response.

> Marketers need to control the initial customer response.

When the Saturn was originally introduced, the marketers did a terrific job of controlling the initial customer response. Saturn's target customer group was young adults with medium range incomes. That group primarily wanted a sporty looking vehicle that they could feel good about owning. Secondary concerns were price and the ability to, on occasion, transport a group of friends. Saturn's marketers correctly identified the customers' major goal of feeling good about themselves. Their commercials and promotions all tied in with this goal. Saturn's commercials showed young people talking about their car, how they like its sporty look, and how they had purchased the car as a reward to themselves for getting a good job. Only secondarily did Saturn talk about the price or quality of the car.

Saturn's program was great. What did young adults' desire to feel good about themselves have to do with the Saturn car? Very little. But that's not the point. Marketers successfully control a prospect's initial response based on what a customer wants and by not focusing on the product's features and benefits.

Contrast Saturn's program with Oldsmobile's "This is not your father's Oldsmobile" campaign. Both programs were aimed at the same target market. Oldsmobile's campaign didn't work at all because it didn't match up with the goals of its buyers. The campaign identified correctly that young adults wanted a sporty vehicle that wasn't like the sedate Oldsmobile their parents drove. But the campaign appears to assume that young adults are rebellious. Most young adults are not rebellious, and I can't believe the ones that are will have the slightest predisposition to buy an Oldsmobile. Young adult prospects ended up dismissing the Oldsmobile without even checking one out.

Novartis Seeds, Inc. has a target customer group of 7,000 farmers. It sells 180 varieties of seeds and has a 30-page catalog that is expensive. The catalog is also guaranteed to end up on the stack of items to read whenever the farmer gets time, which of course the farmer never has. Novartis' sales have jumped since it stopped sending out the catalog and began sending out a one-page brochure customized for each farmer. The company gets forms filled out by its dealers and reps on each farmer that explains what the farmer plants and what type of land and equipment the farmer owns. Novartis also considers weather patterns, government assistance programs, and marketplace conditions to identify what seeds the customer is most likely to want. This allows the company to identify with farmers' concerns and tailor the brochure to exactly what the farmer is looking for. As an example, when the weather dictates that spring planting is delayed, Novartis sends out a customized brochure on fast growing seeds. The company only mails out the specialized information that matches the customer's exact interest.

Part of the reason Novartis can take this innovative approach is that there is new technology in desktop publishing and laser printers that allows companies to print individual brochures. The other, more important reason Novartis can take this approach is that it realizes its prospects are unlikely to search through their catalog. The proper approach is to catch customers' interest by being directly related to what they perceive is their major goal, and then give the customers only the information they want.

> Marketers need customers to see themselves in their marketing communications.

Back in Chapter 4 you listed your target group's desired motivation. For consumers, the motivation tends to be their desired image, and for businesses the motivation is their main business interest, for example, improving customer service. For businesses the prospect's initial response is straightforward; it is based on the businesses interest. The issue is more difficult with consumers because they have restraints on how well they can achieve their desired image. In the case of the Saturn, the targeted group, young adults with a medium income, has the desired image of someone who is becoming successful. But that image is tempered with the reality that the group still has a modest income level. You don't want to sell this group a cheap sports car. They would reject that image. Instead, Saturn was sold as a first sports car for people who are going to make it big. Saturn only showed young people in their ads, and they never talked about the Saturn being the only car the target audience would ever want to buy.

In the case of Saturn, the target customer group is young adults with a good job. Their desired image is a successful person with a flair for adventure, and the initial response you want your marketing program to generate is "I've made it, and I feel good." Saturn's marketing program worked because it had its target customer group saying, "That's me."

If we go back to the manufacturer of the truck washing equipment mentioned at the beginning of the chapter, its target customer was the owners of trucking companies with more than 40 trailers in its fleet. Their main business interest was getting more customers. The initial response you want to generate is "a clean truck is a sign of quality service." As part of a new campaign, the company started using a cartoon in its literature of a clean, sharply dressed truck driver alongside an unshaven, sloppily dressed driver with the tag line "Who would you hire?" That approach caught the eye of fleet truck owners and they responded by evaluating whether the truck washing equipment could really help their sales.

The same process applies for every type of business. Do teenagers like to come into stores that mirror their interests with decorations, posters, and ambiance that reflects their life style? They definitely do, much more than they like coming into a store that just has clothes on a rack.

> Customers only respond to products that they perceive meet their needs.

Now we need to expand our chart from the end of Chapter 4 to include information on the initial response you want to generate in your customer.

List your target customer group(s): _____

List the predominant personality trait of your chosen sub-segment: _____

_____

List the predominant desired image (consumers) or interest (business): _____

_____

List the initial response you want to generate: _____

_____

You should refer to this chart every time you get ready to prepare a marketing program or new product. It is the cornerstone of every successful program.

Intermediate Selection Process

Buyers quickly pare down their list of potential suppliers in the initial buying process, but they usually go through a secondary or intermediate step that evaluates whether products have the two or three features or benefits that are most important to them. Buyers use this criteria to narrow down their list of potential purchases. From that pared down list people usually make their final selections.

I recently did a brief market study on how people choose the grocery store they shop at. The targeted customer group was middle-income grocery buyers in a suburban area. The desired image of the shoppers, when it came to grocery stores, was "a good provider for their family." The initial response supermarkets want to generate is "good meals with wide selection." The intermediate screening criteria people considered next were location, pricing, and how crowded the stores were. The final decision criteria people used included the quality of the meat department, the store layout, and the ambiance of the store.

People spend very little time on their initial and intermediate selection process, while they will spend a great deal of time on the final decision process. For example, people chose their final two grocery stores quickly but then shopped at their final two choices two or three times before actually deciding at which grocery store they would do most of their shopping.

Marketers need to be focused on the first two steps of the customer's decision process because information for those two steps needs to be communicated quickly. The details people need to make their final decision don't need to be communicated quickly as the people are willing to spend time on that phase of the decision process. One of the difficult parts of the marketing process is that people don't want to talk to salespeople until they reach the final phase of their decision process. Up until then people prefer to left alone. This preliminary buying process is really proven out by trade show leads. Most companies will find after trade shows that their sales force will consider 70 to 90 percent of the leads to be just lookers and not buyers. In reality,

> Marketers have to be alert to steer their customers through the initial and intermediate steps of the buying process.

50 to 70 percent of the attendees at a trade show typically buy within two years. The discrepancy is that people often are at trade shows in the preliminary phase of their buying process and they don't want to be hounded by a salesperson. But that doesn't mean they are not future buyers. I've found that most companies can increase sales 20 to 40 percent by sending out periodic mailings to literature response and trade show prospects. That strategy keeps your name in front of the customer so that they will call you when they are ready to buy.

Let me go back to the Saturn example. Young adults wanted a sporty car that said they had arrived. The secondary concerns, which are really part of the intermediate screening process, were price, ability to carry four people, and a friendly dealership. Once at the dealer the final process involved looking at everything in more detail, how comfortable the seats are, the product's price/value relationship, dealer service, quality of the construction, and so on. Those are questions customers like to talk to salespeople about, but only after they've selected the Saturn as one of their final choices.

Discovering Initial and Preliminary Screening Criteria

Most market research focuses on the customers final decision-making process. That data typically isn't much help in determining how people make their preliminary product or service choices. I follow a simple procedure when I want to find out about people's decision process.

$100 →

1. Find sales leads that are about one to two years old. These can be from trade shows, literature requests, or any other source.
2. Call the people and ask them if they have purchased the product. Continue asking questions even if they haven't bought yet. They still have started the buying process and their answers will be helpful.
3. Ask which products they were first interested in. Once they mention their selections, ask them why. Their answers here will let you know their initial decision process.
4. Ask if they eliminated any possibilities of those first products. Their answers here will give you a better understanding of their intermediate decision process.

5. Finally, ask what products they investigated fully and why. Again, this question is geared at customers' intermediate decision process. Don't be surprised if half or more of the people only choose one product to investigate closely. That is not uncommon, and it explains why understanding the customers' buying process is so important.

The Final Decision Process

The conventional marketing wisdom is that the warm fuzzy information that gets you into the final decision process typically won't close the sale. People claim that what the Internet has proven conclusively is that people want to feel like they are in control of the buying process, and they want to have as much information as possible about the product. As an example, people point to companies like Muller Tire Company in Cleveland that grew in seven years from $2 million to $30 million in annual sales. Mueller did this by simply retraining its salespeople so they could be consultants and jazzed up their stores with an array of interactive informational devices to aid people's buying decision.

I don't buy into conventional thinking at all. Why would marketers say on one hand that people are so busy they can't even read an ad, and then turn around and say that people want to pour through reams of information to decide on what they want to buy? All people want when they finally buy is confidence that they are making the right choice. Mueller's change worked very well for another reason. Tire stores have all types of products. Mueller's salespeople would just talk to the people, see what they wanted, and then answer any questions. This is absolutely the right way to build people's confidence. For example, if you have already decided to buy a premium tire for better road traction, all you want to know is that is a good choice. You don't want a fast talking salesperson to talk you into something different.

Mueller Tire's tactics point out that effective marketers help the final decision process by having a conversation and not a monologue with the customer. The core of infiltration marketing is to become one with the customer so he can have confidence in you. Nothing gives people more confidence than other people agreeing with them. I've done some marketing studies in electronic departments of high-end

> Marketing should be a conversation and not a monologue.

department stores. The best closing line I've ever heard is, "That's a very good choice. I think that product meets all the needs of your situation." This line came after a conversation between the salesperson and the customer that followed this format:

1. What are you looking for today? Customer answers.
2. What are the main features you are looking for? Customer answers.
3. Are there any products that you are leaning towards? Customer answers. Fifty to 75 percent of the time the customer was leaning towards one product choice.
4. If the customer has a choice, 90 percent of the time the salesperson answered, "That's a very good choice." And he closed the sale.

If the salesperson thought the product was way off from the customer's needs, he said, "That's a very good choice for" and then the salesperson would describe the type of consumer that product was a perfect fit for. For example, for a cellular phone the salesperson might say, "That's a perfect choice for someone who stays in the city." Then the sales person makes a comment followed by question. For our cellular phone example he might say, "But I'm not sure it would be perfect for someone who travels a great deal in the country. Is that important to you?" If the customer said no it's not important, the salesperson sold the phone. If the customer agreed it was important, the salesperson would say, "Can I show you a similar phone that will work well out of the city?" That salesperson built confidence, was friendly, and sold lots of product.

I once worked with a fireplace manufacturer whose product had tons of technical features. The manufacturer claimed his product was one of the five best on the market. Do you know how many people wanted to learn about those technical features? Very few. People want a fireplace that works. They want confidence that everything will turn out OK. All I did was tell the manufacturer to stop selling features. Instead, all he had to do was have the salesperson come out after the fireplace was installed and he or she would demonstrate how to use the fireplace properly. The manufacturer wasn't building confidence when he sold features. He was building confusion, and confused people never buy. All we did was switch to a confidence building sales strategy for the final buying decision.

The Mueller Tire Co. strategy called for salespeople to be consultants. This can be a very dangerous concept if Mueller wants its salespeople to tell its customers what to buy. That's not actually what people want. They rebel against salespeople telling them what to do. They want a consultant to tell them they are making the right choice.

> People need to have confidence they are making the right choice before they buy.

This strategy is just as true for business-to-business and professional purchases as it is for consumer purchases. One of the reason companies that are industry leaders stay on top is that they are the safe, confident choice. Small companies need to recognize this and adjust. A small manufacturer of automated office equipment was completely unable to sell its equipment against Pitney Bowes. The company kept driving at its better features and benefits and its lower price. But people kept buying Pitney Bowes. Why? Because they had confidence in Pitney Bowes. The company thought one of its main selling points was that it was so simple the customer could install the product himself. What the company needed to do instead was install the product, give a day's training, and come back every other week for six months to guarantee the product would perform. Unfortunately, the company never did understand the customer's buying process and went out of business.

I don't mean to downplay the importance of features and benefits because they do play a part in people's intermediate decision process, and sometimes they become a key factor in deciding between two final product choices. But their importance is overplayed. The key point to remember is that you can't engage customers effectively when you are talking

> Concentrate on your buyer's goals and not on your features and benefits.

about something they don't want to hear. That's a monologue. A conversation happens when you are talking together about something customers want to know. You need to gear you efforts to the customer's buying process and not get caught up in you own product or service.

In 1996 Hewlett Packard decided that small businesses were the ideal target customer for its $400 to $1,000 printers. The initial response the customer needed to have was "It's going to work." Hewlett Packard has a good name but couldn't generate this response on its own. Companies worried about how to hook up the computer printers—and sometimes servers, routers, and modems—and get everything to work. So Hewlett Packard chose to sell its products through value added resellers (VARs). These resellers coordinate an entire system for the customer and are responsible for making everything work. Businesses also have a secondary concern that they use in an intermediate buying choice. That concern is whether the customer is buying the right printer for its needs. Hewlett Packard addresses this concern by offering a range of printers for every application. Finally, Hewlett Packard built confidence by having its products available through many VARs and by having an established reputation as a high-quality manufacturer.

Using a distribution channel gave Hewlett Packard another customer, the distribution channel. Hewlett Packard wanted to create the initial response in the VARs of "I can give good service with this product." Hewlett Packard provided a series of tools to make this happen, including specialized training, financial incentives, and access to technical information. After the VAR knows its customers will be happy, its secondary concern is "Can I make money?" Hewlett Packard offered its distribution network a wide variety of marketing aids and went so far as to print direct-mail pieces with reseller's name and logo on them, and Hewlett Packard was even willing to mail out literature kits for VARs. Hewlett Packard closed the deal because of the confidence it generated by being very thorough with every aspect of its offer and through its well-known brand name.

What about all those information hounds that want to know everything? They can go on Hewlett Packard's small business Web site and find out anything that they want to know. But Hewlett Packard knows what sells in this market: not detailed information, but guaranteed performance. Keep your focus on what the customer really wants, which rarely is simply a product's features and benefits. Customers want to meet their goals, and you need to communicate in just a few seconds that your product is just what they are looking for.

> Your job is to convince buyers that you have exactly what they are looking for.

CHAPTER EIGHT

MATCHING YOUR EFFORTS WITH PROSPECTS' BUYING ACTIVITIES

Most marketers and salespeople worry about customers when they are ready to buy. This overlooks entirely a process people go through before actually buying a product. As the last chapter pointed out, waiting until people buy is waiting too long. As an example, people start the buying process for refrigerators by looking at ones that other people have, looking at various models in a few stores, looking at kitchen remodeling projects, or by looking at different models at a home show. Then after a year or so of scouting things out, the person buys the product. The fact is that customers decide either what to buy or narrow their choices long before they actually make a purchase.

What happens when you go into an appliance store and tell the clerk you are just looking? They leave you alone and look for someone who is going to buy today. I can guarantee you that more than 50 percent of the people who are just looking at refrigerators are going to buy one in the next two years. And the store clerk just let the person walk out. On what activities do most appliance stores concentrate their marketing efforts? On frequent sales, advertising, and direct mail? The "lookers," the key to infiltration marketers, are simply ignored.

I have found that people who are "just looking" are in the preliminary stages of a buying decision. The key is to get these people's names and then get involved in their buying process. What's involved in buying a refrigerator? Color matches, a special space-age look, a great icemaker, easy access for an elderly person, a big freezer, extra freezer shelves, a low price, high efficiency, and probably several other factors.

The company who wins the sale is often the company that first answered a customer's key concern.

The marketing secret for the new age is not to wait till someone is ready to buy to start marketing but to start your efforts the minute a person starts the buying process. People who walk into an appliance store need many more service options than a salesperson asking if they need help. The store could offer a whole series of services to get customers involved early in their buying process. These services could include color coordination by an interior designer, a form people fill out about their refrigerator needs that a computer analyzes and then offers purchase recommendations, classes on cooking, proper temperature control for storing food, or ripening store-bought fruit. The store that features what the customer wants is a pro at infiltration marketing and will succeed.

> Marketing has to start having an impact when customers start their buying process.

$1,999 ➤

Funimals, as in fun with animals, is a new retail chain of pet stores that's totally different than any other store I've seen. The store has nine different animal cartoon characters that teach children the values of tolerance, kindness, and sharing with their pets. Besides a learning center, the store has animal performers, hamster races, and store tours for kids to learn all about different pets. The store encourages people to bring their pets into the store to make sure they are properly groomed and cared for, and the store has all its pets, including reptiles, birds, and fish, at eye level so children can see and learn about them.

$2,000+ ➤

Most people don't buy on their first visit. But that is not the point. They come and turn into loyal customers. Funimals has been growing more than 20 percent per year and is going to open nine new stores between 1999 and 2002. The entire entertailing concept works because it invites people to come for the fun and is non-threatening, which means that no salesperson is hounding them, and then they just stay and buy.

This principle also applies to business-to-business marketers. I once worked with a company making fasteners. Hundreds of companies make and sell fasteners, and business is very hard to acquire from another supplier. One question engineers have is what grade of fasteners to buy: Grade 2, 5, or 8. Each grade has different characteristics depending on the fastener stress created by the application. The company supplied prospects with a computer disk that helped them decide what grade of fastener to select and also offered them other options that might work better in their application. This put the company at the center of the engineer's initial analysis of what type of fastener to use. Often, but not always, the engineers who used the company's disc ended up specifying its product. ◄— **$2,000+**

Infiltration marketers need to adjust their focus to the preliminary stages of a buying decision and place their marketing messages when customers' buying activity occurs. This chapter explains how marketers can effectively communicate with customers during the initial, intermediate, and final decision process.

> Content before commerce is the quick way to increase sales.

The Initial Process

A few years back I called on a manufacturing plant after our product was knocked off the budget priority list. The reason we lost the sale was that somehow the manufacturing manager had gotten fed up with the final assembly equipment and decided it had to be replaced. Why? Well the equipment had been breaking down for years on a semi-regular basis, and the manufacturing manager finally decided that he couldn't take another breakdown. Marketers make a big mistake when they think that people make all types of rational decisions when deciding to start buying. That is almost never the case. People have a sequence of events that leads them to decide to buy something. This is true for virtually all purchases. My wife, for reasons I've never understood, comes to the decision we need to redecorate the house. Small business owners go years with a poor marketing program before they suddenly decide the time has come to energize their marketing approach. Mothers will stay loyal to the same brand of detergent for 10 years and then, without noticeable reason, are suddenly ready to change brands.

Why do people decide either to buy something or make a change in their buying behavior? I'm not sure, and I don't believe anyone really knows. Sometimes there are clear-cut reasons for a purchase, such as your car breaks down, a manufacturing plant needs to add capacity, or an office needs to increase its computer networking capacity. But people have a remarkable capacity to make do with what they have, until something flips their switch and they move into a buying mode.

> There is no way you can predict when someone will start his or her buying process.

The important point for the infiltration marketer is that, for the most part, you have no idea when people are going to switch into a buying mode. So you need to do two things: have your name in many key places, and have as many ways as possible to discover customers who enter the buying mode.

I worked on a product that improved the life of metal cutting tools used by manufacturers. The tools represent anywhere from 10 to 25 percent of the production cost of certain metal parts. Our product saved anywhere from 5 to 20 percent of a company's tool budget, which meant savings of anywhere from $10,000 to $200,000 per year depending on the size of the prospect companies. This sounds like an easy sale, but it was unbelievably difficult. People wouldn't buy the product unless they had already determined on their own that cutting tool costs was a high priority. Without that internal stimulus, the companies wouldn't even try our process out.

One reason I like infiltration marketing is that it lets you think in a different way that offers insights that create cost-effective marketing tactics. When you decide how to keep your name in front of your prospects you only need to consider the target customer group and what initial response you want to create. Going back to the Saturn example in Chapter 7, the target group was young adults with good jobs, and the initial response was "I feel good about myself." Then you just need to make a presence in places where young adults go to feel good about themselves. Bars, nightclubs, clothing stores, music tours, and vacation destinations like Club Med are all areas where Saturn could place its marketing messages.

The music industry does an excellent job looking for its audience in new ways. Semisonic is an alternative music group who recorded the hit record "Closing Time." Its bass player is an expert fly-fisherman, and the bands recording company (label) used that fact to get the bass player interviewed in *Men's Journal*, *Hooked on the Outdoors*, and a variety of other outdoor magazines. Rapster Master P's label gave his band a big push by running ads on *South Park*, a trendy cable TV show. The R&B group Melky Sedeck features a sharply dressed couple as singers, and their record company pitches the group to fashion magazines like *Vanity Fair* and *Cosmo*. The music industry also hands out sampler albums at skateboard events and gives review copies to virtually any Internet music reviewer. Another

$100 →

major strategy used is to place songs on movie soundtracks that record companies feel will be popular with music buyers.

I recommend people prepare a marketing strategy based on how potential customers will see, read, and hear about you. Many small business owners have told me that they want to spend their money on "true" sales prospects. The trouble with waiting for people to be sales prospects is that most potential buyers in the market will have already dismissed your product or service from their selection process. When marketers let this happen they are left with a small pool of prospects. You want to work first to engage the largest pool of prospects you can, as that will end up giving you the best profits and highest sales levels. I've listed below some of the options you might use for each category.

> Your prospects need to see, read, and hear about you.

Prospects can see you:

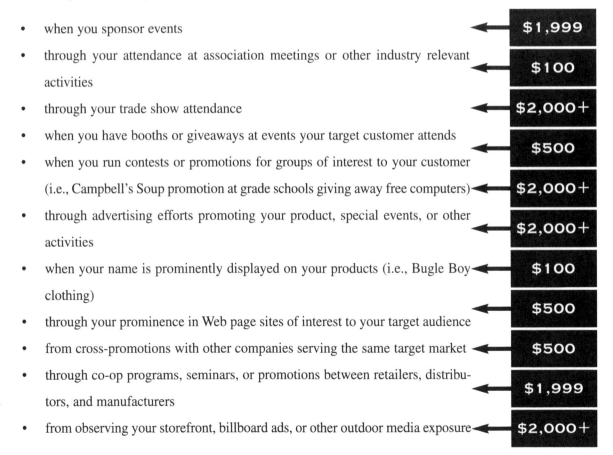

- when you sponsor events — $1,999
- through your attendance at association meetings or other industry relevant activities — $100
- through your trade show attendance — $2,000+
- when you have booths or giveaways at events your target customer attends — $500
- when you run contests or promotions for groups of interest to your customer (i.e., Campbell's Soup promotion at grade schools giving away free computers) — $2,000+
- through advertising efforts promoting your product, special events, or other activities — $2,000+
- when your name is prominently displayed on your products (i.e., Bugle Boy clothing) — $100
- through your prominence in Web page sites of interest to your target audience — $500
- from cross-promotions with other companies serving the same target market — $500
- through co-op programs, seminars, or promotions between retailers, distributors, and manufacturers — $1,999
- from observing your storefront, billboard ads, or other outdoor media exposure — $2,000+

Prospects can hear about you:

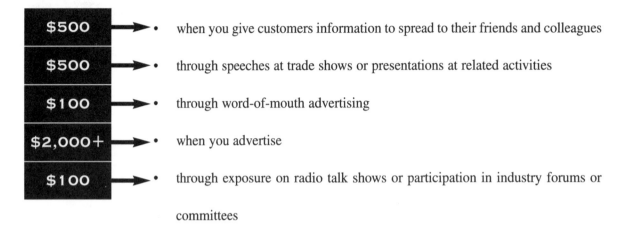

- **$500** — when you give customers information to spread to their friends and colleagues
- **$500** — through speeches at trade shows or presentations at related activities
- **$100** — through word-of-mouth advertising
- **$2,000+** — when you advertise
- **$100** — through exposure on radio talk shows or participation in industry forums or committees

Prospects can read about you:

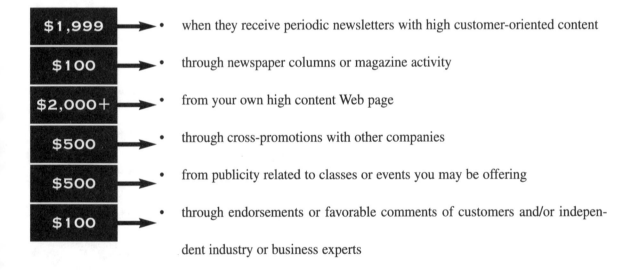

- **$1,999** — when they receive periodic newsletters with high customer-oriented content
- **$100** — through newspaper columns or magazine activity
- **$2,000+** — from your own high content Web page
- **$500** — through cross-promotions with other companies
- **$500** — from publicity related to classes or events you may be offering
- **$100** — through endorsements or favorable comments of customers and/or independent industry or business experts

CROSS-PROMOTIONS

I've mentioned cross-promotions or strategic alliances previously in the book. Many small businesses don't have the promotional power or are just too small to effectively keep themselves in front of customers. Then cross-promotions become by far the most effective way to increase your number of prospects. That's because people are not always systematic about how they move forward with the purchase process. If my wife wants to redecorate, for example, she might start at a furniture store, a wallpaper store, looking at draperies at J.C. Penny's, going to a home show, or talking to an interior decorator. There is no way to predict what she will do first. The result is that any one company only gets the initial call from a small percentage of the prospects. If you want to increase sales without a cross-promotion you'll need to spend more money to significantly increase your market exposure. It makes much more sense to pool your leads with other companies. Sharing leads won't cost you anything.

> Cross-promotions are the most effective way for small companies to expand customer awareness.

Cross-promotions are used in almost every market. MCI offers frequent flyer coupons from major airlines to larger customers. Almost every neighborhood has small service providers like dry cleaners, shoe repair shops, and tailors offering discounts to each other's stores. Gift stores, restaurants, orchestras, and theatres also routinely run cross-promotions because they work, they don't cost very much, and they enhance the image of all the participating companies.

Primo's, a chain of coffee stores in the San Francisco area, teams up with Sweet Charlotte's, a local candy maker, with several stores. Primo's sells Sweet Charlotte's candy and gives away free samples. The Sweet Charlotte shop gives customers coupons for espresso, as well as sells coffee beans in bulk. The promotion works well because both companies are known for having high-quality products, and the two companies are even considering opening a joint store.

Hedrick Co. is a small financial planning consulting agency. It teams up with six other small business consultants to produce a joint newsletter. Combining with the other companies gives the newsletter high content and varied expertise that it otherwise just wouldn't have. The newsletter is mailed to clients of all six companies, which creates a win-win situation for everyone involved. An additional plus is that the coordinated effort increases the credibility of all six companies.

Maxis is a software company with a line of children-oriented software. It teamed up with Mother's Cake and Company to do a cross-promotion that gave free software to schools. The cookie company put a Maxis coupon on its packages and Maxis advertised the joint promotion

> Cross-promotions increase your market exposure while increasing your credibility.

with a point-of-purchase display at computer stores. Sales increased 13 percent during what was a very low-cost program.

Intermediate Buying Process

People actually check products out during the intermediate process. Not actually a thorough evaluation, but they look at products based on what's important to them to make sure the product or service meets their needs. As an example, if someone

> A database marketing program can increase sales 25 percent or more.

is going to buy a copier, they may initially look for a model with high dependability that's very fast. When they go into the intermediate phase they know they need seven or eight other features, such as the ability to print on odd size papers, reduce extra large documents, copy onto transparencies, sort and staple copies, and print up to 75 copies at a time.

During this stage marketers need to make information available to customers in a friendly, easy to understand, high content format. Since customers have a variety of different criteria, it's important for marketers to customize communications to each customer. You can easily create communications targeted at just one customer with database marketing, which is a marketing tactic that uses a computerized database of information on customers. Once marketers have a database with customer information, they can send a customer communications about its product and company that appeals to the specific interests of the customer. I've found that using even a simple database program with a series of programmed messages consistently increases sales a minimum of 25 percent.

$500

1. Select a database or contact management system to put on your computer. Some of the software I've found that works well includes ACT, which is my favorite system for small companies, Fox Base/Fox Pro, and Filemaker Pro. There are many other systems that also work well. The only system I've tried and didn't like was Microsoft Access.
2. List the major categories of concerns customers may have and try to group them into sales groups. What you are trying to accomplish here is establish different customer types and collate the literature that is right for them. For example, a manufacturer of pipe couplings might break customers down by application, which includes mining, construction,

drainage, and sludge transfer applications. A database program will also **$500** allow you to select customer groups by more than one criteria. For example, our pipe supplier might have customers segmented by both application and whether prospects leave pipes in place for extended times or instead reconfigure their pipes at least once a week. The piping manu- facturer would send mining companies who move pipes every week newsletters, press releases, and other information that is tailored for them.

3. Establish a coding system in your database so you can easily identify what **$100** group a prospect belongs to. This is easily done with most database or contact management software.

4. Establish a mechanism for having prospects indicate their interest. I per- sonally like to offer prospects a selection of stories, articles, or other infor- mation in newsletters or other mailings. The customer just has to check off what articles they want. Their choices help you determine what group the **$500** prospect belongs to. Another tactic that you can use is to offer seminars or classes and ask what type of class the prospect would like information on.

5. Select information that is tailored for each type of prospect. It might take the prospect twelve to twenty-four months to buy so you need to have information for three or four mailings. These mailings don't have to offer information exclusively from you. You can use reprints from interesting magazine articles or other information the customer wants. **$500**

6. Periodically mail to prospects newsletters or other information that is tai- lored to their need.

You can also help customers find the information they desire by providing an easy to search Web page or a CD that customers can use. Your Web page should contain as much information as possible. To make the page effective you should have an easy to use directory, or better yet, a search feature

> Learn more about your customers so you can send them information they want to read.

where people can just enter in the word or phrase. Fast searching capabilities are essential because customers are only interested in certain items and they don't want to spend much time locating them. I've also found that encouraging questions on your Web page is a big help to customers in the intermediate buying process. Let cus- tomers e-mail you a question, then you can e-mail the answer back, providing only the exact information that the customer wants.

Pillsbury's and Green Giant's (which is owned by Pillsbury) Web sites are great examples of how to handle the intermediate sales process. Pillsbury started with cooking tips for its products so busy moms and dads could prepare quick, nutritious meals. But Pillsbury quickly found that customers like information related to the time of the year. For instance, people want tips on cooking appetizers during the months of November and December when people do a lot of entertaining. Pillsbury also found that some people like spicy food, while others like pasta, and so on. Once Pillsbury understood how important time sensitive tips were to their customers, it even started signing up customers to a variety of electronic newsletters based on their interest. Pillsbury has tips for planners who prepare cookies three weeks before Christmas, and tips for last minute people who start preparing cookies on Christmas Eve. The result is Pillsbury learns about its customer while selling to them. Pillsbury's goal is to learn more about each customer in order to do a better job of serving them in the future.

$200 ➙

> The Internet is effective at providing information to prospects you've already located.

Your goal in the intermediate step is to give customers as much help as possible to answer the specific questions they have before deciding to buy. Make your information easily available, and easy-to-search for specific requests. I personally have found this is a very cost-effective use of the Internet. Put your Web page address on every piece of literature you send out. People will go there when they have questions.

The Final Decision Process

The final decision revolves around prospects developing confidence that they are making a good choice. Testimonials, money-back guarantees, or successful past experiences are some of the time honored ways companies have built up customer confidence in their product or service. A strong database marketing program is a more recent tactic for building customer loyalty by repeatedly and consistently communicating with target customers. Large companies have started adding one other tactic to their arsenal—developing a branding strategy. Small companies can also develop a branding strategy that will build customer confidence.

Branding refers to establishing in the minds of customers a clear-cut, enduring, distinct impression of your company. You want your customers to have a clear idea of what your company stands for, values, and will provide to them. Creating a memorable, indelible impression does just that. An example of good branding strategy is Lands' End's. At one time they just sold a line of outdoors clothes. Now they offer safaris, khakis, and other services that strengthen the consumer's image of Lands' End as a leading outdoors retailer. Adding entertailing elements to your store, creating events, and sponsoring celebrities are all various ways companies improve their branded image. Fortunately for small companies, they have a variety of inexpensive ways to create a brand image.

> Branding builds a clear cut, indelible impression in your prospect's mind.

Between the Bread is a catering company in New York City. The company wanted to develop an image as a high-quality caterer with innovative menu choices that were attractively presented. The company started with a symbol people wouldn't forget—they delivered every dinner in a logo-marked white box tied with color ribbons. They keep the ribbon motif on their menus; that helps people remember the caterer.

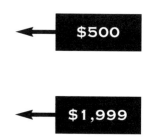

The Nicholson-Hardie Nursery wanted to fashion itself into an upscale destination store. The nursery stocked top-of-the-line tools, carried rare and expensive plants, and sold under its own name a topsoil and potting soil that is friendly to plants in its North Texas location.

A branding strategy isn't that difficult to execute, provided you pay attention to it every day. The steps to a good brand are:

1. Decide what image you want to have. Don't think this step is so obvious. Over half the small business owners I talk to don't know what image they want. Be sure your image matches the interest of your target customer and helps create the initial response you want your customers to have. (See Chapter 6.)
2. Create something distinctive that establishes that image. Between the Bread's ribbon is a great example of a simple, memorable symbol that drives the company's brand into the customer's mind. Pringles's tube for potato chips was another great branding tactic. You can use your company

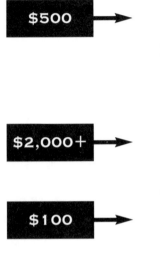

$500 ⟶

name, look, or logo as a vehicle to create a symbol people will remember about your company.

3. Choose three or four different service or product enhancements that strengthen your branded image. Between the Bread could have had business specials or sweetheart dinners to improve their image as someone who provides individual attention. The Nicholson-Hardie Nursery had special tools, plants, and its own custom potting soil to help create its brand. Pringles had a special shaped chip and even put out a small size can for lunch to emphasize the product was a great snack.

$2,000+ ⟶

4. Verify that everything your company does shows your key symbol and established look and reinforces the image you want to project. Then work hard to keep that same image working for you so your customers will remember you.

$100 ⟶

> Branding builds consistency, which builds confidence.

Tandem Computer has long been known as a producer of a top quality server for large banks' computer networking needs. But customers didn't accept some of Tandem's newer capabilities including data warehousing and Internet transaction processing. Tandem wanted to develop a branded image that would help it sell more products in these new markets. Tandem decided that the key to its branding efforts was to focus on its history of business critical transactions. This proven history was just as important to Tandem's new prospects as it was to customers of its standard product line. Once that decision was reached, Tandem concentrated its marketing efforts on its past success in business critical applications. Tandem built that brand image with advertising, collateral materials, and fail-safe product features and benefits.

Consistency on your part builds confidence in customers that you need to close the sale. All of the tactics in this chapter—going into the customer's world, building a relationship through database marketing, and developing a brand image—all work together to build customer confidence. Engaging the customer with the tactics discussed in this section puts you in contact with the greatest number of possible prospects and helps you convert as many of them as possible to customers. You can complete all of these steps for just a small amount of money. This is why infiltration marketing will soon become the only way small companies will be able to thrive in today's competitive market.

SECTION THREE

Arousing the Interest of Prospects

Chapter Nine:
FINDING OUT WHAT CUSTOMERS
WANT BUT AREN'T GETTING

Chapter Ten:
COMMUNICATING YOUR
MESSAGE IN A HURRY

Chapter Eleven:
PRODUCING AN IMPACT

FINDING OUT WHAT CUSTOMERS WANT BUT AREN'T GETTING

Typically companies offer products, retail concepts, or services that are similar to ones already out on the market. Companies might tweak the concepts occasionally, but rarely do they make significant changes. Then suddenly someone comes out and with a whole new concept that customers turn into a "red hot product." The whole Dummies series of books is a great example of what can happen with a breakthrough concept. Before the Dummies books, computer books were for computer nerds who wanted to know every detail of a computer's operations. That's not what the general public wants. They just want to know enough to use a computer for a specific task. That's what the Dummies books provided, and now they sell more than $1 billion worth of books per year.

Creating a breakthrough product doesn't need to be complicated or expensive. It is something small companies successfully do all the time. One of the reason companies don't create the innovative products they should is that they tend to focus on the routine marketing tasks. Marketers can almost always find new innovations if they follow a few simple steps that reveal what customers are really after.

1. Discover customers' objectives for purchasing a product. Customers buy to meet their own objectives. The *DOS for Dummies* publishers realized the main market for computer books were people who didn't understand computers and only wanted to know enough to get by. The book gave clear, easy-to-understand instruction. The book is designed so that new users,

when stumped on what to do next, can just check out a few references to find the answers they need.

Another example is woodworking equipment that has special features for making kitchen cabinets. The company's marketers will probably focus their marketing on how to make a better kitchen cabinet. The customer's real objective is to have a great looking kitchen. The company will generate more business when they add features that can do special shelving for over sinks, pantry organizers, plant holders, or organizing kitchen racks.

> New concepts can become a "red hot product" when they give customers exactly what they want.

2. Rank features and benefits and how happy people are with each. This is a traditional tactic that typically isn't used as often as it should be. Marketers often understand the priority of the features and benefits when a product is introduced, but then they don't continue to follow how customers change their views from year to year. You can use simple questionnaires that ask potential customers to rank, by likelihood of purchase and perceived value, a variety of products or services available in the market. Then ask them why they ranked one choice first and another choice last.

> The reasons people rank a product first or last provide key insight into what customers really want.

I've found that the reasons people rank a product first or last give you real insight into what the market wants. For example, an all-wheel drive mountain bike has many features including the durability of the component parts, the efficiency of the drive mechanism, how easy the all-wheel drive feature is to repair, the ratio of the front wheel to rear wheel (which dictates how long front-wheel drive waits before kicking in), and the aesthetic look of the product. Bike riders rated durability, ease of repair, and performance as high priorities. But riders listed bikes as their first and last choice primarily by how neatly the all-wheel drive features were added on to the bike. Christiani All Wheel Mountain Bikes was recently introduced at a major bike show. It drew huge crowds and rave reviews because the all-wheel drive mechanism was hidden inside the bike's tubing.

3. Look for underserved customers. Some products have buyers who are dissatisfied with the products or features on the market. You might be able to come out with some great new products if you can find and solve the

problem that makes some users unhappy. Typically those features are ones that need to be improved. A few years ago I was listening to a radio talk show that had on Tom Kelly, the manager of the Twins, as a guest. Tom took about three calls from women who wanted to know how the Twins could get the grass stains out of their uniforms. The mothers wanted to know because they couldn't get grass stains out of their children's clothes. I don't know who else was listening, but a year or two later consumer product companies released stain sticks and pre-wash liquid stain removers to get out stubborn stains during washing.

4. Find needs that customers aren't aware of. I've uncovered some of the best product opportunities by just following customers around for a day as they are using your product or evaluating your service. Then simply ask them why they do certain things, or what they'd like a service person to do differently. This technique can uncover product deficiencies that people have learned to accept. I've introduced products that have obtained a 50 percent market share after only six months because of new features I've discovered with this technique.

> Marketers hit a hot button when they find problems that customers have learned to live with.

When I do seminars I like to ask people how many of them are satisfied with their hot water systems in their homes. Everyone always says yes. Then I ask what they do before they get in the shower. The answer is they hold their hand in to feel the water's temperature. Why do they take that step? To be sure they don't get burned. Even more amusing are the different steps people take when someone else in the house flushes the toilet while they are showering. Nobody likes their hot water system after I ask only two or three simple questions. Examples like this abound for every target market group. You just need to get out and find them.

In the previous section of the book we discussed how to engage customers by appealing to their goals and following their buying process. This section covers how to use that engagement to create a strong link with the customer by arousing his or her interest. You do that by giving customers something they want and can't get anywhere else, or by giving them exactly what they want. This chapter discusses the four steps you can use to find a way to make your product or service the ideal customer choice.

Understanding Your Customers' Primary Buying Criteria

Ford initially marked the Pinto as carefree, small, and romantic. The product wasn't selling well and Ford prepared a list of questions for Pinto buyers regarding the type of car they were looking for. Ford found that Pinto buyers responded positively to statements like "I wish I could depend on my car more" and "I am more practical in car selection." They responded negatively to statements like "The kind of car you have is important to how people see you." Ford changed its campaign to appeal to the more practical aspects of their customers and the Pinto sold well.*

Marketers constantly strive to add value for the customer. But as the Ford example points out, you only add value when you give the customer something they want. In Chapter 7 you completed this chart for your client's initial screening process.

List your target customer group(s): _____

List the predominant personality trait: _____

List the predominant desired image (consumers) or interest (business):

_____

List the initial response you want to generate: _____

> Marketers only add value when they meet customers' objectives.

This chart tells you what you need to do to get your client to notice your product or service and investigate it further. In the previous chapter we discussed the Saturn car, whose target customer group is young adults with a good job. Their desired

---

* Source: *Beyond Mind Games*, by Rebecca Piirto, American Demographics Books, Ithaca, NY, 1991, page 27.

image is a successful person with a flair for adventure, and the initial response Saturn wants its marketing program to generate is "I've made it, and I feel good."

Saturn's program got people in the door to evaluate its product. But then the ideal product, store, or service will get the customer to say, "This is exactly what I want." Marketers want to have features, benefits, or other special services so your company survives the intermediate buying process. Your program will increase sales dramatically when those special features tie right into the customers' goals or objectives. Some of the features that customers could feel are important when evaluating the Saturn in the intermediate buying process are:

1. Comfort—comfortable for both the driver and the passengers.
2. Music system—having the option of both a CD music system and additional speakers.
3. Economy—good fuel mileage and low maintenance costs or initial price and resale value can both be considerations.
4. Performance—how fast the car goes and how well it handles the road.
5. Appearance—both the exterior and the interior appearance as well as the number of color options.
6. Brand identity—prospects may be predisposed to either buy or not buy a General Motors car.

Saturn's marketers can't provide features to meet the objectives of every possible customer and still keep a reasonable price. At the same time, Saturn probably has to provide a minimum level of customer satisfaction for each feature or the car simply won't sell. The extra money— the special focus on one or two customer objectives—has to be spent on meeting the customer objectives that matter most.

> Marketers need to be selective in choosing the focus of their marketing programs.

Marketers use two tactics to discover what objectives are most important to their target customer group. One is to ask prospects that recently bought a car to list the cars they actually considered buying. Then you ask the prospects why they had decided that any of those two or three cars would be a wise choice. People will tell you only the one or two things that really matter. For example, companies shopping for a piece of contact management software will have just one, or at most two, reasons that they used to select their final software choices. Some small business prospects might want a system that is flexible and can be modified by each salesperson for his or her needs. Larger companies might want a software system that is the same for each salesperson and that can deliver information to salespeople by modem on current inventory levels, shipping dates, and annual sales by customer. These simple objectives, a system that can be customized for a small number of users, or a system that can scan and deliver key factory information, are the ones marketers need to focus on. I have found that you can get a reasonable understanding of your customers' main buying objectives by interviewing 20 to 30 customers. Small companies should go through the process of interviewing customers every year to determine the key objectives they focus on for their final selection.

The other tactic is to give people a questionnaire with statements similar to the ones Ford asked prospects about the Pinto. Ask people to rate statements 1, 2, or 3: 1 being important, 2 somewhat important, and 3 not important. Some statements might be:

- A high quality music system is: _____ rate the feature 1, 2, or 3.
- High miles per gallon is: _____ rate the feature 1, 2, or 3.
- Number of color options is: _____ rate the feature 1, 2, or 3.

I don't like this approach as well as the first because the data can be somewhat confusing. People might list five statements as important, when in fact one or two criteria will dominate their decision. This method calls for a much larger group of responses and is not as flexible for small companies.

Strata 2000 is a new restaurant concept being introduced by Golden Corral, a grill buffet, low-end steak house. The marketing group at Golden Corral found out that customers felt fresh food tastes better, and they want to go to restaurants where they could be confident that the food was fresh. Golden Corral first realized the importance of this feature with the success of their Brass Bell Bakery kiosk. This was a fully functioning cooking area inside Golden Corral's restaurants. Customer's could see the mixing, rolling, and cutting of dough and smell the fresh aroma of bread coming out of the oven. The Strata concept takes this a step further and showcases to customers food preparation from unprepared produce and meat to the final product.

Prior to the Strata concept, traditional buffet-type restaurants have been stuck in a routine of stainless steel tubs and round plastic crocks. People wondered about just how fresh the food was. Some customers even believed the buffets used the freezer-to-fryer cooking concept. With the Strata concept, customers know that the food is cooked fresh because they see it happening. A nice additional bonus for customers is that there is a lot more color and action in the restaurant and the whole look jumps right out at the customers. The results have been so spectacular that Golden Corral is in the process of converting its entire 454-unit chain to the new concept.

> Golden Corral's restaurant redesign focused on just one customer objective—fresh food.

RANK FEATURES AND BENEFITS

Features and benefits play an important role in the customers' decision-making process. Customers often have features they must have. For example, a young mother might have as a key feature for a car the ease of putting a baby in the back seat. Sometimes people aren't always aware of the features they need until they don't have them. This step is really just a safety valve to ensure you don't leave out or downplay an important feature. Figure 9-1 contains a sample questionnaire for a new phone system.

Figure 9.1

MARKET SURVEY—NEW PHONE SYSTEM

Feature	Yes	Somewhat Important	No	Rank the top five features
Low cost	_____	_____	_____	_____
Brand name	_____	_____	_____	_____
Ease of installation	_____	_____	_____	_____
Ease of use	_____	_____	_____	_____
Appearance	_____	_____	_____	_____
Intercom capabilities	_____	_____	_____	_____

Ability to add music	_____	_____	_____	_____
Switching capabilities	_____	_____	_____	_____
Fax and modem interfaces	_____	_____	_____	_____
Service	_____	_____	_____	_____
Warranty	_____	_____	_____	_____
Customer repair potential	_____	_____	_____	_____
Recommendations	_____	_____	_____	_____

Are you satisfied with the phone system you are currently using? ___ Yes ___ No

You can use this chart to make a list of features that you must have and that have to perform well for customers. You need to concentrate your marketing messages on the features that are important to your customers.

> Rating features and benefits minimizes the chances you'll give customers a reason not to buy.

US West Direct is a publisher of yellow page directories. Up until just a few years ago, US West Direct called up customers with a standard sales pitch on the yellow pages, with numerous options to choose from. Salespeople would cover an array of options such as full-page ads, color ads, multiple ads, and so on. US West's representatives were focusing on the products and prices it had to sell, not on features their customers wanted. The company found it was confusing its prospects with too many choices, and as a result the company was missing out on a large number of sales opportunities. US West Direct looked into what features were important to different customers so it could simplify its product offering. What it found was it had several categories of clients, all who had different features that were important to them.

US West Direct found that niche marketers liked smaller ads in numerous locations. Growth-oriented companies wanted full-page ads with different phone numbers so they could know which ads were pulling the most responses. US West Direct put feature packages together so it had the features and benefits that each market wanted. Salespeople started asking a couple of qualifying questions to categorize the prospect and then only talked to the prospect about the yellow page package that was right for him or her. Salespeople started talking less and selling more. US

West Direct took this customer relationship building experience one step further by entering the customers' qualifying answers into its database so that next year the salesperson would not have to requalify each account.

Look for Underserved Customers

The first sections of the chapter, on finding customers' prime objectives and ranking features and benefits, are tactics most companies use and are needed to keep a company competitive. The last two tactics, looking for underserved customers and following customers around in their activities, are tactics designed to create breakthrough strategies that will give you a huge jump on your competition.

If you go back to Figure 9-1, you'll notice that the last question asks people if they are happy or unhappy with the product they are using. I mentioned earlier in the chapter about how moms were interested in how the Minnesota Twins keep their uniforms clean. Companies like Proctor and Gamble who make detergents like Tide and Cheer couldn't solve that problem without taking the color out of clothes. But what they could do is come out with a stain stick, a stick that mothers could rub on to stains before washing

> Customers will jump on your band wagon if you solve their problems.

without removing the color. When people have a problem with a product category, they always look to see if a new product has solved the same problem. Your company will leap right to the top of an unhappy prospect's list if you eliminate his or her main problem.

Kenneth Johnson had dropped out of college and was wondering what to do. He heard from several of his friends that they were unhappy that the only delivered food they could get was pizza. After a hard days work they didn't want to cook, didn't have the energy to go out, but didn't exactly want to order pizza. So he started Dial-A-Waiter, a restaurant delivery service in Wichita, Kansas. He talked six restaurants into letting him handle take-out orders and started promoting his service. At the end of 1998, Dial-A-Waiter had 10 drivers delivering food from 40 restaurants. The charge is just six dollars, which in most cases is less than the cost of a restaurant tip. Dial-A-Waiter also gets a 30 to 35 percent discount from the restaurants, which produces a tidy profit. This is a great idea, and it came from seeing what customers were unhappy about.

There are many ways to get this information. One is to ask people if they are happy or unhappy about a product on your survey. If you offer people a check or gift for filling out the survey you can obtain their name, address, and phone number. Just call them up and ask them why they are unhappy. They'll usually give you a straightforward answer. Another tactic I've used with great success is to ask questions on warranty cards. Some questions are about why the customer selected the product and what they considered the product's most important feature. I also like to ask what new features they wished were on the product. About one in seven or eight warranty cards would come back with a suggestion that could be incorporated into a new product. Another tactic I used once was at an association meeting. We gave away dinner for two to the person who could guess what people at the meeting would consider a product category's biggest problem. People entering the contest had to first write what people at the meeting would feel is the industry's biggest problem. The second question was what percentage of people in our contest would list the right answer. We had 88 out of 112 engineers enter the contest, which was good exposure for us, and they predominantly mentioned just two problems.

> Any small business can conduct simple surveys and questionnaires.

Follow Customers Around

I've found that following customers around for awhile is a great way to discover product ideas. Not long ago I was sitting at the mall waiting for my wife. Four teenage girls were nearby and they were complaining about how all the stores were pretending to be an Old Navy store. The girls wanted some of the "far out clothes" they saw on an MTV video. The girls walked out of the mall and I'm sure they forgot immediately about how they felt mall stores could be improved. People often have little concerns that they won't tell you in a survey or questionnaire. I noticed in my van today that I had to lean forward to see what gear I was in. I've leaned forward for years, but I only noticed today that I couldn't normally see what gear I was in.

One day I was in a dental office and the dentist had the patient at a 45-degree angle and was twisted around like a pretzel trying to treat the patient. I asked the dentist why he didn't lower the patient so he could work more comfortably. The dentist said that the patient, who was over 60 and a little heavy, was uncomfortable when she was laying flat. I asked the dentist if this happened often, and he told me that yes it did, on one or two patients a month. He also mentioned that his back would ache all day after he spent more than half an hour on a patient who couldn't lie flat. We in the marketing department had never heard this complaint before. But we got the same answer when we went out and talked to five other dentists. We came out with a dental chair that had a special headrest that allowed the head to be laid back flat while the patient's torso was at a 45-degree angle. The chair was very popular with doctors with a large percentage of older patients, even though the chair had a 20 percent price premium over standard products. Ideas that come from following these steps are often "forehead slappers," which is a description for a program or idea where people slap their forehead and say, "Why didn't anyone think of that before."

> People only articulate a percentage of the problems that really bug them.

The Pregnancy Calendar was developed by a trio of women who listened to many of their pregnant friends ask people when they should expect morning sicknesses and whether they could eat certain foods. The three friends asked other friends if they'd like a calendar that covered exactly what physical changes and characteristics they should expect during pregnancy. The response was overwhelmingly positive. By 1998 the calendar had sold over 1.25 million copies in its various versions. The trio of friends then realized that new moms weren't sure what to expect with their new babies, so they developed the Baby's First Year calendar. That product has sold over 500,000 copies. Not bad for three women who still only work part time at their business.

Great marketing doesn't just pay off incrementally, it pays off exponentially. A marketing program that's 20 percent more effective can produce 100 percent better results. The time you take to make the customer say "that's exactly what I want" can quadruple your sales on the very same marketing budget. Harley-Davidson is a good example. It was on the verge of bankruptcy when it started its

Harley Owners Group. That group re-established the company's connection to its customers, but, more importantly, it gave Harley a clear idea of just what its customers wanted: big, oversized engines with that familiar Harley rumble and the historic Harley bad boy image. Customers bought Harley-Davidson products once they gave the customers exactly what they wanted.

> Paying attention to the details of what customers want produces big sales gains.

We need to add to our marketing chart what two or three features of our product will produce a hot button response in prospects and get them to choose our product as a final purchase candidate.

List your target customer group(s): _____

List the predominant personality trait: _____

List the predominant desired image (consumers) or interest (business):

_____

List the initial response you want to generate: _____

List your "hot button" features: _____

CHAPTER TEN

COMMUNICATING YOUR MESSAGE IN A HURRY

When you have the right message, the marketing results can be astounding. At a dental company we typically received 100 to 200 responses from a full-page ad in a dental magazine. When we introduced a new product for cleaning root canals, we generated 8,000 responses, 10 times the highest number of inquiries the magazine had ever received. We achieved this result after discovering that our product was an ideal solution for curved root canals. Our competitor used a rotating file, which could break in a curved canal. The dentist might need two to three hours to remove the file, which was bad for the patient and embarrassing for the dentist. Our system used a vibratory file, which performed well in a curved canals. Curved root canals were a hot button for dentists, and when we hit it we had an overwhelming response.

Having the right message is only half the battle. You also have to communicate the message quickly, often in less than two to three seconds. *DOS for Dummies* is a fabulous example of quick communication. After a nontechnical computer user tries just once to read a software instruction manual, the title *DOS for Dummies* sounds like manna from heaven.

The goal of infiltration marketing is to end up with a core group of loyal customers that treat you like a friend. Probably no company does this better than Harley-Davidson, who is not just a friend of the customer but a member of the family. Most companies don't have a loyal core group established and they need to communicate with customers in order to start the engagement process. The art of communication has changed radically over the last 20 years. The importance of the written word has declined drastically, and visual messages now completely dominate most effective marketing messages. Marketers are also faced with having to effectively communicate in less than three seconds, which can only be done visually. Creating a visually

> Visual images are the only way
> to communicate quickly.

appealing image with a short supporting tag line that quickly communicates a benefit is a crucial step in any marketing campaign. It is especially important to small companies who simply can't afford the same type of advertising budget that big companies have to promote their name and image.

The visual image shouldn't be of the product itself, but instead it should relate to the goal and mindset of the customer. Wheaties communicates the message "Breakfast of Champions" with the picture of an athlete that is currently in the news and is an example of a goal-oriented message. A hat store logo of a fancy hat with the name Millie's under it is an image that is both distinctive and memorable. Perrier uses its name, bottle shape, and label graphics to convey an upscale image. Adcom Air Express specializes in delivering point-of-purchase displays to retailers around the country. Adcom has a point-of-purchase display as its visual image. That image does a key marketing task: identifying exactly what Adcom does.

$1,999

A savvy example of quick communication is Apple Computers introduction of its new personal computer, the iMac. Apple has always appealed to rebels, the people who don't want to join the traditional PC crowd. In the mid 1990s, Apple started looking and acting like an IBM clone, and its profitability plunged. The iMac is totally different from any computer seen in the past. It comes in translucent colors and has a futuristic shape that announces that it is the image of the next generation of computers. The visual look was so stunning Apple didn't even need a tag line. The result in late 1998 was that the iMac accounted for 7.1 percent of all computer sales. And Apple wasn't just getting orders from loyal Apple customers. Thirty percent of iMac buyers were buying their first Apple computer. This is even more impressive when you remember that Apple was a company that many stock market analysts had declared dead in late 1997.

This chapter discusses creating a memorable image and name that quickly tells a story, communicating in a straightforward manner that customers can relate to, and introducing infiltration marketing tactics into your marketing messages.

Creating a Memorable Image

A company's image has to do several tasks in order to stand on its own without an advertising budget. First, it has to identify what the company is about. Second, it has to help its target customer realize that the product is for them. Finally, it has to produce the desired initial response in the customer. Apple Computers' iMacs didn't have to let people know it was a computer since Apple is a well-known computer company. But its color scheme and design made it obvious that it was for younger people who want to have fun with their computer, and its fancy look lets the owner project the image of someone on the cutting edge because of its futuristic look.

> A small company's visual image has to tell the whole story.

Small companies don't have a big advertising budget and they need a symbol that will do everything for them. An infiltration marketer needs the best of all images because cross-promotions and strategic alliances don't provide much benefit if people don't recognize your logo and associate it with who you are. Your visual image is even better when it reveals your distinct product or service advantage. An effective image that customers remember cuts your marketing expense. Silicon Graphics is a big company with highly regarded products. Its logo, which is six triangles arranged in a pie shape, doesn't really say anything, and Silicon Graphics has to promote its name and products constantly in trade magazines so people will remember its products. Compare Silicon Graphics to The Model Stone Company, which sells rocks and stones for landscaping to consumers and landscapers. Its logo has a stop-sign shape with the One-Stop Shop slogan inside. The logo is distinctive and something you can remember. Another example of a memorable brand name is Gadjit, which appears in bright colors with letters that look like they were handpainted on. Gadjit is the name used by MacFarland Corporation. The colorful Gadjit name covers a variety of unique products like a banana hook, a pasta strainer/server, a child seat belt safety guard, and a window gift vase, which is a vase that attaches with suction cups to windows, mirrors, or other surfaces. Gadjit is a good brand name because it gives the customer an idea of what the product is. The type style and color of the logo are bright and fun and add to the brand's image. The manufacturer includes colors from the logo on its products to further establish the brand's identity.

A good logo can be had by even the most mundane companies. Sunshine Answering has a smiling secretary as its logo. Work Place Solutions uses as its logo an engineering drawing, an image that tells customers that it provides temporary draftsman. Retail Site Selectors is a marketing firm that helps companies locate new retail sites. These companies are all examples of companies who developed a distinctive name and logo strategy for an ordinary business. Kindercare is another example of a memorable name. It has two effective visual images. One is a school tower with a bell, and the other is a drawing by kids of a mom and child going into a school.

You start creating your own effective logo by answering these four questions:

1. What feature do you want to communicate about your company?

   _____

2. What do you what the name and logo to accomplish? _____

   _____

3. Who do you want to appeal to? _____

   _____

4. What image do you want to relate? _____

   _____

Let's take a look at how Bob's Grinding Shop, a company that makes form tools for screw machine shops, would create its logo. The first thing that Bob wants to communicate is that his business's specialty is form tool grinding. Bob also wants owners of screw machine shops, who are Bob's target customers, to immediately understand that Bob provides form tools for their business. Finally Bob wants to relate that, though he is small, Bob's is still a high-quality shop. Bob can change his name to Bob's Form Tool Grinding, and his logo could be an engineering drawing of a screw machine part. If the name and logo were in engineering blue ink, Bob's logo would stand out and his customers would remember his company. I'd also recommend using an unusual part for the drawing, say a part on the Hubbell telescope, to make the logo more memorable.

> Don't take your visual image for granted. Most people will forget everything about you except your image.

Your logo should be something that helps people relate directly to what your company is. In Bob's Form Tool Grinding we showed an engineering drawing of a screw machine part. That's an image designed to tell about one of Bob's features, the ability to produce high-quality parts, but it also is an image the screw machine shop owners can easily relate to. Instant Flat Repair is a product that uses pressurized foam to refill a flat tire on the highway. Instant Flat Repair's visual image is of a car broken down in the rain. People relate to that image as they can picture themselves in that situation. I know I sure don't want to get a flat tire in the rain. Another logo I liked was of an air freight delivery system with a slogan "We stretch to make things happen." Their image was of a baseball outfielder coming out of his shoes, stretching way out to catch a ball. It was great image for a company whose business is bailing companies out of shipping problems.

> Orosi LLC is a group of young guys who love to play and happen to own a kayak helmet company. The company is named after the Orosi River, which is one of the top kayaking rivers in the world. They had a fun logo where they have ribbons floating overhead to look like a river. The colors and fonts both show dash and style as do their helmets, which have metallic finishes and sport names like Hawg, Lizard, and Kool Khat. In other words, the company sells pizzazz. And the message starts first and foremost with their logo. The owners started on a shoestring but were still able to increase sales from $40,000 in 1996 to $400,000 in 1998.

Straightforward Communications

Virtually all consumers cast a wary eye on marketing messages. They will stop listening to you the minute they feel you are only interested in selling them a product. As an infiltration marketer you need to learn how to communicate in a nonthreatening manner and how to have your prospects confident that you are telling the truth.

To be nonthreatening you should start by being friendly and not preachy. Messages should also relate to the customers' needs and wants, not your features and benefits. Quaker Oats has a message on its breakfast cereals: "Thinking about a heart-healthy breakfast?" That message relates directly to customers' goal of having a healthy lifestyle. Compaq Computer's ad message, "Better answers," is an example of a company worried about its product's features and benefits. I think Compaq would be better off showing a computer net-

> Virtually all buyers cast a wary eye on marketing messages.

You strike a chord with a customer by meeting his or her needs.

work specialist sitting at a desk with a copy line: "A little security when the buck stops at your desk." Or I'd go with a smiling guy with an empty complaint bin on his desk drinking a champagne toast with the tag line "To the best of times." These approaches would have a much better chance of striking a chord with the customer.

GIVING CUSTOMERS CHOICES

One of the best ways to convince customers you are really on their side is to give them choices and options.

Marketers need to create conversations with the customer.

Churbas is a highly successful boat and motor dealer in Canada. Once you explain to a Churbas salesperson what type of boat you are looking for, they'll show you the models they carry that fit your needs. They'll also tell you what models other dealers carry and send you over to their competitors so customers can evaluate other models. Churbas believes that it's not important to get each sale. What is important is that the customer gets the right choice. Many people are surprised that Churbas has had a fast growth over the last five years. But not me, they are building a loyal customer base that looks at Churbas as a true friend.

This principle is just as true for industrial and business-to-business marketers. I walked into a Sir Speedy printer that I use regularly and asked about a presentation display I wanted done. The printer said he could do it but that I'd be better off going to one of his competitors. I appreciated that piece of advice and that's the reason I always go to this printer first. Did the printer lose business by sending me to a competitor? Not in the long run. He will profit several times over by helping me out.

Industrial marketing is the same way. Tell people what you can do and steer them to the right purchase for them. I've found that a name like Bob's Precision Grinding tends to irritate customers. It doesn't really give them a choice because they don't know what the company does. They are much happier when they can tell by your materials exactly what you do. Bob's Form Tool Grinding, with the subtitle for screw machine shops, is exactly the type of name people like. That puts prospects in charge of the choices that they are making. Prospects do not like stumbling around not knowing what to do. Companies that help customers clarifying their choices have a marketing advantage. Prospects also like clear information on what a product should be used for. People will buy a sleeping bag with a tag on it that says best for 20 to 80 degrees F long before they will buy a product without clear markings.

Offering customer choices is one of the reasons I favor strategic alliances, cross-promotions, and any other type of partnership arrangement. Teaming up lets you offer customers the choices they want to have.

TALK DIRECTLY TO THE PROSPECT

Conversations with customers require you to talk directly to them. This means you must keep track of the characteristics of each customer and send them only the information that relates directly to them.

> Partnerships give you a better chance to offer customers what they want.

Accrue Software didn't exist in 1996. By 1998 it had 50 big-name accounts including Eastman Kodak, Dreamworks, Motorola, and Sun Microsystems. The company did this with a great program that talked directly to the customer. Accrue manufactures software that helps people understand how people come onto and then navigate their Web pages. Accrue started off by identifying four customer groups where it felt that its software would have value. The customer groups it chose were financial services, larger retail stores, media companies, and publishers and high-tech firms that have many customer-related types of services.

After choosing its customer groups, Accrue went on the Internet and looked at Web pages of companies in the customer group. Accrue was able to look at the Web pages, determine what the companies were trying to accomplish, and pick a list of target customers where its software provided the most benefit to the customer. Accrue then had its inside telemarketing force call the companies and get the name of the key buyer at the company. Then they qualified the customer with additional questions so that Accrue could break out each target customer into subgroups.

Accrue's next marketing effort was to conduct special educational seminars around the country for each different market. They conducted these along with several other Web-oriented software companies. After the seminars, when Accrue had substantial customer information, they started calling on customers with a customized presentation that spoke directly to the customer's situation. What about advertising? Accrue doesn't believe in it. They don't think a blanket message connects with customers.

> Careless marketing can ruin your chance for a lasting customer relationship.

I talked to a small business owner the other day who needed more sales and had decided to send out a direct mailing to 5,000 potential customers that he hoped would bring in some business. This usually doesn't work well as most customers don't read direct mail. There is a danger in randomly sending out messages. People pigeonhole companies the same way they do products. If you keep putting out blanket mailings, the customer might look at you as just another firm trying to sell them a product. When that happens you can lose any chance you have for developing an infiltration marketing relationship.

Adding Infiltration Marketing Tactics to Your Marketing Message

When I talk to a company about marketing its products or services, I know they are initially looking at me thinking that I'm trying to decide how much I can charge them. People feel this way all the time when they make a purchase where they are not sure what the price should be. People come to the marketplace with a preconceived notion that marketers just want their money. An infiltration marketer's goal is to convince prospects that they are in the market for the long run and whatever promotes the market helps them, and that in the end what helps their customers will end up helping the infiltration marketer. There are many tactics that convey this message, including:

- making customers realize you have an interest in their success;
- showing you are just like your customers;
- doing things that help promote the overall market;

- letting customers decide how you can help them;
- selling your product or service inside high-content programs that help educate customers to make their own choice.

Making customers realize you have an interest in their success. I take on very few marketing projects each year, while before I used to scramble from month to month to get one contract after another. I made only one small change. I stopped offering a specific service and instead offered to take over a certain marketing responsibility for a percentage of sales or profits. For example, I agreed to intro- **$100** duce one product to the agricultural market for a percentage of sales on a long-term contract. I don't even propose specific programs any more, but only promise that at the end of 12 months I will increase sales. This has a much bigger payback to me because it is a long-term return. And the customers are happy because they see that I only do well when they do well.

> You win when the customers win. That is a success secret that will never fail.

Show you are just like your customers. Orosi, the kayak helmet company I talked about earlier, boasts the tag line "We love to play." Its owners also happen to be kayakers and lovers of adventure. This is a common theme in many of the businesses selling to people in their early 20s. They believe people prefer to buy from people like themselves, and their management are typically in their 20s and 30s and love the same adventure as their customers. Other companies also place a major emphasis on being just like their customers. Harley-Davidson's management drives Harleys. Consultants often participate in the management or boards of companies in the industry they are selling to. Golf club equipment manufacturers have long used golf reps with low handicaps who love nothing better than to get out and play with the club pro.

Doing things that help promote the overall market. Jean Griswold started her company Special Care because she wanted to provide helpers to people who couldn't handle household chores or who just needed someone to stay with at night. Griswold's primary motivation isn't money; she wanted to help people who otherwise had to go into nursing homes. She doesn't have a franchise fee because she wants her concept to spread. At the same time, she runs her potential franchises through a rigorous questioning process so she gets franchisees that care more about helping people than they do about making money. Griswold, who really is an infiltration marketer at heart, says that she only wants franchisees for whom

$100 ➤ helping neighbors ranks higher than turning a profit. "Of course" she adds, "they do make money. They make lots of money."

Letting customers decide how you can help them. Indus is a company that sells asset management software, which is software that helps manufacturers run their plants more efficiently. Indus offers its prospects access to CareNet, a Web site designed to allow customers to call up and tell the company how it can help them. The site also lets clients access frequently updated product information, pose questions to customer and technical service representatives, and find solutions to specific problems. The site also lets customers post tips for other customers, even if the tips are not directly related to Indus products. Prospects are also encouraged to make suggestions for new products or product and service improvements. Indus charges a small fee for access to CareNet. The first month they had 30 users, after ten months they had 600. One of the things that customers like best about the system is that they can post a production problem on the Web site and get an immediate answer. Sometimes the answer comes from Indus personnel, and sometimes the answer is from other people.

Selling your product or service inside high-content programs that help educate customers to make their own choice. USAA provides financial services to U.S. military personnel and their families. USAA doesn't just send out marketing messages selling its services. It knows its clients and what age their children are. It sends out information booklets to its customers based on their age and status in life. USAA sends booklets on managing credit card debt to teenagers and young adults, financing a college education to parents of young children, and booklets on estate planning when people retire. USAA's internal marketing motto is that everything it does has to say, "W e are here to serve you." USAA is a $7 billion organization and it retains 97 percent of its customers. They convince customers to be loyal by being a loyal, helpful friend to their customers.

If you want to communicate quickly, first you have to create a strong visual message, then you have to communicate directly to your prospect, and finally you need to introduce elements of infiltration marketing into your messages. It seems like a pretty easy task. But if you look through any major magazine you'll see that only 50 percent of the ads even begin to meet this requirement of an effective message that communicates quickly. The trouble is that marketers consistently think too much about their product and don't think enough about their customers. You'll never have that problem once you become an infiltration marketer because you'll start spending a significant amount of your time with customers.

CHAPTER ELEVEN

PRODUCING AN IMPACT

The Palm Pilot, a very small computer that sits in the palm of your hand, produces a strong immediate impact on people fascinated by the latest high-tech gadgetry. They are amazed at how small the computer is. People talk about the Palm Pilot, its small size, and how it can input data from a person's own handwriting. People are fascinated by the product, and that fascination continues until people are ready to buy one for themselves. The sustained buzz the Palm Pilot has generated has made it one of the most successful new products of the 1990s.

This section of the book concentrates on arousing the interest of customers in the intermediate buying process. Your goal is to keep your product in line for the final selection process. One of the problems for marketers in the intermediate phase is that it can last quite a while, sometimes for a year or more and sometimes even longer. Your job is to make sure the customer remembers your company for the entire intermediate buying process. Traditionally this has been a difficult time for marketers, primarily because they don't know what prospects are actually in the intermediate buying process. The reason that marketers can't identify prospects is because people don't like to identify themselves as prospects for fear of being hounded by salesmen. Interacting with prospects while they are in the intermediate buying process is a tactic in which infiltration marketers excel because they communicate in a nonthreatening manner. They keep improving their relationship with customers until they are actually ready to buy.

The last two chapters discussed stimulating customers' interest by offering them features and benefits they want and aren't getting and breaking through the clutter in the customers' world by communicating quickly and effectively. Marketers are still faced with the problem that people have busy lives and can forget your product or service even when you execute the first two steps correctly.

Marketers have to compensate for the busy lives of customers by creating a major impact on customers so they do remember you.

Creating an impact is also an important task for retailers and other suppliers that furnish consumable products that people buy all the time. Marketers of consumable products often misunderstand the buying process of their customers. People make a purchasing decision when they decide which store or business will be their primary supplier. The customer will then buy from that supplier for a long period of time until they decide to switch suppliers. Customers are really only making a new buying decision when they consider switching suppliers. Marketers of stores or consumable products need to create an impact strategy to get customers to consider switching primary suppliers.

> Infiltration marketing tactics excel in keeping customers interested until they are ready to buy.

Unfortunately, instead of creating an impact, most retailers concentrate on offering price discounts. That strategy reduces retailers' profits and doesn't create the new loyal stores that the customers want. For example, Cub Foods and Rainbow Foods are two major supermarket chains that compete in several major markets. Their strategy for gaining new customers is to run big specials. Rainbow will run big pricing promotions on certain products almost every weekend. Cub will do the same. And they might win over a few new customers for a few purchases, but they won't be landing a new loyal customer. The stores' marketers need to follow an infiltration marketing strategy that makes their store the customer's first choice for shopping. To find the right impact strategy, stores have to discover a way to help their customers meet their goals.

Men's Warehouse sells high-quality men's clothing, including suits and other work attire, at discounted prices. The store does have an impact in the market due to its huge advertising budget. That is an expensive marketing tactic, and one that most smaller retailers can't afford. But Men's Warehouse needs the big budget because it hasn't otherwise been able to discover an effective way to create an impact on its customers.

Men's Warehouse does a lot of things right with their marketing program, but they just can't get over the hump without advertising. Its situation shows why creating an impact strategy is important. The men's clothing market is a tough market today. Casual wear is starting to be the outfit of choice at businesses throughout most of the country, and the demand for suits is declining. People are buying fewer and fewer suits and traditional men's retailers are failing. Men's Warehouse has fought back with some solid marketing tactics. They use relationship marketing in their ads with George Zimmer, the company president, guaranteeing satisfaction. They offer good service, pressing and altering garments for free at any store around the country. But Men's Warehouse still needs a big advertising budget, and they still haven't caught the interest of the public.

> People won't forget you when you create an effective impact strategy.

Men's Warehouse hasn't been able to create a big impact with traditional marketing tactics. Men's Warehouse can create the impact it needs by forgetting about selling suits. It needs to realize that its customer want to look good for a reason, which is to impress people, whether it be girlfriends, peers, bosses, or subordinates. Men's Warehouse will start to create a big impact when it starts to find out the answers its customers want to know about impressing other people. Here are just a few examples of what information Men's Warehouse could find out for its customers.

- What clothes tell women about men. This can be in terms of personality, ambition, sensitivity, how a man will treat a woman, and any other pertinent personality traits.
- How to dress to show leadership and command respect.
- What men should wear if they want to fast-track their careers.

The changes in the men's clothing world over the last 10 years offer unlimited opportunities for Men's Warehouse. Dress for success, the old standard that Men's Warehouse customers lived by, is history. It's time for Men's Warehouse to help their customers define their new world. It could team up with some men's fashion and business magazines, like *Esquire* or *Fortune* magazines, and record what the new standard is. It could run a contest for the best-dressed men in America. It could offer insights into the new work dress code for various parts of the country. It could run surveys about what clothing styles impress women. Men's Warehouse will start to produce an impact the minute it starts to think like a customer and give customers the information they want to know. Creating that impact is all Men's

$2,000+ ▶ Warehouse needs to do to become the undisputed market leader in men's dress clothing. Small retailers can create a strategy that will have a strong impact on their market as soon as they start to understand their customers' real goals.

This chapter covers several ways to create impact, including becoming the "buzz," being the focal point of a market, and being looked at as a resource for your customers. Your goal is to go beyond what database marketing can do for you, which is to keep your name continually in front of customers, and instead move to the point where customers are so interested in what you do that they actually call you up for your advice.

> Small companies can create high impact strategies in their chosen markets.

Creating a Buzz

People were pushing their way into a booth at a recent European bike show. Everybody was looking to see a hot product, which in this case was an all-wheel drive mountain bike that looked sharp and caught everyone's attention. The bike was to be introduced in the fall of 1999, and the first 40 bikes were going to the top riders on the mountain bike racing circuit. Everyone wanted to see the product.

$2,000+ ▶ That's a buzz. Everyone in your market is talking about your product. You have to have the product, event, or other documentation to make the buzz last, but there is no doubt it is a great marketing tool. The buzz about a product can develop on its own, but in many cases marketers can catalyze buzz with a little cleverness and ingenuity.

Francis Rogallo is the original inventor of the hang glider. He worked on the invention for 20 years, tried marketing kite versions of the hang glider, and tried selling the concept to larger firms, all without any success. His concept did, however, get picked up by NASA as a method for bringing satellites back to earth. *Popular Mechanics* magazine did a little article on the product, mostly based on NASA's work, but it also showed Rogallo's full size hang glider. Rogallo insisted that the statement "Don't try to design or build one yourself" be included at the end of the article. The hang glider was a product for daredevils, and in effect, Rogallo told the daredevils hang gliding was too dangerous for them. That daredevil defying statement created a 10-year buzz on hang gliding that to a certain degree still exists today.

Rogallo didn't deliberately try to create a buzz, but it sure happened. The hang glider example points out that you don't create a buzz by thinking along traditional lines. You have to go way outside traditional thinking to come up with new, unique tactics that get people talking about you. Steven Jobs with the iMac computer and the Palm Pilot creators know how to create a buzz with product design. Francis Rogallo created the buzz with secrecy and mystery. These are just two of the tactics you can use to create a buzz. What the tactics have in common is that they offer consumers a product, idea, or marketing strategy that is much different than anything they've seen before.

$100

> Secrecy and intrigue are what build buzz.

About six months before the movie *Titanic* came out, the buzz in the media was that the movie would bomb at the box office. Too long, very late, re-edited multiple times, and extraordinarily expensive were just a few of the movie's problems. The critics were licking their chops about cutting the movie to ribbons. *Titanic*'s early buzz was definitely negative. Since a couple of bad opening weekends can kill a movie, how did *Titanic* survive and go on to be one the epic films of our times? One of the reasons that *Titanic* had a fast start was all the "unauthorized" Internet reviews that started coming out well before the movie reached the theatres. The buzz started to turn when some of the Internet sites that focus on gossip in Hollywood had spies sneak into showings of the rough cuts of *Titanic*. They came back saying, hey this movie's not bad, in fact, it's pretty darn good. This buzz was not from competitive Hollywood directors or paid critics, it was from the people themselves, who are of course the real judge of what sells. By the time the movie came out *Titanic*'s buzz was positive and it became the best selling movie of all time. What made this whole strategy unique was the idea of ordinary people challenging the conventional wisdom of the experts. People love to give critics a little comeuppance, and *Titanic* was a perfect vehicle for people to let critics know that they really aren't the experts they think they are.

$100

Your job is to instill the seeds for buzz and occasionally nurture it along. But buzz is conversation among people in the market and you can't force it along. You have to let the people build it on their own. To build buzz you need to have something unique and different that people think is worth talking about. Next you have to expose the product in a way that people will talk about. Then you need to add secrecy and suspense, and if possible, make the product or service hard to obtain. In the end you just need to give people something to talk about. *Titanic*'s positive buzz would never have happened if all the negative buzz hadn't come first. That negative buzz created interest when the people on the Internet said, "Those critics and Hollywood don't know a thing about this movie."

Being unique or different. You can't be ho-hum like everyone else and expect to start conversations. You have to be a little different. This doesn't mean you have to be a big company. A gardener in North Dakota started promoting the concept of English rock gardens in North Dakota as part of his line of services. He held classes at garden stores and people came because they had no idea of what an English rock garden was. The gardener tripled his business by offering something people found intriguing.

$100 ➡

> Pastor Josh Hunt is a Baptist preacher in New Mexico. People weren't coming to his church, and he felt the reason people fell away from the church was that they found the services boring. So Pastor Hunt introduced a new concept into his sermons. He didn't give the people the final answer of what every Bible story or religious message meant. He left items open to interpretation so people could discuss the lesson among themselves and learn on their own. The strategy was clearly different. Most pastors use sermons to tell people what Bible messages actually mean. Pastor Hunt feels that religious teachings leave a lot of room for discussion and that his congregation wants to be involved in deciphering the messages themselves. Pastor Hunt's church has tripled in attendance since Pastor Hunt changed his strategy, and the congregation keeps coming back energized to talk about the lessons.

I also wouldn't be a bit surprised if Pastor Hunt's congregation is learning more about their religion than they would if they were just listening to a traditional sermon. Pastor Hunt planted the seeds for conversation by doing something totally different and unique. Or in the popular term of the late 1990's, Pastor Hunt started thinking "outside of the box."

Earlier in the book I discussed stores like Oshman's, the Solar Living Center, Funimals, and MARS that use the entertailing store concept, a store where people can come and enjoy themselves even if they aren't ready to buy. Those stores create a buzz because they are different. Restaurants like the Rain Forest tie into this same concept of providing an unusual destination people want to discuss. Buca Restaurants in Minneapolis started as one small restaurant. Its concept was a parody of traditional Italian restaurants, with pictures of Frank Sinatra on the walls and Italian memorabilia everywhere, They also served meals family style, with huge portions of Italian food that were shared by everyone at the table. The restaurant only opened for dinner, didn't take reservations, and warned people to dress warmly in case they had to wait outside. ⬅ **$500** The restaurant had limited hours and long lines that created a buzz in the market. The restaurant is now a chain of four restaurants, and, not surprisingly, the restaurant is so busy that you actually do have to wait outside in a line.

> Marketers need to think in nontraditional ways to create a buzz.

Exposing the product in an interesting way. Zubas, those wild, colorful, casual pants that were quite the rage a few years ago, were created by two guys who worked out in a gym all the time and found that blue jeans were just too tight. They created Zubas so they could have a pair of comfortable pants, and they made the pants colorful so they would stand out in the marketplace. They had trouble initially selling their product so they started giving them away to pro wrestlers and football players in order to gain market exposure. Zubas became the buzz when Lawrence Taylor of the New York Giants was seen wearing a pair on the sidelines of a nationally televised football game. Breathe Right, the little nose bandage that helps people breathe better when their nose is congested, used the same tactic. The product was from a small company that couldn't afford an advertising budget. They offered their product free to football teams, telling the teams that their product would help the players breathe better when they had a cold. Breathe Right became the buzz after Jerry Rice of the San Francisco 49ers started wearing the ⬅ **$500** distinctive I shaped nose bandage one week when he had a cold.

Little Earth Productions is an environmentally aware firm that makes belts, handbags, and other items out of recycled plastic, license plates, and other throwaway items. To promote its products, the company gave away free bags to Miss America contestants, with each contestant getting a bag made up with items from

$500 ➤ their own state. Some of the contestants loved their bags and started showing them around, and the bag's sales started to take off. Now Little Earth is selling over $3 million in bags per year. My favorite story is about a company called Thump that makes underground clothing that can only be found at special boutique shops for young people. Thump raised money by throwing rave parties in abandoned build-ings. They charged people to come to the parties, and then they also sold them

$500 ➤ clothes. The whole atmosphere of defiance was a perfect route for exposing their product to their target audience.

> Giving unusual products away to key people is a good way to create interest.

Adding secrecy, suspense, and intrigue. When VW announced that it was returning the VW bug to the market, it announced it would start taking orders a year in advance of pro-duction so people could get on the list to buy the product. No one even was sure what the actual product was like and baby boomers that fondly remembered the VW bug were talking

$500 ➤ about it. VW announced the first year's production was already sold out and the buzz just built. It was a great introduction strategy. Unfortunately for VW, the new VW didn't have the survivalist charm of the first bug and the product now is going nowhere, but they did create quite the buzz. Secrecy and intrigue was also a factor in creating the bungee jumping buzz. The idea of a company sneaking off with clients and dropping them from bridges and buildings certainly had plenty of drama that was exactly the type of intrigue that attracts people with a real sense of adventure.

$100 ➤ Kinetix was a small struggling software firm when they put the dancing baby out onto the Internet. The dancing baby is the computer image of a small baby in a diaper who dances across the computer screen. The dancing baby first showed up on the TV show *Ally McBeal*. Computer-savvy individuals started picking up the dancing baby off of other people's Web pages, modifying the baby, and sending their version back onto their Web pages for other people to see. The var-ious babies then started to be picked up and placed into file attachments that people would e-mail to their friends. It became an in thing for people to have the dancing baby on their computer. Kinetix did nothing to promote the baby until it was a full-blown craze. Only then did the company take credit for the dancing baby through press releases and reap the benefits of the dancing baby through increased business. Another product that created a big buzz was the fabric bracelets with the embroidered letters W.W.J.D. The letters stand for What Would

Jesus Do. When kids at churches first started wearing the bracelets, people didn't know what the initials stood for and that made the bracelets almost a secret code for teenagers. Almost overnight the company making the bracelets went from zero to $10 million in sales.

Becoming the Focal Point of the Market

Netscape grew to its early position of market dominance in the Internet browser market by giving away its software so that new Internet users, who were not skilled computer geeks, could easily surf the Web. Netscape dominated the Web for several years, and they made money by selling computer servers and software to large companies and ISPs (Internet service providers) who wanted to communicate with the people out surfing the Internet. AOL, Netscape's biggest competitor at the time, tried to control people's access to the Internet. AOL never scared Microsoft, but Netscape did, because by giving away products and allowing people the freedom to go wherever they chose, Netscape ending up being the focal point of the market. Only Microsoft with its great size and unlimited resources could dent Netscape, and they only succeeded by "persuading" its computer OEM accounts to offer its browser as a standard feature on their computers.

> You are a focal point when customers look to you for everything they need or want.

The McAlpin's Signature Home Store in Cincinnati has created a new type of home store, which it calls the seamless home store, that attempts to make itself the focal point of customers' home decorating process. Traditional home stores group merchandise by categories such as couches or dining room tables, and then place each group of products in its own area. McAlpin's has stopped compartmentalizing merchandise and instead has put a store together exactly as customers will use each product. Instead of all the towels being together in one area and the sheets being in another area, McAlpin's shows individual rooms, such as bedrooms, with window treatments, bedding, furniture, and accessories all together in one location. McAlpin's wants people to see exactly how the products will look in their home. The store offers a wide variety of different type rooms. Its recliners, as an example, aren't all located next to each other but instead are scattered around family rooms with different decorating styles and motifs. McAlpin's goal is to create a sense of surprise in the store as people go from one room layout to the another, all designed to give people ideas of how they can decorate their homes. The layout calls for more space than a traditional store, but the customers love it. It gives them a sense of what might be possible in their home. McAlpin's first store has been a great success and it is planning on opening additional stores across the country.

One of my favorite tactics is to get customers to help design their products. Ohio Art Company, the manufacturer of Etch a Sketch and other toys, sells primarily to the five big toy retailers. Ohio Art works closely with those retailers to develop the products the retailers think will sell. For example, one of Ohio Art's big new product successes was the Grant Hill Pro indoor basketball net. It was created specifically for one retailer who believed the product would be a big seller. Ohio Art prides itself on being able to work cooperatively with its retailers to take advantage of market opportunities that its customers see. That's a good tactic for Ohio Art because it helps them create products that retailers want to carry, and it provides a service that toy giants like Hasbro and Mattel can't match.

$1,999 ➡ Becoming a focal point is another reason I like companies to sponsor industry-oriented advisory groups. It allows your company to be a focal point for discussion on industry developments. Being an important participant in industry associations, conferences, and joint product development projects also keeps a company at the focal point of industry activities. Accountants, lawyers, and invest-

$100 ➡ ment bankers who work with new entrepreneurs use this same tactic when they serve on the board of directors of entrepreneur or new venture clubs. That keeps them at the focal point of their customers' search for information about starting a new business.

Another good way to become a focal point is to concentrate on providing information about how products interact. For example, when you stain your deck you have all sorts of things to be concerned with, such as type of cleaner to use, the

Marketers become focal points when they offer customers opportunities for interaction.

proper way to power wash the deck, what stain system to use depending on how the sun shines on the deck, how cold your winter is, and how far off the ground the deck is. The store or service that gives out helpful cards that describe the perfect products to use for the customer's exact climate has a big advantage. I saw some cards in a hardware store about four years ago. When I finally got around to staining my deck, I went back to that particular store. That store was across town and I hadn't entered the store for four years at the time I made my purchase. But I wanted to be sure I bought the right products and I was willing to go out of my way to get the information I needed.

Other ways to be the focal point are to sponsor clubs and other groups related to your business. Restaurants use this tactic when they sponsor get-acquainted dinners for singles. Sewing stores, hobby stores, and landscaping businesses may all sponsor a club or group related to their business, and sporting goods stores often will sponsor golf trips, tournaments, or vacation trips that feature snorkeling, diving, or other sporting activities. You are a focal point for your customers any time you offer them extra events that they want to attend.

Becoming a Resource for Your Customers

> People remember resources for hard to find information.

Amazon, the leading Internet bookseller, has a sky-high stock price, and I constantly read that people are amazed at the high stock price since Amazon has never made money. But Amazon isn't just trying to sell books. It's trying to become the best available information source for books. It hasn't made it there yet, but it's trying mighty hard. If it ever gets that designation, there is no limit to how many products it can sell.

Kendle International conducts tests for pharmaceutical companies. As Kendle has increased the number of tests it runs, it has started to compile information on what areas of research tests are being conducted. Kendle started to realize that some areas of research were overcrowded while others were being neglected. Kendle uses this knowledge in a consulting capacity, helping companies design and fine-tune their strategies, suggesting new activities they might want to pursue based on the level of research activity being conducted in each area. Most of the time Kendle doesn't charge for its consulting. It offers this service free so it can be resource for its drug companies. Kendle also fosters its expert status by having employees serve on the boards of professional groups, write articles for professional publications, and speak at conventions and association meetings. Kendle's strategy is paying handsome dividends, revenue was growing at a 200 percent rate in 1998, which is the type of growth you can generate by giving things away free.

There are many variations of this strategy. Coca-Cola offers its fast food chain customers much of its market research on the purchasing patterns and needs of various market segments and even makes recommendations on how the chains can improve their business based on Coke's customer research. Accountants, lawyers, and consultants sometimes offer a free walk-in clinic where people can discuss a problem, or they will participate in workshops or seminars to pass out information that customers want to know. Another way to execute this strategy is to carry a large variety of parts, old products, or unusual products that are otherwise hard to find. People remember that store in case they run into an emergency and need a hard to find part.

> Stores that stock hard to find products are a valuable resource.

Recoton Corp. was originally a small electronics distributor that only carried a small line to sell to electronics stores. The company was having trouble selling to new retailers because of its limited line but wasn't financially able to add new products. The company decided that most retailers ran into problems connecting wires and jacks and other items that made products work well together. Ninety-five percent of the time the standard connectors worked fine, but the other 5 percent created big problems for retailers. Recoton started adding a full line of connections and wires that could solve any connection problem. Retailers started to rely on Recoton to solve their problems, and

$500

Recoton used that reliance to add retailer customers. Recoton kept expanding and eventually became the retailers' one-stop source for electronics accessories. Recoton became the resource the retailers needed, and its sales have skyrocketed.

Creating an impact marketing strategy is an extremely effective way to increase sales. It often doesn't cost much because it creates a reason for customers to come to you. Customers won't forget you once you create a buzz, become an industry focal point, or become a resource for the market. That top-of-the-mind customer awareness can be produced with infiltration marketing for very little money, or you can produce it with a million-dollar advertising campaign. I think your choice is clear. You need to create an impact strategy, and you need to create it now. Otherwise you'll be losing sales and/or spending far too much money on marketing to your customers.

Demonstrating that You'll Deliver on Your Promises

CHAPTER TWELVE

CREATING IMMEDIATE CREDIBILITY

Open up the Yellow Pages in any town or the Industrial Directory in any state and you'll find a minimum of 10 competitors in virtually every category. People don't thoroughly evaluate every possible choice they have, that would take too much time. Instead, they look for a company that they will feel comfortable buying from. You can improve the customers' comfort level by projecting the image your customers are looking for. The four factors that influence how comfortable a person feels are the company's image, how safe a person feels buying from a company, a product or service's price/value relationship, and customer service. Once marketers discover what factors positively influence their target customer group, they simply have to gear their marketing messages and tactics so customers will feel good about doing business with them.

Oakley, Inc. is a $233 million manufacturer of ultrahip eyewear and footwear. Its target market is the young "excitement is everything" crowd that favors fast sports, high adventure, and living life to the extreme. Oakley has come under fire from a series of young firms such as Black Fly, Volcom, Hurley, Split, Exekiel, and Shorties whose founders are young and brash entrepreneurs. Its competitors, in other words, are managed by the people who know their targeted customer group inside and out because they are members of the targeted group.

The new companies have a big advantage in the customers' perception because they are managed by one of their own, while Oakley is managed by a 48 year old. Oakley was losing out on all four counts. It didn't have the image of being a company that lived by the rule "excitement is everything."

Its products weren't a safe purchase because how could older people possibly understand the needs of young adults who wear belly rings. Oakley's prices were high because their products weren't highly regarded in the market. And Oakley's products weren't sold in the small underground type shops favored by the rebellious youth. In those shops customer service is perceived to be high because customers are always talking to someone who is like themselves (instead of a 40-year-old store manager). Oakley could see an image and customer perception problem quickly developing.

> Customers have to buy your company first before they buy your product or service.

Oakley had to change its marketing methods immediately to gain back the trust of its customers. It fought back by turning itself inside out. Designers used to sit at headquarters and turn out what they thought were ultrahip styles. Oakley looked at its styles as gold and thought they set the market trends. But after a disastrous 1997, the company hired what they call "hunter-gatherers," which are teams of employees who go all around their customers' world looking for new things, new shapes, new concepts, and new gadgets that strike a chord with their customers. These "hunter-gatherers" had a key influence on what the next products should look like. Oakley also shortened up its product development cycle so it could get out products with new looks before the looks went cold. Fast development with the latest looks paid off for Oakley. Its sales jumped 20 percent in 1998, and it has re-established itself as being in-touch with its market.

\$2,000+ ➡️

Oakley's reliance on "hunter-gatherers" helped it produce the products that the market wanted. More importantly, it demonstrated that Oakley was willing to follow the market and become a part of the market once again. That's the image every infiltration marketer needs to create. Everyone in its customer group could feel good about buying from the company again, and Oakley was back on top in a difficult, rapidly changing business.

> The customers should feel that you are selling the products or services they would have designed themselves.

The reintroduction of the Volkswagen Beetle, on the other hand, was a disastrous campaign. Just who was the bug designed for? Baby boomers nostalgic for the VW Beetle? They were into bigger cars with plenty of ambiance. Young adults of today? There wasn't a chance in the world that young people were going to want a car their parents might have driven when they were young. I can't think of anyone who really felt that the VW Beetle was the one car they would design.

Image

People like to feel that they and the companies they buy from are one and the same. People like to be with people like themselves, and people behave the same way when they buy products. Of course, consumers are all different types of people, which is why you need to identify your target customer group first, determine what image those customers are looking for, and then deliver and reinforce that image throughout your entire business operations. Examples of this are consumers who like buying from high-priced stores, engineers who want to be technological leaders, people who buy from a company that's fun, and people who buy from companies with a stable conservative approach. When you match customers' image of themselves, you establish immediate credibility.

> People like other people who are just like them, and they like companies that reflect themselves.

Bloomingdale's is a great practitioner of this principle. Its customers want to stand out, be aloof, and feel superior to the average person. The perfect picture of a Bloomingdale's customer is someone who walks down the street ignoring everyone while everyone turns and stares at him or her. Bloomingdale's matches this image perfectly. The stores have a spare modern art feel that seems to shout out "I'm sophisticated." Its stores aren't jammed with merchandise and the inventory may seem limited, but the inventory it has is special. Bloomingdale's doesn't bring in just anything, only the items that are perfect for its target market. That image connects immediately with its target customer group.

You need to have both style and substance for credibility. I recently helped choose an industrial firm for designing a product that would be sold into machine shops. The first firm we visited was in a loft of an older building. The building layout was creative, unusual, and eye catching. Every room in the building had creative design elements, the people looked like designers, and every brochure, business card, and even the mugs in the place had a design element to them. The company was very impressive and we might have chosen them except that our

◄ $2,000+

product was for machine shops, where the owners have dirty fingernails and like the rugged, durable look. The firm did a great job of creating its image, it just didn't match the image we wanted.

> A company's image needs to reflect its customers' self-image.

The firm we hired had a more utilitarian look to its brochure, and all their design work was understated rather than flashy. Their products blended in and looked like they had substance. Our target market valued simplicity, durability, and dependability and this design firm had it. Both design firms had a great approach. They differed in that they weren't serving the same target customer group. The first company specialized in consumer products, the

$500

second in industrial products.

Names, logos, typesetting of your literature, and store layout should be carefully chosen to reflect your image. Another company who has done a great job with its image is Old Navy. The company has practical, moderately priced clothes that concentrate on value. The Old Navy name, and even the typestyle of the name, are solid and conservative, the stores aren't fancy, and the layout looks like a moderately priced store. Everything reinforces the store's image, and that helps people

$1,999

understand whether the store sells the merchandise that they want.

KidSoap is a soap that is good for kids. It is free of DEA (diethanolamine), biodegradable, and hypoallergenic. KidSoap's goal is to help kids wash regularly, but its target customer group, kids, isn't really all that interested in using a safe soap. So KidSoap is creating an image that kids want, which is something fun. Each bar of KidSoap features miniature toys ranging from collectible racing cars for boys, and dolls, rings, and charm bracelets for girls. The soap also comes with action scenes that stick to bathroom walls and fun bath toys for the kids to play with. The company also has a Web site where kids can win Beanie Babies, Michael Jordan memorabilia, and many more toys that kids like. The soap gives off bubbles in the bath, and the product comes in a fun package. KidSoap helps parents learn about the dangers of DEA, which causes cancer, and teaches parents what types of ingredients in children's products they should avoid. But the company knows that

$2,000+

the product won't sell unless the kids see it's meant for them, and the company went to great lengths to be sure that happens.

The Customer Needs to Feel Safe

Customers of all types of products are risk adverse. They don't want to buy a product that will somehow backfire on them. This is one of the reasons companies keep buying from the same supplier year after year. That may not be the best decision, but at least it won't get you in trouble. Most marketing tactics are positive and reflect an effort to do something to gain customers. You also have to take steps to be sure you don't do something that makes purchasing your product risky. In the Oakley example used earlier in the chapter, the risk is that people would buy a product that had fallen out of favor with the customer's peer group. For industrial products, the risk could be that someone will be criticized for making a new choice. For a product purchased from a TV ad, the risk is that the real product will be nothing like the one shown on TV.

> Customers are highly motivated by fear of loss and avoid risk whenever possible.

Infiltration marketing tactics go along way towards creating a feeling of safety because the company is constantly out in the market learning about customers. If you are visible everywhere in the market, people will believe you do in fact know what you are doing. For example, a company selling horse-grooming products went to horse shows for three years before people accepted that its products must work and started buying the product. Oakley customers had lost confidence in the company when they felt it had distanced itself from its customers, but their confidence came back when they realized the company was relying on its young team of hunters who were out participating in their world everyday.

$1,999

Creating a feeling of safety depends on the industry and the individuals involved. An engineer specifying new equipment is interested in buying from a manufacturer who is successfully supplying other companies in his or her industry. A small company executive looking for a human resource consultant will look for someone with an affiliation with a Human Resource Association or who has an impressive client list. Business purchases are often heavily influenced by the risk adverse strategies of the people making the purchase. Often business-to-business purchases are decided more on how easily a person can show he or she made the right choice than on what really is the best purchase option.

Traditionally, marketers have tried to figure what the customers' biggest fears are, and then determine what can be done to alleviate those fears. But that's really not the best action. No matter how many fears you eliminate, customers can come up with new ones. What is more important is to have the customer feel comfortable and have confidence in you. Then they will buy. Confidence in you is a natural byproduct of infiltration marketing, and that confidence removes much of the prospect's buying resistance.

> When customers trust you, they will buy.

Steve's Earth Engine makes cedar slat composting systems that sell for about $150. Sales were slow, and Steve Watson, the owner, couldn't get any support from gardening and environmental groups because they didn't believe Watson was really committed to the environment. Watson overcame this with a multiphase approach. He approached the City of Minneapolis and offered to have his product made by a jobs program for inner city youth. To help the jobs program, Watson convinced the City of Minneapolis to put stickers on all their recycling bins offering composting bins for $60. He then had the jobs program subsidize a $45 price for schools who wanted to sell Steve's Earth Engine composting bins as a fundraiser. Once Watson's product was being promoted everywhere, the State Horticultural Society asked him to be their guest speaker at a quarterly meeting. Watson's status shifted suddenly from being a shaky entrepreneur to a leading environmental proponent, **$500** ➤ and sales continued even after the jobs program was over.

The Bank of Collierville is a small bank that was being knocked around by encroaching banks from the big city. The Bank wanted to re-establish its role as civic hometown bank. The bank created a lighted replica of a historic building in Collierville and gave it away free to new depositors. They also let local churches sell the replica to raise money. The bank's tagline was "Where they have their branches, we have our roots." The small bank raised deposits over $500,000 just by showing it **$2,000+** ➤ cared about its community.

Oldsmobile has taken a different confidence building tactic: one-to-one communications targeted at just one individual. Oldsmobile toured 110 cities with the "Intrigue Virtual Mystery Tour." Oldsmobile has an interactive screen that people fill out, and then Oldsmobile prints out, on the spot, a brochure that covers the points that are important to that person. Oldsmobile falls a little short with this effort because it still is trying to sell a product that the consumer feels is designed by Oldsmobile. I believe Oldsmobile could take this even one step further. Rather than ask people what features are important to them, on the interactive screen I'd  have a variety of people that had told Oldsmobile what they wanted in a car. Prospects could pick the person who they felt was most like them, and then Oldsmobile would tell what that person wanted and which car Oldsmobile designed to meet that customer's needs. This would let people know that the cars were designed with the help of real people who will actually buy the products.

> Putting real customers in the product or service design loop gives a big boost to a company's credibility.

Pricing

Consumers are very aware of characteristics that let them know the pricing structure of a business. For example, a big law firm is expensive. Stores in large malls are more expensive than stores in small strip malls. Manufacturers with well-known brand names often have more expensive products. Customers have a preset price in mind when they begin looking for a product, and they will respond to companies who they view as being in their price range. Consistency is what builds credibility, and pricing is a very big part of that consistency.

Your image all starts at a price point. But you also need to be careful. People do not like being ripped off, and they will get upset with a company that they feel overcharges them. Marketers need to carefully plot out their strategy to get the price point right for the market while still providing value for the customer. A great example of a pricing strategy that was well executed is mountain bikes' pricing which has increased over 300 percent in the last five to seven years. The manufacturers started with top-end mountain bikes at $300 to $500. Today the top bikes sell for anywhere from $800 to $2,000, and sometimes up to $3,500. And everyone is happy. More mountain bikes are sold today than have ever been sold before. Following mountain bikes' evolution shows how marketers can properly position their products with price so everyone wins.

Top-end mountain bikes started out costing about $300 to $500 and were geared toward the gung-ho adventure crowd that likes to hike 50 miles into the wilderness. The bikes were sturdy and rugged. After a few years it was obvious that the target customer group of rugged individuals wasn't large. At the same time that bike companies were worried about the market's size, the sports utility vehicle (SUV) market was taking off. High-end Jeep Cherokees were selling fast to high-income young adults who liked to appear rugged but actually had no intention of ever taking their SUV off into the wilderness. This was the target customer group that the mountain bike manufacturers wanted.

> A pricing mistake can destroy all the credibility you've work so hard to build.

The mountain bike manufacturers had to be careful. They had to add features to appeal to their new target customer group, but not in a way that would offend the hardcore mountain bike riders. This was important because if the mountain bike riders didn't feel the new bike was right for them, the product also wouldn't be right for the new targeted customer group. After all, the mountain bike only appealed to young high-income families because the bike appealed to the rugged mountain bikers. The first major changes manufacturers introduced in mountain bikes were greatly improved bearing, gear, and drive systems. This had a big benefit to mountain bike riders because it greatly increased the energy transfer from the rider to the bike. That meant the mountain bikers could ride up steeper and longer inclines. That made the mountain bikers happy.

At the same time, the new drive system allowed the recreation riders to pedal with a lot less effort. Riders could bike for longer times and not feel nearly as tired. They could go up steeper hills and long inclines without having to get off their bikes. They could go out on a three-hour bike ride and come back feeling good about themselves. Both parties accepted the new $600 to $800 price because the improved performance in the bikes was dramatic. The market now started to expand, taking on more of the upscale recreational riders who liked the image of riding a mountain bike. The important point for the consumers was that the bike manufacturers charged a higher price but offered a superior product that consumers felt was worth the money. People considered the bike companies to be consumer oriented because they delivered a significantly improved product.

This first step bike companies took in improving the drive train components was important as it set the stage for the market accepting much smaller advances in the future as being efforts by the industry to promote performance. The next level of improvements were new component materials. Composites, alloys, and other exotic materials that were both lower in weight and stronger than steel were used on high-performing bikes. The mountain bikers again were happy, as they are always seeking added performance. The recreational riders were happy, even though the new materials didn't give them much benefit. They could still see that the new materials cost more, and they were willing pay more to buy the same products that hardcore mountain bikers were buying. This market group was also probably happy to see that fewer people could afford the bike, as it made owning the bike more of a status symbol. The bike manufacturers didn't care that only the high-income segment of the market could afford the new bikes because the price made the bikes that much more appealing to the young upscale riders they were targeting. The prices went up again, but everyone was happy because the new bikes helped meet their needs. The bike manufacturers delivered value for the increased price, and they created products that helped their customers achieve their goals.

Over the last couple of years the recreational riders have become far and away the biggest segment of the high-end bike market. Now the bike manufacturers could add seats with springs, shock absorbers, and a whole variety of comfort features that recreational riders loved but that would be disdained by the hardcore mountain bikers as being too soft. But it didn't matter anymore because the desirability of owning a top-end mountain bike was already firmly established in the recreational bike market. The new features were great for the recreational riders who appreciated the new features, and the true mountain bike riders kept buying the older models. Again the mountain bike companies delivered value for the price.

> Customers appreciate companies that deliver value and dramatically improved products, even if the price is higher.

I used this example because its target customers hold high-end bike manufactures in very high regard. They look to them for leadership and feel very strongly that bike manufacturers are out to help improve the bike rider's world. I'm not sure how deliberate the mountain bike marketers' strategy was, but it was brilliant nevertheless. Increased price, increased value, and industry improvements have to go hand in hand. Mountain bikes tripled or quadrupled in price but no one had sticker shock.

Buyers are highly critical of companies that raise prices without adding any true value-added features. One of the interesting marketing points over the last few years is that prices have been going up very little for any one individual item. But consumers are buying more products and more expensive products just like mountain bikes. That's why our economy is going so well. People are buying better and better products. And it's why America's economy is once again dominating the world. The Japanese may be able to run a better factory, but no one is able to create value-added features that improve a customer's world like American entrepreneurs.

Customer Service

Customer service was a heralded marketing strategy in the '80s and '90s. While I agree you need good customer service so you don't lose the customers you worked hard to get, I don't think customer service is an aggressive or particularly effective marketing strategy for getting new customers. Consider Wal-Mart, one of the stores that does have great customer service. It made its mark by going into small towns and offering great value for the price. It's the value it delivered that allowed Wal-Mart to grow. When it came to the larger cities, Wal-Mart had nicer stores and better store layouts than K-mart. It also had better customer service, but what was the true selling point? I believe the point that made Wal-Mart successful was the company delivered value.

Marketers can maximize the benefits of customer contact to ensure they are projecting a consistent image. For example, if you are a mountain bike company you can't have a practical customer service operation like a lawnmower company. You need to project a fun, adventuresome, cutting edge image. I'd start by having a help booth at all the major events the company attends. This would show that you are accessible. You want young, upbeat, real bike riders to answer technical service calls. And you probably want to send out free products to people who have a problem, even if you solve it. I have a friend who has a truck that had more than its share of breakdowns. The dealer gave him four tickets to the Monster Truck Bash in the Metrodome. Those tickets were a perfect complement for a truck owner. Look for things you can do for customers that reinforce your ties with them. Don't just think in traditional terms of customer service. Think of the things you can do to positively impact customers.

$2,000+ ➤

$500 ➤

Terry's Automotive Group sells used cars as well as providing service for cars. They weren't getting much service business from their used car buyers, which led them to think customers weren't pleased with its service. So the company started to offer a gift pack of a coffee mug, cap, and key chain to each used car buyer. which isn't all that much of a gift. Then after two weeks, the company sent out a Service Saver Card and offered especially high discounts on first-time visits. Service business from the used car buyers increased 40 percent after the company started to treat the customer a little nicer, and it reinforced the company's image as selling well-maintained used cars.

$500

BT Products is a manufacturer that produces warehouse trucks. The company then created BT Compass, a logistics planning software that helps companies cut the cost of their inventory handling process. What BT Products is doing is helping its customers improve the one area of their business that BT Products impacts, inventory handling. But customers didn't accept the image that BT Products was concerned about the companies' inventory handling goals. BT Products responded to its customers skepticism by delivering the message with customer service. To set a new system up requires customized information about the plant, the layout, the type of trucks, the size of the pallets, and other highly specific information so the system can design a layout with the highest throughput. BT Products provides a custom form to collect the information, but it also provides an in-houses consultant to help the company implement the system and enter the data correctly. That extra customer service minimized problems, kept the customer happy, and just as importantly, solidified BT Products's image as a company trying to improve the industry's inventory process. That image will help the company sell both current and future products.

> Sometimes a little extra customer service can boost sales over an entire product line.

$2,000+

Credibility is at the core of infiltration marketing. Every move you make is designed to gain credibility. Concentrating on your image, pricing strategies, and customer service will build credibility with your customers and prospects. Building customers' confidence will make the marketing process that much easier. If you don't build this credibility, or if you lose it due to a mistake, you'll be just another traditional marketer trying to generate business using high-cost, traditional marketing tactics.

CHAPTER THIRTEEN

OFFERING ANSWERS TO CUSTOMERS' GOALS

People do not buy products or services because of features and benefits. People buy products because of a goal that they have. Your sales will increase once you convince customers that you can help them meet their goal. A good example of this is a popular advertisement for a sports utility vehicle that shows a vehicle on top of a mountain. No one believes the vehicle drove to the mountaintop, but that's not the point. The buyer's goal is to be someone who thinks big, likes adventure, and who either is or will be on their own mountaintop someday. The customer's goal is support his own self-image, and the sports utility vehicles, which are oversize, full of luxuries, and present a dominating image are designed to support people's goals of having a power or success image.

The marketer's job is first to understand the customers' goals, second to design the product, service or store to meet those goals, and third to make sure customers' goals are met by a product, service or store. The product, service, or store all have to be designed so that customers immediately grasp that this product is for them. Back to our sports utility vehicles. Ford created the very popular Expedition, which is just an oversized Explorer, which was just an oversized Bronco. You see the Explorer and Expedition everywhere, but they aren't advertised much. They don't have to be advertised. Big equals power in the eyes of sports utility vehicle buyers, therefore, big is better.

This chapter deals with creating an overall package, including the product or service, advertising and promotion, and other marketing activities that deliver goal-oriented messages to the customer. Infiltration marketing is all about creating a chain

> Effective marketing always starts by understanding your customers' goals.

to the customer, forged link by link. Companies create this link by going into the customer's world rather than by blasting marketing messages at it. You are firmly entrenched in the customers' world when you completely understand customers' goals and then deliver a product or service that helps them achieve those goals. Sometimes those goals are primarily psychological, such as in the SUV market. Sometimes they are functional goals, as in the market for drafting equipment that prepares engineering documentation for new products.

And sometimes the goals are a combination of both psychological and functional goals, as in the refrigerator and the home furnishing markets or the quality control inspection market.

> The "you buy—I sell" school of marketing doesn't work anymore.

Most consultants walk into your office with an attitude of "you buy—I sell" that doesn't take them too far. The consultant who succeeds walks in, finds out the customer's goals, learns about the company and its markets, and then comes back a week later with a proposal that fits the customer's objectives. Buyers want solutions that are specifically geared to them, and marketers need to convince buyers that a customized solution is what they are buying. What are the client's goals for a consultant? The obvious one is that he or she has a problem that needs solving. There also may be strong psychological goals. A client may want to feel good about him or herself and want to believe that he or she is an effective executive. Does telling the client that his problem is simple and that you have just the service to help him make him feel good? I don't think so. A better approach is to acknowledge that the client is in a tough business and that his or her problem is going to require some research and

$100 ➤ thought before you can make a proposal. The second approach reaffirms the executive's worth. After all, the reason the executive couldn't solve the problem is

because he or she was in a difficult situation. The executive was wise to bring in a consultant. What self-image is created in the executive when a consultant minimizes the problem? Probably that the executive is too stupid or too lazy to solve the problem on his own. That is a very bad marketing approach.

> Psychological goals, when present, always dominate a buying decision.

My aunt was an artist who occasionally did portraits. She was well know in her market and received a good price for each portrait. She could do a portrait in eight to 10 hours. She had people come for two-hour sittings every two weeks. She never did any work on the portraits when the clients weren't there, and she would never accelerate her schedule. She knew that for her clients, a portrait was a reinforcement of their status and that a long, drawn-out process of completing the portrait only added to that goal. My aunt had more requests for portraits than she cared to do. She did excellent work, but she also understood a customer's psychological goals when securing a portrait.

◄— $100

Besides being the country's largest retailer, Wal-Mart is also awfully good at understanding how people's emotional response can effect even the purchase of everyday necessities. Look at the difference between Wal-Mart and Target. Both stores are well laid out, have quality merchandise, and provide excellent customer service. Target promotes its product in a feature/benefit manner by talking about sales and merchandise selection and customer service. Wal-Mart's ads concentrate first on showing that regular folks work there. They are just like the people next **◄— $2,000+** door who are there trying to help you save money. Wal-Mart's programs seem to scream out "We are your friends and we want to save you money." Wal-Mart does much better than Target because they are smart enough to appeal to people's emotions, while Target concentrates on selling features. Target and Wal-Mart have the same message—save money—but Wal-Mart delivers the message with a personal touch. Wal-

> Wal-Mart talks to customers, Target talks at customers. To customers, that's a major difference.

Mart's program wouldn't work if the store didn't deliver on its promises, but it is strong enough to differentiate it from a competitor that has a similar operation in every other way.

There are four types of customer goals that dominate every purchase decision.

1. A cost/benefit or utilitarian approach where people evaluate how well a company's products or services performs a function.
2. Psychological goals where people are heavily influenced by how the product affects their psychological needs, such as making a safe choice or supporting their self-image.
3. Lifestyle goals, such as adventuresome, sports loving, entertaining, golfing, family oriented, or active senior citizens.
4. Fun-oriented goals; people are always interested in fun, and much of their time is spent earning money so they can spend it to entertain themselves.

Cost-Effective or Performance-Related Goals

People buy products like soap, detergent, plastic wrap, and cake mix because it meets certain criteria. This is true even more for industrial purchases, especially for items that are used every day and that are necessary but don't overly effect a company's actual performance. In a case like this, companies are interested in keeping costs as low as possible. When you think beyond the cost of your product and find other ways to cut a customer's cost, you'll differentiate your competitors and increase sales.

W.W. Grainger sells maintenance, repair, and operating supplies to industrial companies. W.W. Grainger's mission is to provide low-cost distribution of supplies to its customers. This is a tough, competitive business. Grainger realized that the cost of buying supplies includes more than its prices. It also includes inventory cost, ordering costs, unused or obsolete inventory, and the cost of bringing a product into a company, recording its presence, and keeping track of it, all of which together Grainger calls the supply management process. For a mid-size manufacturing company these costs can be as high as $500,000 to $1,000,000 per year. To help customers keep their cost down, Grainger put together a team of its employees to go into a company and evaluate the total supply management process. Grainger then recommends how costs can be lowered and helps companies set up a monitoring process to ensure that recommended actions actually are producing cost savings.

> Grainger understood its customers buy hassle-free, low-cost supplies.

In most cases Grainger finds major flaws in at least one of the key areas, such as tracking inventory use. Often companies tie up two or three people, and sometimes more, tracking these supplies. Grainger will set up a system that can be run by one person, and even install one of their employees at the plant to handle the procuring and tracking process. It is not unusual for Grainger to save a company 10 percent or more of their total cost to install a Grainger employee at the company's locations and to increase the company's business 100 to 300 percent.

$2,000+ ➡

Grainger starts the process of selling a service by performing an initial assessment free. Then it comes back and charges for a more thorough study. In the end though, it makes most of its profits by selling more supplies. Grainger has a built-in credibility because it has served most manufacturers for many years, and people appreciate Grainger's evaluation of their operations. One important point to note is that Grainger's offer made sense to its customers because Grainger would get increased sales as a result of cutting the customer's overall costs. You need to be careful when you offer a free service that you do it in a credible way that makes sense to a customer. Consider these two offers: Get a thorough car inspection for $49.95 or a free car inspection. If your car needs work, the $49.95 will be applied towards the cost of repairs if you decide to have it repaired there. That offer makes sense as you are offering a discount if people decide to get their car repaired, plus the $49.95 offer seems like a reasonable price for a thorough electronic inspection. The free automobile inspection sounds suspicious. Either the inspection is lousy or the garage will try to get you to spend money on repairs.

Both buying supplies and getting a car repaired are performance or feature/benefit-related decisions. Both the Grainger and auto garage example point out that marketers can never ignore people's emotions and feeling of comfort when purchasing a product. Selling the company itself always comes first, which is why infiltration marketing tactics are so effective. Corporate advertising, a traditional marketing tactic, is not effective because it is a company talking to a customer. Intel's corporate image program of promoting its Intel Inside logo doesn't relate to even one customer goal. Intel takes a much better approach with its promotions department when it puts its World of Computer booth into state fairs. Inside the booth Intel demonstrates how a computer works and what happens in a computer chip. That is a good example of infiltration marketing—it goes into the customer's world and offers an interesting experience.

> Image advertising is not infiltration marketing.

Campbell's Soup is another manufacturer who is constantly trying to provide promotions that understand customers' goals and promote what could be considered a commodity item. I mentioned earlier about Campbell's promotion at schools offering free computer supplies for school collecting soup labels. Campbell's is also under pressure from stores who want to reduce Campbell's shelf space to offer generic soups and other lower cost brands.

Campbell's is fighting back with a strategy that helps both stores and consumers meet their goals. Campbell's has put together a small interactive display, about the size of a microwave, that can help consumers find where a can of soup is on the shelf and can call up and print recipes that incorporate soup as an ingredient. The stores like this feature as it encourages people to buy other products in the store to complete the recipes, and consumers like it because it helps them with their meal planning and preparation. That's an effective strategy, helping your customers with their goals, and as result, Campbell's sells more products.

$2,000+ ➤

Psychology-Dominated Goals

I've talked about the important part that self-image, or a feeling of safety or comfort, plays in a purchase decision. Much of the reason for this is that disposable income is rising fast in America and people are having choices they didn't have before. When my father bought a house, any worries about self-image or feeling good were mitigated by the fact he only had so much money to spend and he had to get the house that gave him the best value in features and benefits that he could buy. Today, with higher income levels people can choose to buy homes that are much larger than they really need, and they have a tremendous number of options. They can afford to live in a real big house to show how successful they are. Or they can live in a smaller house that's less work where they feel more comfortable.

As income has increased, people have bought more and more things. But people are limited to how many things they can actually buy, and they are starting now to concentrate on upscale items that better meet psychological or lifestyle goals. That has shifted consumers away from feature/benefit considerations to buying more for desires or lifestyle. As an example, consider stores such as Imaginarium and Discovery Toys that sell products to increase the intelligence and creativity of children. They didn't exist 30 years ago simply because people didn't have the money to buy expensive items for their children.

> The market is buying high-feature, high-value products today that it simply couldn't afford before.

Everyone buys certain items because of self-image or other psychological reasons. We also buy other products for strictly cost/benefit reasons. Marketers need to understand their customers' goals when purchasing their products, and they also need to know what psychologically motivates their customers. Since consumers will pay more for products that meet their desires, marketers constantly strive to improve the importance of their product to consumers. Campbell's Soup's interactive display is an example of a company realizing that its product is used primarily when people want to serve soup, and its interactive program tried to answer the goal of being a good parent by preparing delicious dinners.

The Palm Pilot came onto the market in 1996 and sold 1 million units within 18 months. The Palm Pilot is the fastest selling computer product of all time. It's even sold faster than cell phones, pagers, and color TVs. Its success came because the founders were able to translate the product into a cultural phenomena featured in TV shows and movies. They achieved that goal because they hit their design goal of producing a computer product that could fit into a shirt pocket. That

> There is a large group of buyers who want the latest product with a "gee whiz" factor.

took the product from being a small computer at a high price to the latest gizmo gadget piece of electronic wizardry that every technophile just had to have.

The Palm Pilot's history started when its founders worked on Zoomer PDA for Radio Shack, which was a very small computer with a small keyboard that was hard to use. The computer also was the first one that allowed people to write on a screen and have the computer read the person's handwriting and convert it into a word processing file. It also had drivers for printers and fax machines that didn't work well, and it cost $700. The Zoomer PDA tried to do too many things for the price, and the product failed.

But the inventors learned some valuable lessons. Most of the users of the Zoomer were business people who transferred data to their own computer. The product didn't need fax and printer connections, and the people preferred to write on a screen and didn't want a keyboard.

Taking out these features gave the Palm Pilot designers a new perspective. Taking out all the features people didn't want left open the possibility that the Palm Pilot could fit in a shirt pocket. The goal was delayed because they stumbled over the slow, poor-quality handwriting software programs that were available and the large computing it took to run them and recognize the thousands of writing styles. The only solution was to teach people how to write in a certain way on the Palm Pilot so it could rapidly recognize the letters. This is the time the Palm Pilot was really born. Teaching people a new handwriting style was a tough goal. But its developers knew that any resistance to learning a new way of writing would be overcome by the "gee whiz" factor of a shirt top computer. That transformed the Palm Pilot into something so unusual and innovative that it became a must-have for its main target customers, business people who felt they were on the cutting edge of technology.

The company hit its target, creating a monumental new market of which it is the clear leader. All because it was smart enough to realize sales would come faster if it met its customers' desire to appear to be technologically savvy. As a bonus, Palm Pilot's development cost was only $3 million, compared to the rest of markets development cost of over $1 billion. Once the company focused on customers' psychological desires, it was no longer necessary to spend millions on unnecessary, difficult features that didn't add to the product's "gee whiz" factor.

> Development costs can be slashed when you concentrate on meeting people's desires.

Lifestyle-Based Goals

People lead a wide variety of different lifestyles, including families growing fruits and vegetables on a hobby farm, city families with kids in dozens of activities, single people in business, blue-collar workers who go to the cabin every weekend, and senior citizens who do volunteer work. This, of course, is just a small percentage of the number of lifestyles people pursue. Each lifestyle has a different set of goals that people perceive to be important. People who live on hobby farms probably are focused on environmental goals, families in the cities may focus on doing whatever they can to make their children's lives better. Single people may be interested in things that make them attractive to other singles and things they can do or places to go where they can have fun and meet other singles.

Infiltration marketers want customers to clearly recognize that their lifestyle goals are matched by companies' goals. Restaurants probably do this better than any other business. People can quickly recognize a business-oriented restaurant, a restaurant for young singles, a family restaurant, and a romantic restaurant. Another market group that does a great job is youth-oriented companies like snowboarding manufacturers, where it is quite clear they are appealing to rebellious youth anxious to do anything they can to be different than anyone over 25.

Youth, of course, are a relatively easy group to appeal to because their lifestyle is dramatically different. Family-oriented customer groups with children are harder to connect with because they don't have as many distinguishing characteristics that apply to the whole group. But marketers can still connect to their customers. For example, minivans were a great product that quickly and clearly identified with the family lifestyle. McDonald's connects to families with their playrooms. Bunk beds are another category that is clearly directed at families. Other companies, however, don't do an effective job connecting with their cus- ◄— **$2,000+** tomers. How do furniture manufacturers target the family lifestyle? They tend to be focused more on price or décor style. Outside of kids' bedrooms, the furniture companies haven't really hit on a way to match people's lifestyles.

I'm sure furniture manufacturers and retailers feel it's too difficult to match lifestyles, but I think they are wrong. Single people who have apartments may be looking for a certain type of furniture, and families may want furniture that kids can climb, like a family room jungle gym. I'm not sure what furniture buyers who have different lifestyles are looking for, but I do know that furniture manufacturers aren't offering people choices in a way that is connecting to them. The point is that just because marketers in certain groups aren't doing lifestyle-based marketing doesn't mean they shouldn't be. There are plenty of opportunities for businesses to grow by being the first to connect with the customer.

> Marketing to lifestyle goals is frequently not done, leaving room for innovative marketers.

A Whale of a Tale children's bookstore target customer group is families with small children. It wants to promote the interaction of children and parents through reading. So the store wants to match the parents' goal of having close interaction between parents and children. To project this image, the store sets up many small separate areas in the store where parents can read a book to their child. They have wooden trains separating sections where kids and parents can sit together. They have little specially made doll houses and castles. All of these are separate areas where a

$1,999 →

parent can sit with one or two children. The bookstore knows what it is selling—bonding between parents and children.

This same principle applies to industrial marketers or where the main concern is the driving force behind a business rather than lifestyle. Some companies are marketing driven businesses, like trucking firms or contractors, who are always having to find and replace customers. They tune in to messages that help their business get more customers. When marketing to these companies you need to concentrate on looking like a company that markets products and services that helps customers meet their goals. For instance, how would you market quality control equipment to a marketing-oriented company? Not by focusing on fail-safe measures or 100 percent quality inspection. That is a minor focus at a marketing-oriented company. You need to concentrate on things that will help the company market more of its products. You'd want to talk about a software/printer system that shows what tests have been performed on every product shipped. That would be a tool salespeople could use to show customers. Or you could demonstrate how your equipment is specially configured for rapid changeovers so the company can match even the most specialized inspection request from a customer. Or you might discuss how you could provide a detailed inspection report for every production run that a company can share with its customers. You need to focus on the things your product can do to help a customer market its own products.

> Business-to-business marketers need to focus on the driving force behind a customer's business.

Fun-Oriented Goals

People like to have fun, and no matter what your market, you should be constantly looking for ways to create a fun environment. Restaurants like Rainforest Café are fun, and a little more fun can even be introduced onto a Web search engine, as Yahoo has proven. Yahoo is considered the search engine with the human touch. More consumers go through the Yahoo search engine than any other engine, even though many experts feel it is not the best one on the Internet. Yahoo does nothing more than being likable. It has a friendly layout, Yahoo clubs, and seems to provide primary links to sites that are fun. Another example of the importance of being related to entertainment and fun are the recipes on cereal boxes. Just take a look at the use of recipes. Wheat Chex, Rice Chex, and Corn Chex all have a Chex Mix party recipe on each box. I think most people know about the mix and even use it occasionally even though it is not promoted that much anymore. People remember Chex Mix because it is associated with parties.

Campbell's Soup, which does a lot of things right, has an awfully hard time trying to have fun. If they come up with some party menus or fun appetizers, I think they could accelerate their sales even more. I know one businessman who has a rather dull business. Everywhere he goes he wears a cowboy hat (which is unusual in Minnesota). People think the hat is fun, and they never forget the guy. He tells me he feels a little self-conscious at times but is happy because everyone remembers him. That's a mighty small investment for an effective marketing program.

When Nintendo first created its electronic game system, it had a tremendous amount of trouble creating a game people liked. Apparently the computer whiz kids didn't have much imagination when it came to producing a memorable game. So Nintendo went out and hired an artist to create a game. He was to build something fun that had a lot of adventure. The artist created Mario, the ultrapopular game that established Nintendo as a market leader. He had no idea how to produce the game. But that didn't matter. The computer programmers produced the artist's vision into a game and Mario became a cultural phenomenon.

Resonating with your customers' goals is a critical part of marketing. Infiltration marketing is really designed to help you understand what your customers' goals are. Once you know that, marketing becomes an easy proposition because people will look for you when you help them meet their goals. No matter what you sell or who your target customer group is, you can count on one thing: They all have goals they are trying to meet, and you'll get the sale when buyers believe you help them meet their goals better than anyone else.

CHAPTER FOURTEEN

ESTABLISHING THE PRICE/VALUE RELATIONSHIP

Today's consumers are conditioned to buy only when they feel they are getting a good deal. Otherwise, they wait for a more favorable offer. Studies by groups such as McKinsey & Co., out of Cleveland, Ohio, have found that 25 percent of customers buy based on price alone. Companies that discount price without an inherent cost advantage are doomed to failure because competitors will always match the lower price. Marketers need to make a profit, and providing a long-term, attractive price/value relationship encourages customers to buy—without promotion.

Pricing is an area where marketers consistently fall down and ruin their relationship with customers. In 1992 Congress passed laws regulating the pricing of cable TV because consumers thought they were being gouged. In 1996 additional laws were passed regulating cable TV prices. This is amazing as cable TV provides home entertainment, and it should be one industry that is closely aligned with customers. But instead it has fostered a "me versus you" attitude that hurts everyone. Resistance to price levels is showing up everywhere. A luxury tax on boats caused sales to fall dramatically. Lawyers, who are suppose to be advocates for their clients, are roundly criticized for their high fees. Consumers are calling for legislation to curb automobile and life insurance costs.

At the same time, other industries raise prices successfully and keep customers firmly on their side. Sport utility vehicles and pick-up trucks have risen rapidly in price with few complaints. Snowboard, ski, and skateboard manufacturers have consistently convinced customers they have a good price/value relationship despite rapidly escalating prices. Personal services such as fitness trainers, home cleaning services, and caterers have been able to increase prices while still keeping closely connected with their customers.

Marketers need to learn how to create profitable sales prices while still increasing customer loyalty and satisfaction. Infiltration marketing tactics help build value because they are in a sense a branding strategy. But marketers still need to carefully follow pricing guidelines to avoid pricing pitfalls. Once you avoid mistakes, you can then turn pricing around and use it as aggressive strategy to build customer loyalty, all without alienating customers.

> Infiltration marketing is a comprehensive strategy that establishes a brand name.

This chapter covers how to prevent pricing errors, how to sell increased pricing to customers, and how to create a tempting price point that will entice customers to buy today. This chapter will be covering long-term strategies that create value. Some of these will be promotions, such as package pricing, while others will be adding features to tie the customer to you more closely to justify higher pricing. Chapter 15 will cover the use of short-term promotions to increase sales while still supporting your company's image.

Raising prices is not something marketers should be afraid to do as long as they create added value. Your company will simply not grow if you don't constantly move forward and offer more value and service, which in many cases dictates that you must learn how to effectively raise prices. Customers are willing to pay more if you give them exactly what they want. You are wasting your time if you go into the market, learn what the customer wants, but then are afraid to capitalize on your knowledge by refusing to raise prices.

Snorkel Stove Co. in Seattle, Washington manufactures kits for hot tubs that are heated by a wood-burning stove. The kits sell for about $2,000. Snorkel has few competitors, but it doesn't increase prices because the owner is afraid the phone will stop ringing. By keeping prices down, Snorkel isn't able to get out into the market and learn just how its products could be better. Snorkel also isn't able to develop a strong brand identity or have an aggressive program tying itself to other companies serving the adventurous outdoorsman, nor is it able to put together an ambitious program to find new customers. Snorkel's sales shuffle along at about $700,000 per year.

> Prices need to go up if you are going to add more value for your customers.

Preventing Pricing Errors

KNOW YOUR TOP PRICE POINT

Cable TV found itself in trouble because it forgot that you have to decide what your top price is before deciding on what services to offer. Cable TV had a group of viewers in cities that had trouble getting good reception. They only wanted cable for the free commercial channels (ABC, NBC, and CBS). These customers, many on fixed incomes, had a top limit of only $6 to $8 per month. Cable TV's approach was to bundle a large number of "free" channels like TBS, USA Network, and WGN TV into a service that was anywhere from $14.95 to $19.95. Then cable TV tried to explain to their fixed-income customers that they added more value and that the customers were getting a good deal. All that didn't matter though because the top price those people would pay was $8 for the low-end service.

No matter what your market is, people have a limit on what solving that problem is worth. People are only willing to pay a top price of $250 to $300 for a standard push lawnmower no matter what features it might have. You need to know this price first before you come out with a product or service to be sure that you meet your price point. Otherwise you may over engineer a product, provide too many features and benefits, or build the product with quality materials that the market just won't pay for.

Lawnmower companies have been in an interesting dilemma over the last few years. They have been hit by a series of environmental edicts to lower the pollution from lawnmowers. These changes add cost to the lawnmower, but they don't change the top price people are willing to pay for a standard push lawnmower. Lawnmower manufacturers have responded in four ways. First, they all banded together to develop a product solution to lower pollution. This cut the development cost to each manufacturer, plus it cut the actual per unit upcharge the environmental systems would cost. Next, they pulled some of the more decorative features off the lawnmowers to cut cost. The lawnmower companies have also started to sell more products through home improvement stores like Home Depot that take a lower markup than the hardware store/specialized equipment dealers that lawnmowers have traditionally been sold

Marketers need to scramble when their costs go up and their prices have to stay the same.

through. Finally, the lawnmower manufacturers introduced new models with new features, such as mulching mowers, allowing the top acceptable price to creep up toward the $300 price point.

PRICE RANGES ARE IMPORTANT

People become accustomed to buying products at a certain price range. When you blur those ranges you confuse customers and they don't know if they are getting a good price or not. Ford sells three low- to moderately-priced cars, the Escort, Contour, and Taurus. Prior to 1998 the prices of the three cars overlapped. That price strategy blurs the distinction between the cars and hurts each product's differentiation. In 1998 Ford switched strategies, pricing each car in its own separate range, and developed new positioning themes for each car, from a young buyer theme for the Escort to the affordable family car for the Taurus.

Customers generally put products into a price range based on quality, a brand name, features, product looks, or some other factor they have been conditioned to in the market. As an example, a graphic designer that does brochures will typically have a creative cost of $2,000 to $4,000, a full-fledged advertising agency will be in the $10,000 range, while an Insty Print or Sir Speedy will be in the $500 to $1,000 range. The quality of each piece and level of service will be different, with Sir Speedy offering a traditional, simple layout based on a layout and copy that you provide. The graphic designer will do the entire layout but will need from the client copy and positioning statements before being able to complete a layout, while an advertising agency will do a positioning strategy, prepare copy, and do a creative layout. A graphic artist who offers to team up with a marketing consultant for a positioning strategy and charges $6,000 to $8,000 will be outside traditional price ranges and be considered either a lousy advertising agency or a high-priced graphic designer. That's not a good place for anybody to be. The graphic artist has to offer a more comprehensive service at the high end of the graphics arts range or gear up to be a specialty agency that either offers limited services that are hard to find or customized services for a special market.

I recently was on a marketing assignment to figure out a new positioning strategy for a bike pump. The manufacturer had been in business for over 50 years and once was the leading manufacturer in the business. But the manufacturer had gotten complacent, stopped being a vital player in the market, and sales had plummeted. I found that the industry's pricing range had changed and the company's pricing had left a gap in the new market price ranges. The company manufactured a gauge pump

> Creating a new price range is a task even large companies have trouble executing.

that put out 150 pounds of pressure and came with a Schrader valve. (When you fill a tire, the Schrader valve is the pin inside the thumblock that lets air in or out of the tire.) For years this was the top-end bike pump. Over the last 10 years bike manufacturers started to raise the price of their top-end bikes and they came out with new tires that took up to 200 pounds of pressure and used Presta valves instead of a Schrader valve. This was part of their effort to distinguish high-end from low-end bikes. Two types of pumps started to take over the market. One were low-end pumps with gauges that measured to 100 pounds of pressure and came equipped with Schrader valve fittings. These pumps sold for 50 percent less than my manufacturer's pumps. The other pumps were high-end pumps that had gauges that measured to 200 pounds of pressure and came equipped with Presta valves. They sold for double the price of my manufacturer's gauge pump. The pumps stopped selling because they were perceived to be a very expensive cheap pump. This is not a good positioning statement. We reconfigured the pumps, going to a 200-pound pressure gauge and adding a Presta valve, and the company was back in the hunt.

IGNORING THE INFLUENCE OF A BRAND NAME

Companies work hard to develop their brand name so people recognize it, value it, and search it out. Consumers are also more confident buying a brand name because they know that manufacturer or retailer will be careful not to ruin a name that it has worked so hard to build up. For example, a brand name like Tide detergent has been built up for years. The manufacturer of Tide is going to be cautious about making any marketing or product moves that could hurt its image. Consumers know that and are willing to pay more for Tide because they know they won't be disappointed. A few years ago an environmentally safe detergent tablet came out from an unknown manufacturer. This tablet could be used for several months before a new tablet was needed. The company didn't have the money to

> The strength of your brand name is an important element of perceived value.

promote its products, and consumers thought the product was too risky to buy. That product would have been a success if came out under the Tide name. That's the power of a brand name, and it can command a 10 to 30 percent premium in the market. When you set your prices, don't just consider how your features and benefits compare to competition, consider also the power of the brand name.

Woolrich has been making outdoors-oriented products for 170 years and is a well-known name among people over 45. When outdoors clothing by retailers like Eddie Bauer and L.L. Bean took off, Woolrich manufactured most of the products in the market on a private label basis. L.L. Bean and Eddie Bauer started their own production once they got large enough and Woolrich got killed when it tried to re-enter the market. Woolrich believed that all it needed was a high-quality product, but that belief was disastrous. What happened was that Woolrich had let its brand name slip, and it couldn't get the same price as the other retailers. Woolrich laid off over half of its employees and closed six plants before it woke up and started to rebuild its brand name with advertising and newer product designs. It could increase sales even faster if it would convert over to an aggressive infiltration marketing strategy.

Raising Prices Safely

All you need to do to safely raise prices is to substantiate in customers' minds that you are increasing the value that they receive for the higher price. Cable TV suppliers got in trouble with buyers of its basic package because more channels weren't valuable for them. One of the reasons marketers use infiltration marketing tactics is to know their customers and what is important to them. Infiltration marketers typically use customers as advisers on new products and services so there can be no doubt the company is adding value.

> You can safely increase prices when customers perceive you've increased value.

Adding value in the customer's eye has two components. The first is to actually increase value, and the second is to make sure the customer understands how you added value. One tactic people frequently use is to come out with a new product or model. Chrysler did this on their minivans. They started with a standard product, the Caravan, then added the Caravan SE, which had more luxurious features, and finally they added the Grand Caravan. In the end the standard Caravan became a very low selling model. But the important point is that Chrysler let the market decide to pay more rather than forcing a price increase on the consumers. Chrysler was protected from a mistake with this strategy. If customers didn't see increased value from the new features, ◄— **$2,000+** they would just continue to buy the standard model Caravan.

Another tactic is to offer a product free for a period of time before implementing a price change. The *Toronto Globe and Mail* wanted to raise its Sunday paper price 25 cents to $2. The newspaper started offering a new and improved entertainment section and a larger business section in its Sunday paper without increasing prices. The paper raised the price about two months after the changes when the paper's new sections had received a great response and people indicated ◄— **$2,000+** that the paper had indeed added value.

You can also add value to customers by taking over some of their tasks. Kingsway Paper distributes shopping bags throughout the country. In order to secure business, even with higher prices, Kingsway has taken over many store tasks. It tells store headquarters usage levels at each store as well as determines the ordering variables that each store should consider. Kingsway makes each sales call with an itemized list of what each store should order based on past usage patterns and recommendations for purchasing changes based on innovative tactics being ◄— **$1,999** used by other stores.

ESA-IRA is a European supplier of hard-to-find information over the Internet. When it decided to raise prices it changed prices to correlate with the customers desired benefit. The company formerly charged for connected time online searching various databases. When it raised prices it changed to pricing for information, where customers paid for the amount of information they received. This gave customers a true look at their cost for the benefit they received. The company found after raising prices that customers stayed online longer, conducted more ◄— **$100** extensive searches, and found the experience more satisfying.

Swardlock Marketing Group of Portland, Maine raised prices by including an additional specification that promises performance. When Swardlock quotes on a project they specify what the project's objective is in real terms to the customer, such as a sales brochure that will help salespeople close on 25 percent of their sales calls. The added specification ties in with the benefit the customer wants, and it allows prices to go up because Swardlock has made itself accountable.

Another tactic is to use flat rate pricing rather than per hour pricing. Lawyers and others use a per hour charge of $150 to $500. Clients are scared off by the high price and are constantly tying to limit the firm's hours, which limits the efficiency of everyone's efforts. Switching to a flat price rate can help lawyers work with a client to set up a cost-effective plan that benefits everyone. Another advantage to everyone is that the client is never faced with unexpected charges that they might not be willing to pay.

Federal Express recently switched to zone pricing, which is a differentiated pricing strategy. Instead of charging the same price for each part of the country, Federal Express charges a different price depending on how far the product is shipped. Federal Express dropped the price for close zones and raised the price dramatically for distant zones. The overall result is a significant price increase from Federal Express, but their strategy made sense to the customers who feel distant shipments should cost more than short shipments.

Other companies will bundle services to add value when they raise prices. For example, Pitney Bowes added features to many of its postage machines and raised their price. But they also offered a new service that allowed customers to increase the postage in the meter by phone. This eliminated long waits at the post office and was a great new service for the price. Overall, the customer looked at the price increase as an even tradeoff; they paid more per month for the machine, but they received a new service that created more value than it cost. Marketers should follow Pitney Bowes's example and coordinate the introduction of very high-value services with the implementation of higher prices.

I've read several articles recently that said all marketers need to do is establish why the prices went up and people will accept higher prices. I don't find that to be true at all. People will only pay more when they receive more value. Our lawn-mower manufacturers can't raise their price $100 because they have to meet environmental regulations. The customers won't see increased value, and they won't pay for it.

Customers don't care if you have a good reason for raising prices. They only care if you add value.

Creating Permanent Value

I've talked about adding features, services, and other products to create value. The best perceived price/value relationships are ones that come from a complete solution to customers' needs or goals. This is primarily because the customer will have a final price to evaluate the service provided. For example, if a company wants to increase sales, it might hire a marketing consultant for a 20 percent commission who will handle everything: brochure expenses, hiring and paying sales agents, calling on major accounts, and staffing trade shows. The customer has a fixed figure of 20 percent for a known goal, increased sales. The customer probably knows his current marketing expenses, and if they were 20 percent he would say this is a fair offer. But what is the customer's response when a consultant offers to do a marketing plan for $15,000? Is that a good deal? That is hard to tell because the customer can only evaluate what other plans cost and can't evaluate what the value will be for him. And what if the customer is worried about whether he or she can execute the plan? Then the plan's value to the customer really becomes uncertain.

> ITI Technologies Inc. is a manufacturer of wireless security systems. When ADT, its largest customer at 40 percent of total sales, informed ITI that it was going to stop buying ITI's products, ITI's response was a classic case of adding value to entice customers to buy. Their strategy was so successful that ITI's sales were higher the year after ADT made its announcement. The classic steps ITI took were:
>
> 1. ITI created a hybrid (both hardwire and wireless) system that could be used in conjunction with any preinstalled security system for easy installation of additional security components. This strategy provided a complete customer solution, which has high value to customers.
> 2. ITI introduced the Quick Bridge product for wireless receivers, which allowed ITI's products to be used with any hardwire security system. This easy-to-install, easy-to-use product was an important benefit to companies who only rarely install security

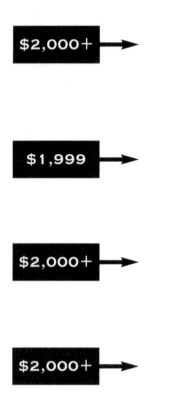

systems. This unique proprietary product provided an important and added value.

3. ITI signed a marketing agreement with Honeywell, through which ITI was able to sell a new do-it-yourself product to Sears stores. Aligning itself with Honeywell gave ITI high leverage with both Sears and Sears's customers. This part of ITI's strategy was to utilize a brand name (Honeywell) to secure both a distribution outlet and to help create a higher perceived value.

4. ITI set up a network of smaller independent dealers throughout the country to handle its products to both commercial and residential service. These dealers provide total installation, rapid service backup, training, and a personal contact, all service features that create value.

5. ITI signed agreements with 30 utilities around the country. The utilities, such as Southern California Edison, Washington Natural Gas, and South Carolina Gas and Electric, were looking for ways to increase revenue to its customer base. ITI benefits from the increased sales and distribution and from the credibility it gained from being associated with such well-known utilities.

> Joining forces with a strong brand name increases value dramatically.

Amazingly, ITI accomplished all these tasks in one year, which shows how much a desperate company can do. In reality, ADT's decision to drop ITI was the best thing that ever happened to ITI. It is a much stronger company now than it ever was before. ITI utilized four great strategies for increasing value: 1) it provided complete solutions; 2) it added unique features that provided benefits that customers desired; 3) it aligned itself with companies with strong brand names for increased credibility; and 4) it created a distribution network that could generate a high service level, and as result, create a higher perceived value for its products.

The one value-added feature ITI didn't use that I like is a performance guarantee. I'm not talking about a warranty but a guarantee of performance. Customers are tired of warranties and other forms of guarantees that don't necessarily assure performance. When companies go out of their way to guarantee satisfaction they quickly connect with customers.

Bank One acquired a failed Texas bank that had sold its trust department. Bank One decided to reopen the trust department. The new managers wanted to make a strong service statement to rebuild its customer base. The managers decided to offer an unconditional guarantee. Any customers, dissatisfied for any reason, could receive all their fees back or any portion of their fees that they felt was fair. Over the next six years only seven customers out of 4,500 asked for their fees back.

That is truly an infiltration marketing guarantee. It makes customers 100 percent clear about whose side the bank is on—theirs. The Bank One example of generating 4,500 new accounts points out one other important fact. Your pricing structure contributes strongly to your image as a company that cares about customers. Infiltration marketing requires you to care about the customer first before counting on the sales coming in. For customers to believe you are serious about being in their corner, they have to believe you are providing products and services that are a great value. Don't be afraid to raise prices as long as you use one and preferably more value-added strategies so your customers will perceive that you've improved your price/value relationship.

CHAPTER FIFTEEN

USING PROMOTIONS TO GENERATE SALES

Most retail and industrial business operate in a manner that suggests "Here I am—come and buy." They might run sales, send out salespeople, or do advertising to lure people in, but they mostly are just there. If a person comes into a store or contacts a business they may get a "Can I help you" or get sent a package of literature. Part of a typical business's strategy is to have a sale or other promotion every now and then. This promotional strategy calls for either price discounts, giveaways of some type, a package price, or a contest. Promotions are a good way to boost sales, but only if you can justify a sound reason for the promotion and if the promotion enhances your overall business image.

Price discount promotions are often inconsistent with the concept of infiltration marketing. You are supposed to be walking hand in hand with the customer. If you can afford to drop your prices, why aren't they lower all the time? That's a tough question to answer. Cub Foods, a major retailer, gets around this problem by offering sales on seasonal items. At Christmas you can buy a wreath for $6.99, which is $5 to $6 less than any other store in the area. This helps reinforce Cub Foods's image of a value leader without compromising its price structure. MCI's five cents per minute promotion also enhances its image. It is a discount, but it is on the slowest phone day of the week. If calls aren't made on a Sunday, the time is lost forever to MCI. So why not offer a super low rate so people can talk to their friends and family. It reinforces MCI's image as the friends and family phone company without undercutting the core value of MCI's service. There are many other reasons to use price discounts sparingly, but the most important one is that it tells customers that you are charging more than you need to.

Toy retailers have started making a strategic change at Christmastime by releasing catalogs of the toys they have. The catalogs go out in the Sunday newspapers and are also available at the stores. Ames, a discount store in smaller towns, sent out a catalog that had 66 pages of toys with their prices listed. Ames's stores tend to be smaller than Wal-Mart or K-mart, and having a big catalog showing a lot of products was a good strategy because it sent the message to customers that they didn't have to travel to a bigger city to shop at a big discount store.

> A price discount promotion tells customers you are charging more than you need to.

Caldor is another smaller discount store. Its catalog talks about its value pricing in the store but doesn't offer any discounts. Caldor's catalog also had a pack of yellow stickers that kids could use to place on the pictures of the toys they wanted. That makes it easy for parents and grandparents to know what kind of presents to buy.

$2,000+ →

K-mart, known for its blue light specials, couldn't resist putting coupons in its catalog. But they also had an overall theme, Toy Mania, and heavily promoted the fact that it carries products from all the main brand names such as Lego, Barbie, and Sesame Street. Toys "R" Us used its catalog to promote that it not only carried the major brand names but also that it had a large number of exclusive toys that you couldn't buy anywhere else.

> Promotions should enhance your company's image.

Caldor and K-mart both introduced catalogs in 1997 and used the catalogs not just to advertise price but to help position their stores and images in the customer's mind. All the stores realized that selection was a more important criteria than price. I especially like Caldor's idea of giving a set of yellow stickers with its catalog. The use of catalogs demonstrates three points. One is that promotions can and should add to your company's positioning strategy. Another is that, like Caldor, you can add infiltration marketing elements into your promotional strategy. The final point is that tactics like promotion, publicity, advertising, and customer service are all being blended together and it's often hard to draw a line between them.

$500 →

Your promotions can have all the elements of marketing promotion wrapped into them, and marketers shouldn't settle for less.

Reader's Digest launched a promotion in the United Kingdom (UK) for its book *Foods that Harm, Foods that Heal* that included many PR, advertising, and infiltration marketing tactics united in one campaign. The key to the strategy was to go on a road show touring various cities. The tour included many of the doctors and dietitians that were featured in the book. Reader's Digest set up clinics at supermarkets where doctors and dietitians would actually evaluate the health contents of people's purchases. Reader's Digest brought enough people along that each clinic seemed like a huge event. Reader's Digest arranged for interviews on radio shows before the clinics promoting both the book and the clinic. Radio stations loved the interviews because the whole concept of doctors analyzing what people actually buy was new. Newspapers also picked up on the stories, and TV networks covered the clinics in their nightly newscast. After clinics left a city, Reader's Digest ran a direct response TV ad program selling the product directly to consumers that capitalized on all the exposure the company had received. The results: *Foods that Harm, Foods that Heal* quickly found a spot in the UK's list of top 10 hardback bestsellers.

> Marketers can triple a program's effectiveness by combining the entire range of marketing tactics into one program.

← $2,000+

Small retailers may not be able to afford the same scale of events as a Toys "R" Us or Reader's Digest, but they can certainly follow the same tactics. Small retailers can network with other retailers serving similar customers and have postcards and flyers displayed at other stores. Smaller companies can take advantage **← $500** of high-speed color printers to print their own customized postcards or brochures every week. Too often retailers print a catalog that doesn't change for several **← $500** years. It's important to change promotional material often, highlighting new and unique items, special events, and other promotions.

Small companies that serve the consumer market should always partner up to cut marketing costs, particularly for newspaper or local magazine ads. Big retailers sign contracts with newspapers and catalogs that cuts their advertising rates up to 75 percent less than what small retailers, advertising sporadically, pay. Small retailers get this rate only if they commit to so many inches or pages of ads for the year and agree to pay for the ads even if they don't run them. This is a risk most small retailers can't take. Why not team up with a group of retailers and take turns running ads under the same contract and place on the bottom of each ad every

$1,999 → company that is in your group, such as the outdoor retailers of Dorchester. Retailers can each advertise three or four times as often for the same price they were paying before, and each retailer will have its name mentioned in each ad. If retailers in the group plan their promotions to coincide with their ad space, each retailer will maximize the benefit of the ad. All the retailers in the group will benefit from increased image and increased business. I think a program like this would be effective even if the retailers didn't get such a huge discount on ads.

Reader's Digest's health clinic promotion was really centered on a local supermarket. This is a promotion any business or store can, and many do, run. Local publicity can be generated through

> Decide on the goals of your promotion and then coordinate as many activities as you can to hit that goal.

local papers, radio shows, and through a variety of other local organizations. For example, the Philadelphia Children's Fair, sponsored by a variety of local children-oriented businesses, receives local media coverage. But it also gives $2 off admission coupons out through schools, day care centers, and park and recreation centers. The Children's Fair could go even further if it allowed

PTAs to use their admission tickets as a fund raiser or gave away a free gift to

$2,000+ → anyone bringing a coupon sponsored by a school.

The Children's Fair and Reader's Digest examples both emphasize that you need to plan a promotion carefully to be sure you are getting all the exposure you possibly can from your marketing dollar. You should start with the objective of the promotion. Reader's Digest wanted to introduce a new book with a different idea to the market, and the Children's Fair wanted to expose consumers to businesses they didn't know about and find out the names of people actively buying products for young children. In Reader's Digest's case, the goal was to sell books. The promotion program first created interest, and then a direct response TV program sold the product. For the Children's Fair marketers wanted wide exposure to viable customers. The Fair's objective was to attract as many people as possible to the fair.

Promotions can be varied to accomplish four tasks: exposing your name to customers, engaging the customer, getting customers' names, and closing the sale. Seminars, special promotions such as gourmet cooking classes, or a demonstration of rope climbing equipment do all four. Other promotions such as a bridal fair or outdoors show primarily expose a product and help marketers get names. The focus of this section is on getting customers to make purchases, and the way to that is by improving your tactics for engaging customers and using innovative promotions that promote immediate action without hurting your price structure or infiltration marketing image.

> Promotions can and do get customers to buy. Innovation promotions do that without compromising a company's image.

Engaging the Customer

Involving your business in the customer decision process. Engaging the customer is always the first step in the successful sales process. For example, if an engineer calls up for information on a piece of industrial equipment, he isn't being engaged. I'll start to engage the engineer if I tell him or her that I'm planning on doing an educational seminar in his area in three months. When I ask the engineer why his or her company is considering using the equipment, the engineer will answer me when I mention that I'm surveying potential seminar attendees to see what information is most useful. And the engineer might even explain what specific topics he would like covered. But you can also engage the customers in such depth that they are committed to buying from you well before they are sure exactly what they ◄— **$100** are going to buy.

Lear Corp. is an OEM supplier to the automotive industry. Lear specializes in supplying high-tech parts to the automotive industry. If Lear waits until a part is fully designed, it is just another supplier involved in the bidding process. Lear's goal is to be involved when the engineering design of the part starts so that its processes and technologies are built into the part. Through its advanced technology center, Lear has 300 people on staff who work directly

> Integrating the customer's design process into your company typically secures the order.

with customers in the design of component parts, and Lear has another 400 people stationed throughout the world. To enhance its position as a partner in the design effort, Lear is building a $10 million testing center where automotive manufacturers can actually test out their product

$2,000+ →

designs. The testing center allows manufacturers to actually see how product development is coming along on a new part.

Many Web pages are taking this same approach, being an all-around reference source for individual topics that range from room acoustics to medical studies. Small companies can provide the same type of engagement. Buzz Tool manufactures prototypes and small production runs, but its main business is building the actual molds used for full production runs. Engineers from prospective customers can come into Buzz Tool's prototype shop and use the equipment or hire a model builder to work with them for a fixed hourly fee. Many industrial suppliers provide programming on the Internet or on disc that allows customers to select the best part for a specific application.

One tactic real estate agents use is to make books or videos of various houses available to customers. Realtors will also do a market study of homes in an area that have recently sold. This tactic, which levels the playing field between the customer and company, is extremely effective. In 1998, two million people utilized information on the Internet about buying a car. They did that so they would know as much as the dealers about what the right price should be. I've found that consulting jobs are much easier to sell when you show people the work you've done for others and tell

> Customers want the playing field leveled and will buy from marketers who level it for them.

$500 →

them the price you charged for that work. The question customers have is, "Am I getting a good deal?" People are reluctant to buy if they don't have an answer. You can also use this tactic by preparing a portfolio of options for customers to look at. For example, a meeting planner had a three-ring binder that detailed many of the different meetings she had worked on. The customer could see options to chose from and could see that the prices being quoted were consistent with what other customers had paid.

Another effective tactic is to let people help you select or design new products. In the Attic is a small gift shop that emphasizes Victorian merchandise. The store has a suggestion box that asks people what new products the store should carry. They box also asks people how old they are and has a special section in the store for people 18 to 25 years old. All the products in the young adult section were

$100 →

based on suggestions. When stores solicit input from people, then buy the merchandise customers suggest, the products do sell. This tactic also works well in industrial and business-to-business markets. Before you introduce a product why not ask customers for their input on the features they'd like to see? Typically they will see many of the same needs you do, and they will respond favorably when you introduce a product with many of their suggestions.

$500

Offering choices for customers' purchase decisions. Marketers typically segment customers by their wants or usage patterns. But within that group are people with differing styles. You can get an edge when you let customers select the purchasing style they want. Customers fall into a wide variety of purchasing styles: people who decide quickly, look for a recommendation, mull over information, or want to see options. Bookstores are frequently set up for this by having an information area where people can come and ask questions. This is always a good idea. Let people select their purchasing mode and then provide them the information just the way that they

> Marketers can accelerate a promotion when they match up with the way customers want to buy.

want it. On Valentines Day, stores should offer a consultant for people in a hurry. The store could also promote having a gift consultant in the store for certain hours. The same policy could apply for a hunting store, or for a men's suit store when it switches to winter merchandise.

$1,999

Service and business-to-business marketers can also have the same strategy. Your business should be set up to ask the customer this simple question, "Do you know what you want, or would you like a recommendation or like to consider several options?" Remember, your job is to be one with the customer, so work with them on their terms. Companies can offer selection disks to prospects that can be used on their computers based on the company's recommendations, or they can order a disc that offers a range of options. Another tactic is to bring in an expert to help customers decide what to buy, such as a university professor who concentrates on cryogenics. The company pays for the expert, who answers questions and recommends the best solution for businesses interested in using a cryogenic process. I've even seen a modification of this tactic used with senior papers of engineering students. A manufacturer of testing equipment can have customers cosponsor a research study on the effectiveness of their equip-

> Everyone wins with an effective promotion.

ment at a university. A professor working as a consultant with the testing equipment company can arrange for a senior to do his or her final paper on a customer's product, and the testing company only needs to supply equipment and supplies.

This benefits everyone. The customer gets a study validating the equipment for his chosen application. The manufacturer gets a customer and an in-depth study it can use for promotion. The university professor and student generate the data they

$2,000+ ➤ need to publish a paper.

Buying Today

Getting people to buy today can be done with a little ingenuity that doesn't sacrifice your price, product integrity, or your image as a customer-oriented company. As I discussed earlier in the chapter, you clearly do not want to offer a steady stream of discounted price sales. Every promotion has to make sense to the customer and should enhance your image. There is nothing wrong, for instance, with an end of the season sale. Customers understand that you have a cost of carrying inventory over to the next season and that selling it for a discount is a better option for your company. They also understand a special buy on merchandise from a manufacturer that you can offer at special savings. For example, when REI (an outdoor retailer) makes a special big buy on Columbia winter jackets, they can pass those savings onto customers with a short promotion. Since Columbia is a leading brand of rugged outdoor outerwear, it enhances REI's image as a leading retailer for people who love the outdoors.

$1,999 ➤ REI making a special effort to bring in a large shipment and then passing the savings onto the customers also reinforces REI's image as being in sync with its customers.

There are many other promotions marketers can run that also promote sales without compromising your market position. Many examples are listed in the remaining part of the chapter. Don't be afraid to come up with new ideas for promotions. This is a fast changing market and your creativity plays a key role in your ability to stay ahead of your competitors.

Enhanced service. In the Attic, the Victorian gift shop mentioned earlier, has

$500 ➤ every gift for Secretary's Day delivered by a women dressed in a black dress with a white ruffled apron. Family reunion specials from a photography studio could include a special portrait of the grandparents. Plumbing companies might include an inspection of the plumbing throughout a home with the installation of new piping. A septic tank cleaning company might offer to run a drain cleaner between the home and the septic tank for people who get a total tank cleaning and inspection during a certain month.

Consumer products manufacturers frequently will tie in retailer dealer promotions, special point-of-purchase displays, or co-advertising dollars to get dealers to stock a new product. These are programs that both help promote the manufacturers' products and help the store promote its image. Industrial manufacturers frequently will offer co-op programs to industrial distributors, or they will bring in special programs for a distributor celebration. Another promotion I like is when service providers give free samples to referrals in return for business. Maid services might offer two gift certificates to customers who sign up for a year's worth of services. Then the customer could give the certificates away as presents to friends and relatives. This promotion helps secure orders, plus it is a referral to another person who might become a customer.

Premium's for high-end users. AirTouch Cellular recently announced that it would offer free nationwide roaming privileges for people purchasing air time for $74.99 or more per month. Cellular rates are dropping, but rather than just drop its price, AirTouch has responded by offering additional services. There are many other examples of businesses that utilize this tactic. People who travel first class on airlines get preferential treatment including free drinks, early loading and unloading, and special dinners. Cable TV suppliers provide free installation for buyers of two or more premium channels. Companies that buy over $5,000 of computer network equipment can typically get free installation. Special billing options and details can be available for high-end users. Federal Express, for example, ships a large number of hospital samples overnight to specialized laboratories. Federal Express sets its billing policies to correspond to the hospital's internal billing procedures to make its billing easier. ← **$2,000+** Twenty-four-hour pickup is another special service that freight companies will offer to their larger customers.

Cross-promotions. The Rand/Ross Bicycle Co. recently signed a deal with Chrysler to produce a Jeep mountain bike. Ross benefits by selling bikes with the ← **$2,000+** Jeep name to the upscale young professional, and Chrysler benefits by associating the Jeep name with a top-of-the line, rugged mountain bike. Another example is Giant Foods on the East Coast. It teamed up with Better Homes and Gardens to offer a free gift subscription to *Better Homes and Gardens* for people who bought greetings cards on Mother's Day. The promotion was a good deal for Giant, who

$1,999 →

generated lots of extra business, and it worked well for Better Homes and Gardens, who had a low-cost method for increasing its readership among its core target customer group of middle-aged and older women.

The Giant Foods promotion is one of my favorite type of promotions and I'm surprised it isn't used more often. Paper Warehouse is a big supplier of party paper products. Other people involved in parties are bakeries, specialty frozen food suppliers, delis, caterers, and even grocery stores. The other related businesses should be happy to offer a coupon for their stores to be used by Paper

$100 →

Warehouse for a Party Pack. In fact, they might all want to share coupons so that a person throwing a party goes to one store and is enticed to go to the others to purchase products.

Promotions based on holidays. Sears has installed gift registry kiosks at some

$2,000+ →

of its stores where people can list what they'd like for birthdays, holidays, or weddings. People can register in advance, and people wishing to buy gifts can just call up someone's name to see if they've registered any gift ideas. Sears is not the only one trying to capitalize on holidays. Stores formerly would just bring in Mother's

$500 →

Day cards to sell. Now they are expanding their promotions in every direction. Kroeger's ran a promotion of free maid service for a year to coincide with Mother's Day. Stores offer special purchases on items like bath and body products geared towards mothers, as well as special phone cards so moms can call their children whenever they want.

Promotions based on special events. Wal-Mart, K-mart, and other retailers buy special supplies for back-to-school sales. Anniversary promotions or programs tied to seminars, classes, demonstrations, or other special events are other excellent times for promotions. Bike-Line is a specialty bike retailer in the Philadelphia

$500 →

area. They constantly have bike races at various locations for their customers. They could charge an entry fee for the event and then give a coupon to cover half the cost of the entry fee back to each contestant.

All special event programs work better when they are tied to a special purchase rather than just standard merchandise. When you get ready to run an event ask your suppliers if they'd be interested in participating in a special promotion to go along with the event. The supplier could contribute goods below cost in return for having its products mentioned in promotion of the event, and have its products prominently placed for sale. You, of course, don't have to limit the items sold to

$500 →

the promotional item. You can use the supplier's low cost as a special draw to customers and still sell other products. When you do this, the lower price is attributed to the supplier and not the retailer, and it protects the retailer's pricing strategy.

Sampling. Giving away samples is often done carelessly, but when done right it can be an effective strategy. They key is to create an environment that enhances the product. For example, Remy Martin cognac targets young trendsetters. Remy Martin sets up events in combination with independent film makers or theatres to have a night where trendsetters come, see some innovative entertainment, and taste a variety of Remy Martin cognac. This promotion not only gets the target market to sample the cognac, it does so in a setting that enhances the brand's image.

$2,000+

Sampling can also be done in a way to enhance the product's usefulness. Sprint has cellular phone kiosks set up within a block or two of its New York retail locations. People could pick up and use the phone free to get a dramatic demonstration of the major benefit of a cellular phone. The kiosks also told people where the nearest retail store was. Both examples point out that sampling is done best when it is done with an advertising viewpoint. You should decide on the ideal setting for an ad that would communicate the values of your product. Those are the same settings that you want to give your samples away.

$2,000+

Special catalogs. Donna Morgan is a small women's clothing manufacturer that sells products to department stores like Dillards. They put together a catalog called "The Little Black Dress Book" that showcased their dinner dresses. As part of the program Donna Morgan also furnished a book demonstrating models in dinner dresses with jewelry and other accessories so customers could see exactly how they should look. The books were given to sales associates at department stores who used them as a sales tool for Donna Morgan products. This program had many benefits for Donna Morgan. It gave a boost to its retail customers, and helped Donna Morgan's brand image as a high-end dress supplier. Sales skyrocketed, and department stores are thinking of opening up little black dress sections in their stores.

$2,000+

Coupons. While straight dollar-off coupons cut into your image, you can use coupons to introduce new concepts or to provide a bonus to your customers. Panasonic, as an example, ran two promotions for its line of batteries. One offered a five-dollar-off coupon on its brand new Shock Wave brand of audio equipment, while the other a offered a five minute prepaid phone call. Customers understand coupon or price discount offers when it involves coupling products together. This tactic works well when you want to sell your full product line.

$2,000+

When I worked for a dental company, we sold a full line of equipment. Our top product had a 40 percent market share, while our other products had anywhere from 7 to 25 percent. We offered discounts for dentists who bought a whole package of equipment.

> Coupons are useful for promoting full product lines.

Promotions are a vital part of every marketer's strategy. They offer a way to highlight your company at certain times of the year. Try not to focus all your promotions on getting sales. Events that expose your company or find customers and enhance your image will pay off in long-term sales increases. But when you do run a promotion to increase sales, make sure it enhances your image and doesn't hurt your image of being customer oriented or damage your product or service's perceived price/value relationship.

SECTION SIX

Replicating Sales Activity

Chapter Sixteen:
BUILDING A LOYAL CUSTOMER BASE

Chapter Seventeen:
SETTING UP CROSS-PROMOTIONS
AND ALLIANCES

BUILDING A LOYAL CUSTOMER BASE

Companies spend quite a bit of money to get new customers, and once a customer comes on board, companies need to make sure they stay. Customer service was a hot topic of the '80s and '90s as a way to keep customers. Customer service is important, but it really isn't enough for you to compete against an effective infiltration marketing competitor. For example, who is going to develop a loyal customer following: Bike-Line Bicycle shop, who stages several races a month, posts the results on the Internet, has demonstrations, lets customers try bikes out, and actively supports all area bike riders, or a bike shop with good customer service? The answer is obvious. Bike Line will win every time. While I'm not suggesting you cut back on customer service, I am saying you need to go much further and actually create a concrete link between you and your customers.

A loyal customer base is built best with a deliberate, intentional infiltration marketing program. This means you need to have a plan to use infiltration marketing tactics throughout the year to keep customers aware of your company. You won't create a loyal customer base by using these tactics on an occasional basis. Other tactics that also increase customer loyalty are offering customers complete marketing information, providing customers a complete solution, and insulating customers from competition with promotional programs.

I'm not trying to minimize the importance of the effectiveness of giving customers a little extra attention with traditional tactics such as answering the telephone cheerfully, greeting customers with a big welcome, and sending out thank-you notes. Those tactics still should be used, but they must be supplemented by a wide array of more aggressive tactics. I consider customer service tactics to be somewhat passive. To use them you have to first get a customer in some other way. Infiltration marketing is all about aggressively going out, finding, and converting

> Good customer service won't be enough to keep customers in the 21st century.

prospects into lifelong customers. The radical shift infiltration marketing makes is that it finds and converts prospects by supporting and promoting their goals. That's a sharp contrast to traditional marketing programs that bombard prospects with commercial messages and heavy-handed sales tactics.

An Infiltrating Marketing Program

Your yearly program should consist of five key steps: getting customers involved, having visibility in the customer's world, putting the customer first, staying on the leading edge, and being a leader in advancing customer goals. You will be a leader in your industry and have a loyal customer base if you consistently do all five steps every year. These tactics are not special programs but rather a focus for your business that must continue all the time. I recommend you evaluate your business every six months to see how well you are meeting every one of these steps. You'll find it is easy to slide backwards into traditional marketing tactics if you don't monitor your company's focus at all times.

> Infiltration marketing builds customer loyalty by supporting and promoting customer goals.

GETTING CUSTOMERS INVOLVED

You can get customers involved in any number of ways. You can have them participate in advisory councils, attend seminars, offer support to new customers, participate in events or races, or help decide what inventory you should stock for the next season. Getting customers involved shows your customers you value them and it builds bonds that are not easily erased by competitors. I've mentioned the tactics above earlier in the book, but there are many other ways to involve customers.

$500

1. Review literature and promotional programs before you finalize them.
2. Critique new competitive products and programs.
3. Demonstrate the equipment customers have purchased in the past for your new salespeople and have your customers explain to the new salesmen why your features are important.

4. Serve as participants on panel discussions for seminars you sponsor.
5. Evaluate their interactions with your company and, when appropriate, have them suggest how you can improve your customer service.
6. Test new equipment or products.
7. Participate in a fashion show, either as a judge or a model.
8. Attend celebration parties or other events you host throughout the year.
9. Be a member of a preferred customer club or presidential club (a club whose members meet once or twice a year for lunch with your company president).
10. Ask customers to be involved in building and updating the community and content portions of your Web site.

I know that small business owners have self-confidence and don't always really believe that they need their customers' input. I don't agree with those owners; customers can always help you. But the real reason you want input is because it shows you value your customers, and because it involves them in your business.

> Small business owners need to change their self-reliant nature to be an infiltration marketer.

HAVING VISIBILITY IN THE CUSTOMERS' WORLD

You want your customers to see your name as many times as possible, especially when they are involved in activities directly related to your business. For example, if you are a car repair service business, you want to have visibility in car service-related activities. You might want to do cross-promotions with car washes, battery shops, or gas stations. You also might want to sponsor a car column in the local paper or run a car familiarization class for women at the community education department of your local school district. Another tactic is to offer to evaluate used cars for prospective purchases. You might also buy gifts or prizes to award at events such as cub scout pack blue and gold dinners, high-school bands award dinners, or elementary school graduation parties. As in most infiltration marketing tactics, the only limit you have on ideas is your own creativity. I've listed just a few additional examples below.

1. Passing out free samples at major events.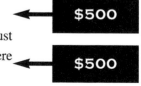
2. Help sponsor events. Small events, such as a school walkathon, work just as well as big events. People appreciate you more at a small event where there are few sponsors.

3. Have complementary businesses pass out or mail fliers or post cards of your business.

4. Run cross-promotions with other businesses that target the same customer group. This cuts your costs and allows you to be in front of customers more often. These can be joint promotions such as a sidewalk sale or a promotion where you and another company helps sponsor a golf tournament for your customers.

$1,999 →

5. Run events that generate publicity in local papers or trade magazines. Contests, especially ones where people have to do something to win, typically produce a positive impact without costing a lot of money. Our car service business could run a contest for kids to write in about their worst car breakdown experience. Classes, seminars, demonstrations, and presentations with guest speakers are all good sources of publicity.

6. Offer premiums or giveaways that are part of a larger company's marketing. For example, our car service business could give away a free oil change to every 500th customer at a grocery store's anniversary weekend.

7. Offer a newsletter of interest to your customer group. You should minimize your commercial messages and instead provide informative, easy-to-read articles.

PUTTING THE CUSTOMER FIRST

Infiltration marketers do not focus exclusively on how to sell more products. They concentrate instead on helping customers get what they need, even if it doesn't involve their products. Cisco Systems is a major supplier to the networking, router, and telecommunications markets. Its Web page started out as product information bulletin board. Cisco's customers kept asking it for new services that would let them share information with other customers. The information they wanted to share or learn about wasn't always about Cisco products, but Cisco didn't care. It was happy to provide whatever information the customers wanted. Cisco gets great marks from its customers for this because it shows Cisco is their partner and not just another company out to take away their hard earned money.

> There are literally hundreds of ways to keep your company visible with your customers.

Your customer has goals related to your product, and your job is to help them reach them. If you own a gift store, your customers' goal is to make someone else happy. Why not help them do that? You can arrange your store by the type of person a gift is for. Or you can have people enter into a computer the profile of the person they are buying a present for and have the computer suggest gifts. You could also add little cards by gifts and suggest who would like each one. The gift store really puts the customer first when it suggests gift from other stores in the mall for certain people. For example, most gift stores don't have many presents for men. If someone is buying a gift for his or her father, the store shouldn't be afraid to send the customer to another location.

> Content comes first, before selling.

A good rule to follow is put content first and selling second. All of your information should be focused on helping the customer. As I mentioned earlier in the book, the most successful introduction I ever had consisted of seminars by leading endodontists. We had only a tiny marketing and sales message component to the seminar, yet people remembered our product much better than they would have if we ran an extensive advertising campaign. You can also employ a variety of other effective tactics.

1. Sponsor leading experts or competitors in return for their offering classes and demonstrations for your customers. ← **$1,999**
2. Help sponsor a state-of-the-art demonstration center with other companies.
3. Provide an open forum newsletter where your customers can write articles that they believe will be of interest to other customers.
4. Hire an expert-in-residence that will tour your customers' plants and offer suggestions on how they can improve operations. This tactic also helps your expert gain exposure and is a great publicity event.
5. Arrange for group transportation for customers to trade shows and other events.
6. Bring in special purchases for your customers that you sell at cost or for a small profit. An example is that at the beginning of ski season the local ski shop brings in samples of high-performance cross-country ski waxes that it offers at a bargain price.
7. Send your customers reprints of good articles that talk about how customers can achieve their goals.

STAYING ON THE LEADING EDGE

Your image of being concerned about the customer, a leader in the customers' world, and keeping your customer well informed works best if your company is always on the leading edge of technology. I've talked quite bit in the book about cross-promotions and strategic alliances from a marketing point of view. Another key tactic for staying on the leading edge is to form R & D alliances. You have a much better chance of staying on the leading edge by working with suppliers of complementary products, even if it is only for periodic plant visits or meetings. You should also always be on the lookout for small companies with new innovative products. You can form an alliance with them. Helping a company with a new innovative product or service helps promote your company's image as a technology leader. Stores have to buy new, innovative products that the market talks about, and service businesses have to be sure to add services as other companies around the country create them. You can only go so far off of other companies' innovations, so you have to be sure to devote time, money, and energy to developing technological advances of your own. I've listed a few additional tactics next.

> Keeping the customer informed also keeps you informed, which will help you create exciting new products and services.

> R & D alliances are just as important as marketing alliances.

1. Sign exclusive marketing contracts for one or two years with new companies with innovative products.
2. Sponsor research at universities throughout the country regarding your product area. You can agree to pay the universities royalties if you use some of their ideas.
3. Conduct a yearly contest for the most innovative new product of the year. Have customers submit nominations and award the winning prize to the product with the most nominations. This is also a great tactic for generating publicity and it helps you know what features and benefits customers are looking for.
4. Have a submission program where customers can present ideas to you for services, promotions, or products. Offer customers rewards of either a cash payment or a royalty if you decide to use their idea. The Lisle Company makes automotive tools and actively solicits its customers'

ideas. Lisle knows that its customers, who are mechanics, are the people most likely to create an innovative new tool. If more than one person submits the same idea, Lisle simply splits the reward among each of the customers who submitted the same idea.

5. Include in your newsletter information on new market developments and new products. Invite some of your best customers to review the ideas and products, and solicit customers' input as to whether they feel the new product's features are worthwhile.

6. Keep tabs on market developments overseas and report them to your customers. All you need to do is subscribe to international trade magazines. You can find the names of those magazines in *Gale's Source of Publications* in larger public libraries.

BEING A LEADER IN MEETING CUSTOMERS' GOALS

You want to be the leading source of informational content for your customers, plus you want to do things that help customers meet their goals. If you sell outdoors camping equipment, you want to offer seminars and parties that feature videos and information about new techniques, new products, and places where people can go to have a great adventure. You probably will want to sponsor trips to those locations. You can charge to attend seminars and trips to recoup your expenses. Customers won't mind paying for these services because they offer high value to them. They'll be pleased you are making the seminars and trips available to them. It's not important that you do things for free, only that you do things that promote your customers' goals.

Advertising agencies and public relations firms should also be leaders in meeting customers' goals, which for the most part are increased sales and profits. Those customers want to hear about new trends in the market, new programs, and new strategies that are working in other parts of the country or in other industries. Ad agencies should be sponsoring quarterly luncheons where they keep people up to speed on what's happening in the market. They could bring in guest speakers and charge an admission. If ad agencies around the country would band together they could probably coordinate a series of luncheons and get speakers and programs at a

> It's OK to make money helping people meet their goals. You don't need to do everything for free.

competitive price. Ad agencies and PR firms should be particularly adept at this step because their function is to communicate with people. There are a wide variety of other tactics you can use to show people you are a leader in helping them reach their goals.

1. Sponsor a fair or mini-convention with other suppliers serving your target customer. Have booths, demonstrations, talks, and entertainment related to your customers' goals.

2. Have races or contests where customers can compete. Post the results and times and interview the winners.

3. Have open forum meetings where customers can share their own ideas with other customers. You can have five or six forums going on at the same time around the room. Ask customers to submit a short summary of what they want to talk about, and then set a schedule of 30 to 40 minute presentations. This tactic works well because people love to receive approval for their work and efforts. Being selected to present at an open forum is validating that the customer knows what they are doing. A variation of this tactic for companies marketing home or yard products is to have an organized tour of the homes or gardens of their customers.

4. Industrial companies can be involved with customers in setting up a high-efficiency production line or foolproof quality control line. A supplier of phone or office equipment might work with a customer to set up a study that shows how productive the office staff is.

5. Marketers can participate in industry forums, panel discussions, or standards committees that are working towards improving the performance in the industry.

6. Clothing stores that target young customers can bring in a variety of small manufacturers for a fashion show and then ask for their customers to rate the clothes and tell the stores which clothes they'd like the store to stock. This is also great publicity for small manufacturers trying to expand their distribution network.

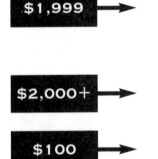

You'll notice that many tactics can overlap several steps, such as holding demonstrations, races, or other events. You don't have to run 10 events per year to have an effective infiltration marketing program. You must, however, have enough so that the customers realize that you are on their side.

> Customers will keep aware of what activities you are planning once they realize that you are on their side.

Providing Complete Information

Providing information on related topics is part of the infiltration marketing step of putting customers first. I want to list it separately because it is effective even if you don't implement any other infiltration marketing tactic. One of the advantages of providing complete information is that companies can't be isolated in the market, worrying about only their product. They have to worry about what's going on in the entire market, which will lead them to discover better marketing tactics. Providing complete information may require companies to recommend competitive products

> You'll have loyal customers when you keep them fully informed of their options.

when they do a better job than their own products of solving a customer's needs. Marketers need to make a radical readjustment to be concerned first about the customer. A truly loyal customer will only develop when a true partnership arrangement is reached. Marketers don't need to have all the solutions and answers themselves; they just need to be willing to help customers get the right answers.

Ron Retzko founded Batteries Plus, a chain of 175 stores in 30 states that does nothing but sell batteries—car batteries, radio batteries, camcorder batteries, and just about any other type of battery you can think of. His store is a one-stop battery store service center for both consumer and industrial accounts. The key to Batteries Plus's service is that it feels that its job is to keep people's machines running, not to sell equipment. The store doesn't replace batteries until it checks out the equipment and makes sure the problem really is the battery. Store personnel tell people when there is a problem that needs fixing that's not related to the battery. All for no charge. The store also builds batteries when necessary, explains how the battery systems work, and reconditions batteries that are worth saving. Each store location is a complete source of battery information. Batteries

$500 ➡ Plus succeeds even with many other companies, including auto service centers, drugstores, discount stores, and a variety of other businesses, selling the same batteries to the same target customer.

Offering a Complete Solution

Batteries Plus is a complete information source, but they are not a complete solution because customers still need to go to other businesses to get their equipment fixed. Businesses that put together the entire solution for customers have an enor-

$2,000+ ➡ mous market edge.

The *Farm Journal* is a trade magazine that serves farmers. The company's target customer group is companies that want to advertise to farmers. *Farm Journal*'s goal is to provide complete access to the farmer market through the entire spectrum of media. The *Farm Journal* also owns AgDay, a syndicated daily TV news show, a weekly newsletter called *ProFarmer*, and a satellite-based agricultural news service called Globallink. The company started a new magazine called *Global Agribusiness* and it has a Web site (www.farmjournal.com). Everything the *Farm Journal* does is geared towards farmers and creating the targeted access to relevant farmers for *Farm Journal*'s customers.

Farm Journal knows that its customers don't just want access, they want access to the farmers that need their products. *Farm Journal* has used its database of 615,000 farmers to produce over 2,000 versions of its magazines. The farmer on one side of the road might get a totally different magazine than the farmer on the other side of the road. This gives advertisers the option to place ads in only the versions that are targeted at the farmers they want to contact. Rather than advertising in a mass mailing, agricultural manufacturers can target their prime customers by using the *Farm Journal*. The company believes it is the place to come for anyone who wants to reach a target group of farmers. That total service makes *Farm Journal* a valuable resource for its customers. *Farm Journal* is especially appreciated because it allows adver-

> Sales will skyrocket when you offer customers the only complete solution.

tisers to buy ads only in magazines going to the select group of target farmers. Other media aimed at agricultural companies force manufacturers to advertise to their entire readership, which is expensive and not what advertisers want to do.

Insulating Customers from Competition with Promotions

Marketers typically talk first about loyalty promotions, such as the airlines frequent flyer programs, when they talk about building loyalty. In reality, your promotion is only good until a better one comes along. The tactics discussed earlier in the chapter are ones that competitors can't easily match, which gives your company a sustainable advantage over the competition. But some customer loyalty promotions go beyond pure discounting and become infiltration marketing tactics.

> Great promotions build customer loyalty.

CUSTOMIZED COUPON PROGRAMS

Roundy's is a supermarket and it has a kiosk for its Saver's Club members. Roundy's keeps tracks of what people in the Saver's Club buy, and when they come into store, they can run their card through a kiosk which will only print out coupons on the items they actually buy. The customers' buying patterns are electronically available at all 75 Roundy's stores. This isn't just a discount program, it's a program that changes for each customer that makes shopping more convenient for them.

PROMOTIONS THAT APPEAL TO CUSTOMERS GOALS

Zeller's is a chain of discount stores in Canada. It offers shoppers a membership in Club Z, through which they earn points for purchases. They can apply those points to get awards in catalogs. This is a standard reward program. What makes it special is that parents, grandparents, aunts, and uncles can also earn points for a child who has a Generation Z account. The kids can select their own awards, check on the Internet for their points, and visit the www.genz.com Web page for updates on new awards. Zeller's program signed up 100,000 kids in the first two days, and the

Companies build loyalty when they target customer goals.

number was expected to grow to 1.5 million members in 1999. That's out of a total Canadian population of 30 million people.

VALUE-ADDED PROMOTIONS

These are promotions that offer soft benefits like special promotions, free tickets to special events, announcements on new merchandise, and free gift wrapping services. Industrial suppliers might offer free installation or training programs with certain size purchases. Copier distributors might offer two-hour repair service for companies that buy more than two copiers, or they may provide cases of colored paper for the same price as white paper.

PARTNERSHIP PROGRAMS

This is a program where a company offers another company's products or promotions. Sprint has a partnership program and offers frequent flyer miles for every $100 of phone calls. You can turn this into a good promotion if you offer your customers gifts or discounts on new products that come into the market from other companies. Two or three times a year a distributor of paramedic products likes to offer new innovative products to its customers as a gift (if it is a consumable product) or a big discount if it is a one-time purchase. That enhances the distributor's image as a partner with its customer and as a supplier of leading edge products. Typically, the distributor can get the manufacturer to give him a good price in return for the extra exposure it will get as the featured product in the promotion. Partnership programs can also be effective when run with companies with the same target customer. For example, kayaking and snorkeling stores could offer discounts on each other's products. This strategy works best when it involves five to six companies and each store rotates what coupons it offers on a monthly basis. For example, a snorkeling store could offer kayaking coupons one month and golf store coupons the next.

Infiltration marketers always have loyal customers because they put the customer first. You might need several years to become an infiltration marketer, especially if you already have an established image. You should include in your yearly market plans a marketing program to increase loyalty. You'll find that a well-designed loyalty program can be a critical first step in being perceived as a company that is on the customer's side.

Loyalty promotions build relationships that last.

CHAPTER SEVENTEEN

SETTING UP CROSS-PROMOTIONS AND ALLIANCES

This chapter features the major, overwhelming benefit of infiltration marketing for all small to midsize companies. When a company enters the customers' world, it also enters the world of other like-minded businesses. When marketers throw their efforts together, they all share customers, which greatly reduces marketing costs and dramatically increases the effectiveness of your marketing program.

This strategy works for every business. The Galleria is a small specialty mall in Minnesota that carefully selects high-end specialty stores that aren't commonly found in larger shopping centers. The Galleria merchants pool their resources for events, share customers, and work in a cooperative manner to get customers coming into their mall. The main reason these stores fail in larger malls is that they can't afford to attract their targeted customer group when they are isolated from other like-minded stores. But the stores succeed in a large way when they are placed together and when they work cooperatively. The stores succeed because the target customer has more fun shopping when many of their favorite stores are in the same location.

Contract manufacturers can pool their talents, as can consultants and service businesses. In effect, this strategy is just repeating what independent manufacturing sales agencies have known for years; the first sale is the expensive sale, other sales of different products to the same customer have relatively low sales costs. An added plus is that this strategy helps a company keep on the cutting edge of product or service design, as they have a better understanding of its customers' world. But the most important benefit of a partnership or alliance is that it provides better service to customers.

Shopping centers have a whole host of services they need. They include daily cleaning, maintenance, landscaping, snow removal, parking lot cleaning and striping, and sign construction. They may need as many as 15 or 20 services, which are all competitively bid out to a variety of small suppliers, often on a yearly basis. Today, full-service companies are popping up that provide all the maintenance services to shopping centers. In some cases the companies do some of the work and subcontract the rest of the work out. In other cases, companies band together in an alliance that has an office staff and coordinator to secure this business for all the alliance members. But in all cases, the new service businesses take care of every shopping center maintenance need. Southeast Service Corp. was one of the first companies to offer this bundled-service approach and one of its early customers was Simon Property Group, one of the nation's property mall management groups. Southeast Services started with contracts to 20 shopping centers, and now it has contracts for 80 centers and the number is still growing.

> The first sale to a customer is always difficult and expensive. The second sale, even of another product, is typically easy and cheap.

$2,000+ →

The bundled-service approach is certainly better for small vendors who band together. They don't have to enter into yearly bidding wars. They also have much higher credibility when they approach non-shopping center prospects when they are a part of a larger entity. But probably the most important reason for the alliance is that it simply gives customers better service.

It doesn't take a lot of effort for a gift store to swap sales fliers with a restaurant. But in many cases, small companies will want to set up promotions with much larger companies. In this case you'll need to know how to go about setting up a cross-promotion, partnership, or alliance. This chapter shows you how to do that, including locating partners, getting your foot in the door, staging proposals, and closing the deal. Appendix A contains a list of a wide variety of partnership arrangements you can utilize, and Appendix B provides a format for a written proposal that you can use when suggesting a cross-promotion or alliance to another company. I recommend that every small business try to strike at least three or four alliances every year. The benefits of an

> Every small company should try to form two or three alliances every year.

alliance or partnership are enormous for both companies, and the deals are easy to strike if you follow the step-by-step approach of this chapter.

Where to Look for the Right Partner

The right partner is a company that has the same target customer group that you do. It doesn't matter if the company is in the same industry, sells the same type of product, or even attends the same trade shows. It just needs to market to the same customer group. Back in Chapter 7 you prepared a chart on the distinguishing characteristics of your customer group, which is reprinted below.

List your target customer group(s): _____

List the predominant personality trait of the chosen sub-segment: _____

_____

List the predominant desired image (consumers) or interest (business): _____

_____

List the initial response you want to generate: _____

One of the examples I used in Chapter 4 was Frontier Communications. Its target customer group was small businesses with four to 12 incoming telephone lines. The subsegment of the customer group Frontier Communications appealed to is optimizers, companies that wanted the very best equipment. The buying group's desired image was a cutting edge technology leader. The initial response that Frontier wanted to generate was: "This system has it all." Frontier wants to form partnerships and alliances with other companies that are targeting the same customers and are trying to generate the same initial customer response that Frontier is working to generate.

> The best partnerships are between companies targeting the same customer group.

One tactic for finding a company to partner with is to look for companies in your industry that have holes in their product line. For instance, Frontier Communications specializes in small companies. It may want to partner with a company that produces phone systems for large companies. That prospective partner may be installing systems at company headquarters but losing out on sales at small regional offices and distribution centers. Combining with Frontier would give the company selling larger phone systems a competitive edge over competitors who can't take care of all of a company's needs. Frontier would benefit by picking up new business at satellite offices of its partners' customers.

Another place to look for partners is to look at companies that work with your products to provide a complete solution. This was the approach small companies took when they offered bundled services for shopping centers. This approach works because customers don't want to be bothered with creating their own solutions. Potential partner companies are receptive to this type of an approach because they typically know they are vulnerable if a full-service supplier should enter the market.

A third tactic is to partner with companies that supply complementary products to the same target customer group. This tactic is especially effective if you partner with a company supplying a product that the customer feels is important to its success. In the case of Frontier Communications, a phone system is probably somewhat important to target customers but probably not one of their leading concerns. To decide who might be a strategic partner, Frontier could find potential partners from suppliers of any office- or sales-related products and services its customers feel are most important.

> Any company selling to the same target customer is a possible partner.

For companies that desire to be on the cutting edge of technology, potential partner companies for Frontier could come from companies supplying the following products or services.

1. Web page development service. The target customers might feel that having a strong, interactive Web page for its customers is a key selling tool.
2. Contact management software. Software that links information about product availability, customer applications, and technical data to field salespeople.

3. Computer networking and modem equipment, linking computers in the office, at outlying company locations, and with salespeople as they make customer calls.

4. Database management programming that manages routine mailings to customers and prospects, prepares customized mailings, and categorizes customers into relevant buying groups.

5. Employee retention programs, including training, non-cash rewards, office layout, and continuing education.

Making Your Prospect Partner List

The next step is to learn all about each industry, who the companies are in that industry, the companies' approximate market size and market position, who your key personal contacts are, and why they would partner with your company.

Medi-Seal is a manufacturer of a special sticker that provides key information about an individual in case of an injury. The sticker has two parts. The first part of the sticker attaches to a helmet or employee badge. This part of the sticker contains information about the person including his or her name and address, key personal contacts, personal doctor, blood type, and other relevant medical information. The second part of the sticker is the cover sticker, which is pulled off to reveal the personal information. The outer sticker, which is a shape similar to a police badge, says "Medi-Seal" on it with the saying "remove for medical information."

> Marketers need to make a database of potential partners for future promotions.

For several years Medi-Seal had a partnership with Trek bicycles. Trek offered the Medi-Seal free with every purchase of a child's bike helmet. Medi- Seal's profile on Trek looked like this.

 ← **$500**

Potential Partner:	Trek Bicycle Company
Business:	Manufacturer of midrange to high-end bikes and bike accessories.
Company Size:	Over $500 million

Market Position:	One of the top five bike manufacturers
Key Personal Contact:	Bike Helmet Marketing Manager
Key to Partnership Potential:	Medi-Seal offers Trek helmets a differential advantage over competitive helmets for child safety. It allows medical professionals to expedite treatment in case of an injury.

Unfortunately for Medi-Seal, Trek stopped offering the Medi-Seal after a few years because Trek found that Medi-Seal's wasn't encouraging enough parents to buy Trek's helmets. Medi-Seal was a one-man, poorly financed company that had a real chance to make it big in the market because its product was promoted by a large bike company.

You can start learning about an industry by subscribing to trade magazines, joining associations, chambers of commerce, and other civic groups, attending trade shows, and getting out to meet the owners of other businesses. When you start receiving trade magazines, send for literature from companies that are advertising or publishing press releases that are aimed at your targeted customer groups. As you receive the literature, start talking to salespeople, distributors, and retailers that are listed as sources of the product. They should be able to tell you what companies are aggressive in the market and likely to be receptive to a partnership arrangement or a cross-promotion.

$100 ➤

The most important activity for you is to get out and meet people in other companies so you can develop key contacts in companies that are potential partners. You have your best opportunity to land a partner if you meet the key people involved in a partnership before you offer them a proposal.

Getting Your Foot in the Door

You need personal contacts to strike a relationship with another company. I've found that making personal contacts can be done rather easily with other small companies, but that it is much more difficult to begin a key relationship within a larger company. I've found that the best initial contacts at large companies are regional sales managers. They are fairly important in the company, but more importantly, they have the ability to champion your product inside the company.

The regional managers have nothing to lose in promoting a cross-promotion or partnership deal. If the company agrees that the partnership makes sense, the regional manager looks like a hero for bringing the idea to the company. If the company turns down your proposal, the regional manager still looks like a go-getter who is trying to find opportunities to grow the company's business.

Small companies often have to work through regional managers to penetrate a big company.

 **$500**

Stage a Long-Lasting Relationship

The one reason many companies are reluctant to enter into a cross-promotion is that they are worried that the other company will be difficult to work with. You can alleviate this concern by starting with a small event first so the other company gets used to working with you. Some of the programs you could run are:

1. Joint classes or seminars. These could be at a local community education program, stores or retailers, association meetings or at trade shows.
2. Marketing mailings. Arrange for a group of three or four companies to include each other's flyers in all their mailings. The cost is low, and each company gains credibility as a larger and more reliable supplier when it teams up with other suppliers.
3. Provide a complete solution for one customer. This tactic is used when you come across a company that needs to purchase products from three or four other suppliers to interact with yours. Instead of just pitching your product, offer to line up a complete solution for the company, and offer to install the entire system. If the customer says yes, contact the other companies and offer them the business. This helps the customer who gets a complete working system, it helps the other companies who get a sale they might not otherwise have gotten, and it helps you because you minimize the chance of a competitor coming in and stealing the business.
4. Co-sponsor an event at a school or mall. If you are a retailer or a local area supplier, you should always be on the lookout for events you can suggest

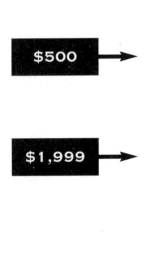

at local schools or malls. Some of these might be free demonstrations you offer at school carnivals, a promotion that gives the school 10 percent of the sales value for every purchase a school parent makes, or offer special classes for school children one week of the year.

5. Joint outings with companies that have the same target customer group. I mentioned earlier in the book about how graphic artists and advertising agencies work together to sponsor a golf tournament for their best customers. You can also host picnics, riverboat gambling excursions, or rent Super boxes for football parties.

6. Offer a low-cost item for a promotion or contest. Sprint offers frequent flyer miles to new Sprint customers. It doesn't cost Northwest Airlines that much money, but it still gives Sprint customers an incentive to use Northwest Airlines. You can put many creative twists on this tactic. A women's shoe store could give away a color analysis (which tells women which colors they will look best in) from a women's clothing store. An informational research company might offer two free hours of research to customers of a consulting company. In all these examples the company whose product is given away gains exposure to new prospects, while the partner company offers customers an extra incentive to buy its products.

7. Work together with a university researcher on a program important to both companies. Companies in any industry have a large number of similar research interests, which can range from understanding consumer buying behavior, to discovering the long-term effects of stress on new compounds.

Try to make your first proposed program as low risk as possible.

There are hundreds of other options you could use that have been discussed throughout the book. The important point is to make sure the first program you propose has low risk. You want to build up your relationship slowly.

You want to keep building momentum with the companies you approach. You can run a second program that still has low risk but is a little more aggressive than your first program and builds a far more lasting relationship. Some of the programs you can propose are:

1. A limited time package offer. Kiss My Face packaged its products together with a new Bic razor for a short time offer that capitalized on Bic's large advertising budget. The promotion also helped Bic, who used Kiss My Face's appeal to upscale consumers to position its new product as a step up from its ultra-cheap predecessors. **← $2,000+**

2. Marketing campaign to a targeted customer. Fishing stores might team up with a resort to offer a free one-week vacation. Suppliers of products for weddings, such as bakeries, flower shops, tuxedo rentals, and wedding planners, might team up to offer a contest for two free nights at a honeymooner suite at a local hotel. **← $1,999**

3. Catalog mailing. Direct-mail catalogs to consumers as well as promotional catalog mailings to distributors or retailers are expensive. Your mailings will be more effective when you team up with other companies going to the same target customer group. Your costs will be lower, and the customer is likely to save a more complete catalog. This is common practice for companies selling to people who hunt, have hobbies, or love to fly remote control model airplanes. **← $2,000+**

4. A major series of events across the country. This practice is used by music and clothing companies that sell to teenagers and young adults. Sporting goods companies will sponsor sporting events such as bike races and marathons, and medical suppliers will sponsor seminars at state medical association conferences. **← $2,000+**

5. An exclusive relationship for certain customers. This is a common practice for companies that private label products. For example, a small company may come up with a great new cooking accessory. To gain quick market momentum it might private label the product to another cooking supplies manufacturer for an exclusive one- or two-year distribution agreement to major department stores. This benefits the larger cooking supplier, who gains an advantage on competitors by being able to exclusively offer certain products to department stores. It benefits the small company who has its product sold through a major, prestigious distribution channel. This will help the small manufacturer make later sales to other retailers. And it helps the department store by offering a product no one else can carry. **← $500**

6. Warehouse and distribution support in certain geographic markets. Often companies need to stock products throughout the country in order to provide good customer service. Instead of using a public warehouse, companies can have the distribution handled by a company that hopefully will become a marketing partner. That cuts the warehouse's cost of the potential partner and helps you create a positive relationship.

7. Combine to offer a full line of products to a category of stores. It's hard to convince retailers to take on a new product unless it can offer a complete category of products. For example, a supplier of expensive children's dresses isn't going to get a midrange priced children's retailer to carry its products unless the retailer has a whole line of more upscale products to attract potential customers. Manufacturers of upscale products would do well to band together to offer retailers a complete solution.

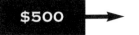

> Your creativity is the only limit you have on your range of potential cross-promotions.

Again, these are just a few ideas you can explore. Appendix A offers more examples of some of the different types of promotions, partnerships, and alliances you can propose to other companies.

Tactics for Closing the Deal

Doing a proposal for a joint program isn't that difficult if your proposal can produce significant results for the other company. What makes proposals interesting to other companies is that they have all of the same problems you do in marketing their products or services. Costs are too high, customers are too hard to engage, and competition is too fierce. But that doesn't mean you can approach a partnership proposal lightly. You need to think through your approach just like any other sales call, and you need to take the time to prepare a written proposal. (See Appendix B.)

Most small company owners have two traits that makes cross-promotions difficult to set up. The first is the owners are primarily domineering personalities who are used to doing things their way. They are also not always real good about taking in a lot of other people's input. That's why you must have a written proposal that clearly spells out all the details of your proposal, along with the details of what tasks each partner will perform. The second trait, which is true of most domineering personalities, is that they are always worried about someone taking advantage of them or getting a better deal. You must be careful when you make your presentation that the situation is set up so both parties equally benefit from the promotion. I've found that you'll never sign a deal with a small business owner once he or she feels you've tried to take advantage of him or her. Marketing managers at big companies are much easier to deal with than small business owners when it comes to worrying about the benefit that each business derives from a partnership or alliance. They typically only worry about whether the partnership is a good deal for them. The drawback to rely on larger companies for partnerships is that a small company often can't produce a big enough promotion to interest the larger company.

> Presenting a partnership proposal requires a win/win situation.

In order to cinch the deal you need to follow three steps:

1. Develop strong personal relationships with a potential partner. Once you find companies you feel would be good partners, you need to contact them many times, pass ideas by them, and generally keep in touch.
2. Establish some successes with the company through small promotions, mailings, or other low-risk partnership arrangements.
3. Show how the deal is fair to both parties. This is the most difficult step. Even if the arrangement helps both companies, one company typically won't go ahead if it feels both parties don't benefit equally.

As an example of how to make things fair, consider the example listed earlier of the shoe store that gives away a free color analysis from a clothing store. Both stores will feel the arrangement is fair if they are both about the same size with a similar image and clientele. If the shoe store is quite a bit larger, it may feel that the cross-promotion benefits the clothing retailer much more than it does the shoe store. The shoe store owner probably won't be willing to move ahead even though it is still a good deal for both companies. The clothing retailer might have to add value to the shoe store before securing a partnership arrangement. The clothing retailer might need to perform color analysis in the shoe store or arrange for free offers from other smaller women's retailers.

Conclusion

I give seminars on strategic alliances and partnerships, and the experienced small business owners are excited because they have many new and innovative tools that they can use to effectively market their businesses and services. Experienced business people are not naïve. They know they have probably made many mistakes marketing their products and that it takes a major effort to entice customers to buy a product or service. There are always a few people in the seminar that are just starting in business that look at me with a blank stare. They often feel marketing only consists of doing a little advertising. They are totally unprepared for the commitment of time, energy, and resources required to implement an effective marketing program. This book has not been about variations of traditional tactics that you can use to improve your marketing. This book is about the tactics every business will need in the future to survive. So set your mind to the fact that you won't be able to compete effectively against competitors who use infiltration marketing. It is simply not possible to last against companies who have half the marketing cost per customer that you have.

I hope that I've prepared you to successfully market your business with three key lessons:

1. Infiltration marketing creates a strong bond between companies and their customers. Start putting less emphasis on traditional marketing methods and start looking for new creative ways to connect with your customers in their world.

2. Forming alliances and partnerships is by far the most cost-effective method of marketing available to small business owners today. These alliances don't have to be formal commitments or official joint ventures. They need just be an agreement between two or more companies to collaborate on many of their marketing activities.

3. You don't have time to delay putting together your own infiltration marketing program. Today, infiltration marketing tactics are being used by only a small percentage of companies. But I expect that to change. You will have a big advantage when you are the first company in your market with an infiltration marketing approach. That advantage will disappear if you are the fourth or fifth company to initiate a new marketing program.

My goal in this book was to alert small business owners and marketers to the fact that their marketing world is undergoing major changes and to offer a cost-effective way to market products and services to retail stores and other types of business. Big companies are starting to adopt many of these tactics for one simple reason: They work better than costly traditional marketing tactics like trade shows, advertising, and direct mail. I believe that you will be armed for the 21st century if you adopt the tactics laid out before you. I also believe you will be left behind if you don't change your marketing approach. I've given you the tools you need to succeed. Your job is to start using them today.

SAMPLES OF ALLIANCES, PARTNERSHIPS, AND CROSS-PROMOTIONS.

1. Group of businesses selling to the same market can create an alliance for merchandising products to retailers, conducting seminars, hosting trade show booths, running contests, or selling complete solutions to key targeted customers.

2. Any size company can sign a marketing agreement to have their products sold through larger companies either through a private label arrangement or under their own label.

3. Small manufacturers with innovative products often sign short-term exclusive distribution agreements with distributors, manufacturers representatives, catalogs, or retailers. The agreements can call for the distributor or retailer to feature the product exclusively, which helps both the retailer and manufacturer enhance their images.

4. Exclusive manufacturing agreements with contract manufacturers often can help underfinanced entrepreneurs launch their products. The contract manufacturer will produce a product for extended payment terms and amortize the tooling expense in return for a one-year or longer manufacturing agreement.

5. License agreements with a manufacturer or marketer that targets a different market than you do. For example, a siphon pump sold to marine stores licenses its product to an industrial supplier for sale to the industrial maintenance market.

6. Joint development agreements, either for a product or market. This is a common tactic when a small company has a great idea but doesn't have the resources to develop the product. The small company will be a partner with a large company in development. If the product is successfully developed, the product will be offered on an exclusive basis for a limited time to the large company, or the large company could market the product.

7. Research agreements with university professors and well-known individuals. For example, if a company needs research done, have a university professor supervise the research, prepare the paper, and present the paper at major trade shows. This enhances a research report's credibility and helps promote a company's cutting edge technology image.

8. Joint sponsorships with trade associations or magazines. Sponsor classes, seminars, Web pages, and other marketing activities. You may even provide free or no-cost services in order to be connected with an association. This tactic increases credibility, gives a company access to a large number of potential customers, and helps the company stay on top of current market trends.

9. Advisory councils with key suppliers and distributors. The councils can be specific to a company's product, involved more in industry-wide advice, and can be sponsored by more than one company.

10. Endorsement agreement with supplier, i.e., with a special process or part. For example, if you were to heat treat a metal part for greater corrosion resistance, you might get vendor funding if you promote heat treatment with induction heating. You can also do joint development with vendors. The vendor might also promote your product as an example of quality parts made with a heat treatment process.

11. Sharing of a sales force, warehouse space, and shipping departments between two companies in different parts of the country. Small manufac-

turers often do this when the two companies are in separate parts of the country.

12. Sharing of office space, administrative help, warehouse space, and marketing leads with a similar business in the same town. This is done typically to save costs, but being in a combined, larger office also enhances a company's credibility.

13. Sponsorship of sports teams, events, musical acts, or a sporting competition. Often companies will team up with other companies or associations to help fund an event. This produces both visibility and credibility for the companies involved. Examples of events where this can be done are bike races, home shows, boat shows, golf outings, and school carnivals.

14. Offer programs for fundraising to schools or other organizations. General Mills's Boxtops for Education program where schools that collect enough boxtops can get free computers, is a good example. The association with schools boosts market exposure and increases a company's credibility.

15. Combine with other companies for a demonstration of a new technology or an improved manufacturing system. Combining forces allows companies to see a fully working system, which attracts more interest than a demonstration by one company and also builds credibility for all the companies involved.

16. Offer your product on an OEM basis to major manufacturers. An OEM (original equipment manufacturer) supplies components to other manufactures who use the components in their product. If your product or service complements the products and services of a larger company, offer to OEM your product as an option the larger company can offer to its customers.

17. Offer to use a store or retailer as a demonstration site for your product. For example, if you sell solar products, you can install one of your products in the retailer's location. That enhances your product, and it helps the retailer sell more products.

18. Offer to put on motivational seminars or demonstrations over the lunch hour at large companies where many of the company's employees are in

your target market. For example, a bike retailer could offer seminars on setting up a bike training program to lose weight.

19. Combine with other companies to offer a full selection of products to retailers or distributors. For example, you could have a line of baby/toddler food that would feed a child from birth till they are three years old. Or you could combine with another tool manufacturer to offer a full line of automotive exhaust tools.

20. Form an alliance with a big user. A company can offer to be an exclusive service or product provider to a company in return for an investment or in return for being able to tell other customers that you are the exclusive supplier for the large company. A smaller company may have to discount its products or offer additional services, but in return they will receive credibility and a valuable sales tool.

21. Form an alliance with other retailers or similar businesses that serve the same target customer group. Pass out each other's coupons and/or promotional brochures, do joint mailings, and offer special events. Each company will gain exposure to new customers at a very low price.

22. Form a partnership with companies selling products to the same personality group that your company's products or service appeals to. For example, if a company sells office products targeted at optimizers (people who only want to own cutting edge products), the company could form a marketing partnership with other companies targeting the same type customer.

23. Join together with other businesses targeting your same customer group to publish newsletters or other materials that are of interest to people in the target group. Joining together will result in a better newsletter, and mailing to everyone's customers will expose each business to new prospects.

24. Offer to sell to another company targeting the same customer one of your products at a very low price in return for the company offering your item as a promotional giveaway. For instance, a magazine may sell copies of an issue to an office supply store like Office Max for 25 cents in return for Office Max giving the issue away to anyone who makes a $10 or higher purchase.

25. Combine with other businesses, associations, or groups to start a club or an Internet chat room related to your business. This again gets your name out in front of what hopefully will become your key customers.

26. Share space with other stores serving the same customer. Two or more retailers in the same space not only cuts cost, but it brings in more customers. Service businesses can also do this to pick up more business. A furnace repair technician, plumber, and electrician could share space and a secretary, and each service business would receive customer referrals from the others.

27. Give or sell your loyalty coupons to another company to pass out for their promotions. Northwest Airlines does this when they allow MCI to give away Northwest's frequent flyer miles with the purchase of a new cellular phone.

28. Bypass normal distribution and form an alliance with installers of your product. For example businesses that build decks for homes typically buy supplies from a lumberyard. An inventor who has trouble selling a special deck building item through lumberyards could allow deck installers to have exclusive sales rights to his or her product.

WRITING A PARTNERSHIP, ALLIANCE, OR CROSS-PROMOTION PROPOSAL

I recommend writing a proposal for most partnership arrangements so that it is clear to both parties what exactly you are proposing and what expectations each prospective partner should have. Don't make your proposal too long. I feel three to four pages is long enough. The proposal is just a starting point for your discussions. After you meet with the potential partner and work out the details of what you are going to do, you should prepare a letter of understanding or a final proposal with all the final details of your arrangement spelled out. Without a final proposal or letter of understanding, people have a tendency to forget exactly what they agreed to, and the result is that a potential long-term partnership starts out on rocky ground.

I recommend you prepare a business proposal in a traditional format because that is what most other companies will be familiar with. The key elements of the proposal are:

- Opening
- Opportunity Summary
- Background
- Recommendation
- Rationale
- Activity List with Implementation Dates

- Expected Outcomes
- Next Steps

This format can be adjusted slightly to meet your individual needs, but you'll find it works well in almost every situation. I'll be using as an example in this Appendix Medi-Seal's alliance with Trek bicycles from Chapter 17. This is not what the proposal actually looked like, but it is what it easily could look like. Each section on the proposal will include how Medi-Seal's proposal to Trek could look. This example should give you a better understanding of what a proposal should look like.

Proposal Description

This section should just be a very brief summary of the proposal. Don't add too much marketing language here. It should simply state that this is a proposal from your company to the name of the other company for the specific proposal.

Sample Proposal Description

This is a proposal from Medi-Seal Corp. to Trek for incorporating Medi-Seal's Child Protection Stickers as a promotional giveaway in each box containing one Trek child's bike helmet.

Opportunity Summary

In most business proposals this is the situation summary, but I prefer the term opportunity summary for a partnership proposal. This is the section that defines what you are actually proposing. If you have one particular event or campaign in mind, you can clearly state what that event is. For example, say you are proposing to promote a training seminar at an upcoming Business Expo jointly sponsored by you and the potential partner as a tactic for generating high-quality leads. Other times, you may have four or five different events or programs that you could jointly run with the partner. Since this proposal is only a starting point for discussion, you can give the partner several options to choose from. For instance, if you and the potential partner both have products and/or services for desktop publishers, your proposal might state that "You would like to run a joint program with the potential partner to generate high-quality leads among desktop publishers. Potential programs that could generate those leads are:" Then you would just list the programs. This approach is often more effective because it sets up the partnership on a collaborative basis rather than a partnership where you are in control of the events or programs.

Example of an Opportunity Summary

This is a proposal to give Trek a differential advantage in the marketplace by offering a free, easy-to-use Medi-Seal sticker with the purchase of any Trek child safety helmet. The Medi-Seal sticker contains key medical facts as well as parent contact information. The sticker gives medical personnel all the information they need to immediately contact the parent and start medical treatment in case of an accident. The addition of the Medi-Seal sticker should provide a perceived benefit to the safety-conscious parents that are already buying bike helmets.

This proposal is to offer Trek a special purchase option on the Medi-Seal stickers so they can be added as a sales feature to Trek's helmets at minimal cost. The expectation is that the addition of the sticker will give Trek a market advantage against other bike helmet manufacturing companies, while Medi-Seal will gain exposure to the broader market that will in the future enable it to sell individual Medi-Seal stickers for other applications.

Background

This section is usually about five to 10 sentences. You should explain a little bit about each partner in the proposal, what each partner contributes to the arrangement, and what each partner gets as a benefit from the proposal.

Example of a Background Section

Trek is a major bike manufacturer that also manufactures bike accessories including helmets. Trek sells through specialty bike shops, many with the Trek name on them. While Trek bikes are restricted to upscale bike retailers to protect the Trek brand name, Trek can sell its accessories to a larger number of retailers. Offering exclusive features gives Trek additional sales tools to expand its retailer network. Medi-Seal manufactures a durable sticker that attaches to a helmet, employee badge, or other hard surface. The inside, permanent sticker lists key medical and personal information, and the exterior, removable sticker displays the Medi-Seal label. Medi-Seal is willing to offer its product at a favorable price (see attached price sheet) to gain the broad market exposure that Trek's brand name and established distribution network can offer.

Recommendation

You need to briefly describe what program you are recommending. You can state that the program is proposed and leave open the possibility of changes, but try to list as many program elements as possible to give the potential partner a good idea of the scope of the program's possibilities.

Example of a Recommendation

It is recommended that Trek start to supply Medi-Seals in its child helmet boxes effective January 1, 2002. That will help ensure that the Trek helmets will be on retailer's shelves to coincide with a big April 1 spring promotion on child bike safety. Bike helmet boxes should have a big sticker on the front announcing that each box contains a free Medi-Seal sticker on the inside, with a sticker on the box showing Medi-Seal's product features. These box stickers will be supplied along with the Medi-Seal sticker as part of the package price listed on the attached sheet.

The April 1 publicity program will include:

- Announcement of the National Safety Council's approval of the Medi-Seal sticker.

- Press releases will be published in all children, parent, and bike-oriented magazines about the Medi-Seal program.
- Bike safety rodeo kits will be sent to all Trek dealers for distribution to schools. The kits will be used by the bike shops to promote bike rodeos at local schools. The kits will include promotion of the National Safety Council's approval of the Medi-Seal and Medi-Seal cards, which will list the information on a Medi-Seal sticker on card stock. (Medi-Seal cards to be furnished by Medi-Seal.)
- Medi-Seal will be featured in Trek's "Schools Out" promotion in June 2002, offering special pricing to bike shops that participate in a co-op advertising campaign.
- Medi-Seal and Trek can cooperatively prepare point-of-purchase materials for bike shops regarding the Medi-Seal and its approval by the National Safety Council.

Rationale

This section reinforces the reason why both parties should be interested in moving forward. It often explains why the proposal is good for both parties and why you are proposing the specific action in your recommendation section.

Example of a Rationale

The National Safety Council has recently informed Medi-Seal that it will be putting its seal of approval on Medi-Seal's stickers. Coordinating this announcement with a major spring promotion by Trek on child bike safety featuring Trek's bike helmets benefits both Trek and Medi-Seal. Trek gets to associate its product with the National Safety Council's seal of approval, which supports its image as a safety-conscious company concerned about children. Medi-Seal benefits from the promotion because it is a small company that needs the exposure that Trek can offer. Both companies benefit from the promotional possibilities of the program.

Proposed Activity List with Implementation Dates

The activity list covers what steps you feel will need to be accomplished in order for the program to work. I recommend you make this fairly comprehensive, as it lets everyone know what needs to be accomplished for the program to move ahead. Without a list people aren't going to get everything accomplished to pull off the program. The list also helps people realize the marketing potential of the program. It also lets your potential partner see exactly what it will have to do to make the program work. You should negotiate with the partner who will accomplish each task, and then list that information in the final proposal or letter of understanding.

Example of a Proposed Activity List with Implementation Dates

STEP 1. COMING TO AN AGREEMENT

1. Medi-Seal will receive a letter from the National Safety Council verifying that it will be placing its seal of approval on the Medi-Seal sticker.
2. Medi-Seal and Trek will come to an agreement to move ahead on the proposed project of adding a Medi-Seal sticker as a promotional giveaway to each Trek child's bicycle helmet.

STEP 2. PREPARING FOR THE MARKETING CAMPAIGN

3. Medi-Seal will submit to Trek several sticker options for placement on the outside of Trek's boxes announcing that there is a free Medi-Seal sticker inside.
4. Medi-Seal and Trek will coordinate the materials and work with Trek's PR agency for the PR program that will be released to support the spring campaign. Trek's marketing department will control the PR campaign.
5. Medi-Seal will submit some ideas to Trek's marketing department for a proposed point-of-purchase display. Trek's marketing department will be responsible for choosing the final display layout and producing the display.

6. Medi-Seal will submit to Trek for approval the card version of the Medi-Seal sticker, which will be available as a pass-out at the bike safety rodeos that are run for schools by Trek dealers

7. Trek will prepare the promotional materials for the bike safety rodeos for its retailers.

8. Trek will coordinate a direct mailing program to schools promoting the issues of child safety and the availability of bike safety rodeos as a school project. Medi-Seal will prepare an original master of a flyer for the mailing relating to the National Safety Council's decision to put its seal of approval on the Medi-Seal sticker. The flyer will also feature information on Trek's spring bike safety promotion offering the Medi-Seal sticker free in Trek's child safety helmets.

STEP 3: IMPLEMENTATION

9. The sticker for Trek's child safety helmet box will be presented to Trek by August 1, 2001.

10. The PR program details will be released to the PR Agency in August 2001.

11. Medi-Seal will provide its ideas for a point-of-purchase display by September 15, 2001. Point-of-purchase display layout will be approved by November 1, 2001.

12. Medi-Seal will provide its proposed version of the Medi-Seal card for approval by Trek by October 15, 2001.

13. Material layouts for major retailer mailing announcing the bike rodeo should be prepared by November 1, 2001.

14. Material layouts for mailing out the bike safety rodeo kits to retailers should be prepared by December 1, 2001.

15. School Program mailing materials need to approved by November 15, 2001.

16. Trek should start shipping children's bike helmets with the Medi-Seal sticker on the inside of the box on January 1, 2002.

17. Announcement about the spring promotion mailed to Trek's sales force on January 15, 2002.

18. Major retailer mailing announcing the spring child safety bike program on January 15, 2002.

19. Bike safety rodeo materials mailed to retailers on January 30, 2002.

20. School mailing announcing child bike safety program on February 15, 2002.

21. Store displays for child bike safety program and the addition of the Medi-Seal sticker to Trek's children's helmets shipped to stores on March 1, 1999.

22. Trek sales force to complete calls on all retailers explaining the new child safety program by March 1, 2002.

Expected Outcomes

This section should reinforce the benefits of why a proposed partner should want to run a program with you. Using bulleted points along with a brief description clearly communicates the program's benefits to the partner.

Example of an Expected Outcome Section

Trek should receive the following benefits from the child bike safety promotion:

1. Trek will be associated in parents' minds with a worthwhile goal: child safety.
2. Trek will have an exciting new program for its dealers.
3. Trek will receive enhanced credibility for its helmets due to the National Safety Council's seal of approval of the Medi-Seal sticker.
4. Trek will have a strong differential advantage over its bike helmet competitors, which should enable it to expand its retailer network.
5. Trek will set a precedent of running programs with schools, a precedent that will help it set up future programs with schools.

Medi-Seal will receive the following benefits:

1. Broad market exposure to parents, schools, and retailers that will help Medi-Seal secure business in other markets.
2. Enhanced credibility for its sticker due to Medi-Seal's association with Trek.

Next Steps

This section describes what next steps you and the partner should take. In some cases you need to decide to go forward and set up a program plan, in other cases you might need to make a joint commitment to reserve a booth or an area for an event, or you might need to get together to talk the situation over further. Typically the proposal is a starting point for discussions, and the next step is really to get together to hash out all the details so you can either finalize the proposal or prepare a letter of understanding.

Example of the Next Step

Medi-Seal and Trek need to get together during the months of June and July 2001 to decide whether to move ahead, and if they decide to move ahead, to finalize the program plan and details.

MARKETING PROGRAM SUMMARY FORM

List your target customer group(s): _____

_____

Check the predominant personality trait: _____ Maximizer _____ Risk Adverse

_____ Judicial _____ Maintaining

List customers predominant desired image (consumers) or interest (business):

_____

_____

List the initial response you want to generate: _____

_____

Describe your company's target image: _____

_____

Describe your program: _____

_____

What is your program's goals _____

_____

How does the program enhance your image? _____

_____

How does the program tie in with the initial response you want to generate from

customers?_____

_____

Are there other companies you could partner with for this promotion? _____

_____

What additional infiltration marketing tactics can you add to the program?

_____

How will you promote the program? _____

_____

Have you added any elements to the program to encourage customers to give

referrals? _____

_____

What outcomes are you expecting from the program? _____

_____

What results will make you feel that the program has been a success? _____

_____

Evaluate the program at its conclusion.

Did the program achieve the results expected? _____ Yes _____ No

What is your overall analysis of how the program worked? _____

_____

What worked best in the program? _____

_____

What in the program didn't work? _____

_____

Would your run this program again? _____ Yes _____ No

INDEX

FIND MORE ON THIS TOPIC BY VISITING
BusinessTown.com
The Web s big site for growing businesses!

- ☑ **Separate channels on all aspects of starting and running a business**
- ☑ **Lots of info of how to do business online**
- ☑ **1,000+ pages of savvy business advice**
- ☑ **Complete web guide to thousands of useful business sites**
- ☑ **Free e-mail newsletter**
- ☑ **Question and answer forums, and more!**

http://www.businesstown.com

Also available from Adams Media

STREETWISE BOOKS

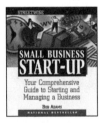
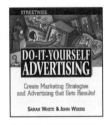